The Lost O

The Lost Oases

A.M. Hassanein Bey

Introduced by
Michael Haag

The American University in Cairo Press
Cairo New York

113 Sharia Kasr el Aini, Cairo, Egypt
420 Fifth Avenue, New York 10018
www.aucpress.com

First published in 1925 by Thornton Butterworth Ltd. in London and Century Co. in New York

Dar el Kutub No. 14108/05
ISBN 978 977 424 980 8

2 3 4 5 6 7 8 9 10 14 13 12 11 10 09 08

Printed in Egypt

Introduction
Michael Haag

In *The Lost Oases*, one of the great classics of desert exploration, Ahmed Hassanein tells how he set out by camel from Sollum on the Mediterranean coast of Egypt west of Mersa Matruh, heading for the oases of Siwa and Kufra and into the unknown. The first man to cross the Libyan Desert, as the eastern Sahara is called, Hassanein began a perilous eight-month journey in 1923 that was to take him round the western shores of the Great Sand Sea to El Obeid in the Sudan, a distance of over 3,500 kilometers, and lead him to the discovery of the lost oases of Arkenu and Uweinat at the extreme southwest corner of Egypt.

At Uweinat Hassanein was amazed to find rock drawings of animals, including lions, giraffes, ostriches, gazelles, and possibly also cows. He was deep in the trackless desert, but what he had found, and photographed, was evidence of a flourishing human existence ten thousand years ago, before desertification drove these mysterious people to the valley of the Nile.

Hassanein's discovery—and indeed the pages of this book—excited the imaginations of later explorers such as Ralph Bagnold, who relied on convoys of stripped-down Model-T Fords (and who in the Second World War would create the Long Range Desert Group, the forerunners of the SAS), and Count Ladislaus Almásy who did his exploring by light aircraft and was the model for the eponymous character in *The English Patient*. But the significance of Hassanein's adventure and the achievements of his life amounted to a great deal more than that.

After returning from his remarkable journey across the desert and his discovery of the lost oases in 1923, Hassanein was offered $20,000 by American promoters if he would go on a lecture tour around the United States dressed in his Bedouin robes. The press in America had already dubbed him Egypt's Lawrence of Arabia; Rudolph Valentino's film *The Sheikh* had been big box office two years before; and the world was still agog at Howard Carter's discovery of Tutankhamun's tomb in 1922. Egypt and deserts were the stuff of sensation and romance, and Hassanein was a hot property, a popular yet mysterious figure to the newspaper-reading public in Europe and the New World. But Hassanein turned down the offer, saying that "my standing precludes earning money in such a manner." And when he did go to America in 1924, it was in an entirely different capacity.

In Egypt, where Hassanein's expedition was celebrated as a great advance in geographical knowledge and as a patriotic achievement, there was a sense of satisfaction that while Europeans had explored Africa by its rivers, it was Hassanein who first successfully penetrated the Libyan Desert, traversing it from north to south, and was the first to cross the Great Sand Sea. "The Libyan Desert is part of our country," he had said before embarking on his journey, "and it is incumbent upon us to ascertain our borders there, so that we may better know our country. By traversing the desert I will have established some of the rights of our nation." Now in August 1923, after returning from the desert, Hassanein addressed a grand reception in Alexandria of princes, ministers, senior officials, and prominent men of letters. He outlined the scientific benefits of his expedition, adding that he had pinpointed precisely the geographical location of every area through which he had passed, not least the oases of Arkenu and Ouenat (Uweinat), making it possible to draw a detailed map of Egypt's western territories. In November that same year in Cairo, Hassanein was feted with a large ceremony at the Opera House attended by King Fuad, who conferred on him the title of bey.

Yet Hassanein always understood that his greatest achievement was his discovery of the rock drawings at Uweinat; they were "the most interesting find of my 2,200-mile journey," he would write in the September 1924 issue of America's *National Geographic Magazine*. He saw that they pointed to the passing of a sophisticated pastoral culture, the victim of dramatic climate change, which he placed at some time before the introduction of the camel to the desert in about 500 BC. But how much earlier than that, he could not guess, adding that "here is a puzzle which must be left to the research of the archaeologists." In *The Lost Oases*, published in the following year, he describes how he tried to hide his excitement at the discovery, and even avoided visiting some other rock pictures half a day away for fear of arousing suspicions among the native Tebu who thought of them as the work of jinns. In fact Hassanein had discovered the first prehistoric rock drawings ever found in Egypt's deserts, the first evidence suggesting that Egyptian civilization may have started in a once greener Libyan Desert and not, as universally supposed, in the valley of the Nile. As Michael Hoffman, the eminent prehistorian wrote in *Egypt Before the Pharaohs* (1979), Hassanein had "uncovered an archaeological mystery whose solution is only now coming within our grasp."

Hassanein would say that Bedouin blood ran through his veins, explaining the lure he had long felt for the desert. But he also belonged to the Turco-Circassian upper class, and by profession he was a diplomat, who had asked the Egyptian Foreign Office for a leave of absence in order to undertake his expedition in search of the lost oases. Now that he was back, he was posted to the Egyptian embassy in Washington, where as First Secretary, and still only thirty-three, he held the number two position after the ambassador himself. Next he was sent to London, the plum overseas posting, where again he was number two, and where also he was awarded the Founders Medal of the Royal Geographical Society. He was recalled to Cairo in 1925 to serve as First Chamberlain to King Fuad, and for the rest of his life Hassanein remained close to the throne of Egypt, an influential and indispensable advisor, not least during the tumultuous years of the Second World War. Yet as a friend of Hassanein's observed, "he would have preferred to have left behind the ceremonies, the trappings and the splendour to live in a tent in the desert. He loved the desert. It was like a garden of contentment for him."

Ahmed Mohammed Hassanein was born in Cairo in 1889, where his father, Sheikh Mohammed Hassanein al-Bulaqi, was a distinguished scholar at the thousand year old mosque of al-Azhar, which was also a university, the oldest in the world. His grandfather was Ahmed Mazhar Hassanein Pasha, the last admiral of the Egyptian navy before the British occupation in 1882. When ordered to hand over his fleet to the British at their naval base in Malta, Admiral Hassanein instead sailed about the Mediterranean for a while before giving his famous reply, *Malta mafish*, "Malta is not there."

In his introduction to the 1925 edition of *The Lost Oases*, Sir Rennell Rodd loosely summarizes Hassanein's early education and career. Rodd himself was a diplomat and author, and had recently been ambassador at Rome and Britain's representative at the League of Nations, while his son Francis, who was Hassanein's friend from their days at Oxford before the war, had written *The People of the Veil*, a book about the Tuareg, which would be published in 1926. After Hassanein had studied for a year at Cairo's Khedivial School of Law, his father sent him to Oxford University where he entered Balliol College in 1910, returning to Egypt in 1914 just before the outbreak of the First World War. There he joined the Ministry of the Interior and served as private Arabic secretary on the staff of Sir John Maxwell, Commander in Chief of British forces in Egypt. In 1917, together with Francis Rodd, Hassanein was sent on a delicate mission to the Senussi Bedouin who roamed on both sides of the Egyptian–Libyan border. Libya was then still notionally part of the Ottoman Empire, and the Senussis, armed by Turkish and German agents, were persuaded to mount attacks on Egypt's western frontier, which required 35,000 British troops under Colonel Milo Talbot to contain them. The Senussis were not a tribe, rather adherents of a fundamentalist Sufi sect who were militantly protective of their independence. After their defeat in battle it was the negotiations in which Hassanein, a fellow Muslim and son of a holy man, played an important part that led the Senussis to adopt as their new leader Sayyid Idris, who was friendly to the British and their allies.

This mission to the Senussis was the practical beginning of Hassanein's long-cherished dream to penetrate to Kufra, the capital of the Senussi sect deep in the Libyan Desert. As Hassanein explains in the first chapter of this book, no outsider had penetrated as far as Kufra other than the German Gerhard Rohlfs in 1879, who was nearly killed in the attempt and had all his instruments and scientific records destroyed. With the war now over, Hassanein met again with Sayyid Idris, and drawing on the earlier trust established between them, obtained his authority and permission to make the otherwise impossible journey to Kufra. Francis Rodd planned to join Hassanein in the adventure, but when he was obliged to drop out, his friend the travel writer Rosita Forbes, a beautiful and vivacious divorcée in search of exotic adventure, pressed her chance. Hassanein cajoled a reluctant Sayyid Idris into allowing the Englishwoman to accompany him on the journey. Disguised as 'Khadija,' she "dressed as a Muslim woman and posed as a female relative of mine, thus ensuring that the Bedouins could not address her or ask about her." On several occasions they came close to being murdered by suspicious Bedouins and were saved only by Hassanein's coolness and quick wits. Once they were challenged at Jalo, where they were asked about some merchants in Cairo to see if they really were Egyptian. Fortunately Hassanein had the answer, and their caravan was given the traditional Bedouin hospitality. At another point, north of Kufra, their expedition missed a vital well owing to Rosita's lack of skill in taking compass readings, and they nearly died of thirst. Hassanein was badly repaid for the effort and risks he took on Rosita's behalf, for as soon as she returned to England she wrote *The Secret of the Sahara: Kufara* (1921), in which she represented herself as the sole organizer and driving force behind the expedition, and described Hassanein in terms that suggested he was nothing more than her hired servant. The book won her the reputation of being an intrepid explorer and made her famous throughout the world. But as the explorer and Arabist Gertrude Bell wrote at the time, "in the matter of trumpet blowing she is unique," adding that "she doesn't know a word of Arabic," and that without Hassanein "she couldn't have done anything." Even Rosita's entry in the *Dictionary of National Biography*, not normally given to critical remarks about its subjects, says that her book "decidedly under-played her companion's share in the expedition and gave rise to resentments which long persisted."

This probably explains Rennell Rodd's remarks in his introduction, where he says that Hassanein had consulted him "in a very delicate matter" in which he proved himself to be "generous in his judgements and, for I know no other way of expressing what I mean, a great gentleman." Rosita had fallen in love with Hassanein, but the details are hidden behind Hassanein's discretion and Rosita's catty remarks. It was said in Cairo that she would climb into his tent and try to seduce him, but that Hassanein refused her. "I was determined not to offend Allah and his mercy," Hassanein is remembered to have said, "for we were in the midst of uncharted desert with the perils of death surrounding us on all sides."

Or maybe something did happen between them, but if so then it would seem that Rosita's false compass readings chastened Hassanein's desires. "On my first trip through the Libyan Desert I took a vow," Hassanein writes in *The Lost Oases*. "We had lost our way and we had lost all hope. There was no sign of the oasis we sought, no sign of any well near by. The desert seemed cruel and merciless, and I vowed that if ever we came through alive I would not return again. Two years later I was back in the same desert, at the same spot where we had lost our way, and landed in the same well that had saved our lives on the previous occasion. The desert calls, but it is not easy to analyse its attraction and its charm." And again, describing his love of the desert: "It is as though a man were deeply in love with a very fascinating but cruel woman. She treats him badly, and the world crumples in his hand; at night she smiles on him and the whole world is a paradise. The desert smiles and there is no place on earth worth living in but the desert." But not if you are with a woman who does not know how to read a compass.

A mystical streak ran through Hassanein and was part of his charm and charisma. In a diary entry for 1927, Jasper Brinton, an American judge on the Mixed Courts of Egypt, described sitting at a state dinner. "I sit beside the wife of the Italian Minister—a dullish party, but enjoy talking to Hassanein Bey, who tells me of his proposed trip across Arabia, 900 miles by camel—a charming and lovable fellow. Spoke much of religion and said that most great religions have come out of the desert—the silence of the desert and its encouragement to meditation. He would be a fine man to travel with."

Clearly Hassanein still had his mind on crossing deserts, but he would never undertake such an expedition again. In 1926 he had married Loutfia Yusri, a beautiful and stylish woman whom he had met in Washington when he was First Secretary to her father, Seifallah Yusri Pasha, Egypt's ambassador to the United States. Her mother was Princess Shevekiar, a woman of immense wealth whose town house in Cairo was of such gigantic proportions that it now houses the Egyptian Ministry of Foreign Affairs. Shevekiar's first husband had been Fuad, before he came to the throne; when he tried to confine her to his harem quarters, she escaped and divorced him.

Hassanein's recreations included fencing, and he had fenced for Egypt in the 1920 Olympics at Antwerp. Now he took up flying, and in 1930 he attempted to become the first person to fly solo from Europe to Egypt. After taking off from Heston Air Park near London he got as far as Pisa, where he smashed up his machine on landing. A replacement aircraft was put out of action by an accident at Naples, and when he was offered an Italian aircraft in its place, that crashed during a trial flight, killing its two occupants. At that point King Fuad lost patience with Hassanein and ordered him back to Cairo, where the palace relied on his presence. He was also valued for the diplomatic bridge he created between Britain and Egypt, the British government honoring him with a KCVO (Knight Commander of the Victorian Order) in 1927, so that he was now Sir Ahmed Hassanein. But as a secret Foreign Office report on Hassanein made clear, "his knowledge of English and charm of manner leave many English people with the impression that he is unfavorable to Egyptian national aspirations. It would be a mistake to act on this assumption."

After the death of Fuad in 1936 and the accession of the sixteen-year-old Farouk, Hassanein was elevated from bey to pasha and was appointed governor of the Royal Household, by which he became responsible for the upbringing and education of the king. Both measures were instigated by Fuad's widow, the still youthful and attractive Queen Nazli. By the terms of the Anglo-Egyptian Treaty signed in the same year, Egypt accepted a military alliance with Britain in the event of war but otherwise achieved total control over its own affairs. But that did not prevent Sir Miles Lampson, the overbearing British ambassador, from patronizing "the boy," as he routinely referred to King Farouk. "I quite realised," said Lampson when Farouk ascended the throne, "that in the next little time things were going to be extremely difficult for the young

Ahmed Hassanein at the start of his attempt to fly solo from England to Egypt

King and that he was going to feel the want of someone to lean upon." But the more Lampson pressed himself on "the boy," the more the king rebelled, and instead it was Hassanein that Farouk admired, almost to the extent of hero-worship at times, trusting him, imitating him, but fearing him as well. He was the only person able to speak to Farouk with entire frankness and sometimes he was blunt, but he always remained entirely loyal to his king.

Edward Ford, who was Farouk's English tutor, wrote of Hassanein at this time: "I sit next to him for most meals and his reminiscences of Oxford are a delight to me. He has a quick wit, great courtesy, an interest in all subjects and is a quite unusual type of Egyptian. Slim, sharply featured, with a sallow colour and grey hair brushed straight back from his high forehead, he has an unmistakable Bedouin look. . . . He has keen penetrating eyes, never looks sleepy and has an air of refinement that the coarse looking Egyptian type entirely lacks. He has never had political inclinations, and, though he is a firm believer in Egypt's right to govern herself and a fervid Moslem, he is quite without that aggressive conceit which marks other ambitious men in this country. Although his culture and his intellect are occidental, his mentality and nature are from the east. He has an eastern courtesy, and, in conversation, an eastern way of leading you off the path you have selected by a sympathetic evasiveness."

Meanwhile Hassanein and the queen fell into a romance, and after he divorced Loutfia amid a spectacular scandal, Hassanein and Nazli were secretly married in 1937 by Sheikh Mustafa al-Maraghi of al-Azhar.

In June 1940 Italy entered the war. With large armies in Libya and Ethiopia ready to strike at Egypt, the Italians posed a serious threat, and the British demanded reassurance that the Egyptian government would not stint in honoring the provisions of the military alliance in the 1936 treaty. A former ambassador to Britain became prime minister, an anti-British minister of defense was dropped, the suspect and uncooperative chief of staff of the Egyptian army was dismissed, and Hassanein was appointed to the important post of the Chief of the Royal Cabinet, which placed him in direct liaison with Sir Miles Lampson, the British ambassador. The arrangements were made in time to meet the Italian invasion in September 1940, and when General Wavell counterattacked in December, Hassanein eagerly phoned Lampson to ask for news and was told of Wavell's early success. "He expressed much gratification," Lampson recorded in his diary, "and said that he would at once tell King Farouk. Hassanein is of course violently anti-Italian and he made no secret of his delight at their reported discomfiture." Which made it all the stranger that in February 1942 Lampson had Farouk's Abdin Palace in Cairo surrounded by British troops and armored cars and demanded the king's abdication for supposedly being sympathetic toward the Italians. In fact Lampson, together with Anthony Eden, Britain's foreign secretary, were playing a deeper game. Farouk was taking himself too seriously as an independent king of an independent Egypt, Lampson complained to Eden, and they wanted someone more malleable on the throne, as well as a prime minister of their own choosing. Lampson's show of force so overawed Farouk that he was about to sign the abdication document, but then Hassanein intervened, and whispered something in the king's ear. Farouk conceded the British demand over the prime ministerial appointment but contritely asked to remain on the throne, an offer that Lampson, caught slightly off-balance, accepted. From Hassanein's point of view, and in this he probably would have found support among almost the entirety of the Egyptian population, it was right that the integrity of the monarchy be preserved, whatever the merits of its occupant. Certainly Lampson's action provoked nationalist outrage at foreign interference, destabilized constitutional government, and introduced a bitterness between Britain and Egypt that would culminate in the Suez debacle.

But long before that, Hassanein was off the scene. Since his days in the desert, he had often said that he had an appointment with death, but that so far neither he nor death had shown up on time. But in February 1946 the appointment was finally met, and he died in a freak motor accident when a British truck went into a skid and smashed into his car on a rainswept Cairo bridge. Thereafter, both Egyptian and foreign commentators agree, Farouk began to lose his grip over affairs. "This was the first of many unfortunate events," wrote one British emissary, "which from then on seemed to dog our footsteps in our relations with Egypt, for Hassanein was the one cool and experienced advisor to the young King Farouk."

He was interred in Cairo's City of the Dead, his remains placed in a domed mausoleum built by his brother-in-law, the outstanding Egyptian architect Hassan Fathy. After a lifetime that took him thousands of miles across uncharted sands, that opened up the remote ages of the past, and that seemed to belong more to a tale from *The Arabian Nights*, Sir Ahmed Mohammed Hassanein Pasha was laid to rest. He was only fifty-six.

THE LOST
OASES

THE LOST OASES

BY

A. M. HASSANEIN BEY, F.R.G.S.

INTRODUCTION BY

SIR RENNELL RODD

IN HOMAGE AND GRATITUDE

TO

HIS MAJESTY KING FOUAD I

WHO

BY HIS HELP AND ENCOURAGEMENT MADE
THIS JOURNEY POSSIBLE

Foreword

I AM deeply indebted to Dr. John Ball, O.B.E., Director of Desert Surveys of Egypt, who has been good enough to summarize the scientific results of my expedition in the First Appendix to this volume. His advice and the instruction which he gave me in the use of scientific instruments were invaluable. I was indeed fortunate in being able to draw upon his great knowledge.

The maps of my journey, one of which accompanies this volume, were kindly prepared by Dr. Ball and Mr. Browne and other members of the Survey Department of Egypt.

Dr. Hume and the late Mr. Moon of the Geological Survey of Egypt classified the geological specimens which I brought back and prepared a report which is contained in the Second Appendix to this book. By their willing assistance they added much to the results of my expedition.

Lewa Spinks Pasha, D.S.O., and Meshalani Bey of the Ordnance Department of the Egyptian War Office were responsible for the cases and containers and other camp equipment which I used. These proved to be satisfactory in every way, and I am grateful for the care and thought which were expended in their preparation.

My old friends Sayed El Sherif El Idrisi and his son Sayed Marghanny El Idrisi again gave me that good counsel and ready help which I had received from them in the course of my trip to Kufra in 1921.

Throughout my expedition I received the most friendly and effective assistance from Colonel Commandant Hunter Pasha, C.B., D.S.O., late Administrator of the Frontier Districts Administration; Colonel M. Macdonnell, late Governor of the Western Desert; Major de Halpert of the F.D.A.; Captain Hutton, O.C. Sollum; Captain Harrison, O.C. Armoured Cars at Sollum; Abdel Aziz Fahmy Effendi and A. Kamel Effendi, Mamurs of Sollum and Siwa; Lieutenant Lawler, O.C. Siwa.

When I reached the Sudan my way was made easy and pleasant by the kindness of His Excellency Ferik, the late Sir Lee Stack Pasha, G.B.E., C.M.G., Sirdar and Governor-General of the Sudan, and I cannot let this opportunity pass of expressing my cordial thanks to all the officials of the Sudan Government along my route, and especially to Lewa Midwinter Pasha, C.B., C.M.G., C.B.E., D.S.O., Acting Governor-General of the Sudan; Lewa Huddleston Pasha, C.M.G., D.S.O., M.C., Acting Sirdar; Kaimakam M. Hafiz Bey, O.C. Troops at Khartoum; Mr. H. A. MacMichael, D.S.O., Assistant Civil Secretary; Captain J. E. Philipps, M.C.; Samuel Atiyah Bey, M.V.O., and Ahmed El Sayed Pifai of the Sudan Civil Service; Mr. Charles Dupuis, Acting Governor of Darfur; Sagh A. Hilmy, S.O. El Fasher; Mr. J. D. Craig, O.B.E., Governor of Kordofan; Bimbashi A. Khalil, S.O. El Obeid, and the officers, officials and notables of El Fasher and El Obeid.

To Bimbashi G. F. Foley, M.C., O.C. Artillery at El Fasher, I am grateful for the verse which adorns the last chapter of the book.

I am particularly indebted to Mr. Harold Howland and to Mr. W. H. L. Watson, an old Balliol friend, for their invaluable help and advice in the preparation of this book.

Introduction

MY friend Ahmed Hassanein has asked me to write a few words of introduction to his record of a remarkable voyage of exploration. It was the more remarkable because the expedition, the results of which have enabled him to fill up an important gap in our knowledge of Africa and to determine with precision positions only approximately ascertained by that great pioneer in African research, Gerhardt Rohlfs, was conceived and led by him single-handed without other assistance or companionship than that of his guides and personal attendants.

A traveller whose work has been recognized by the award of the Founder's Medal of the Royal Geographical Society should need no introduction to the British public. But I welcome the opportunity of drawing attention to his achievement in another field, in the production of a book which will, I feel sure, be acknowledged by all who read it to have exceptional interest, written in a language of which he has made himself a master, although it is not his own.

But first, disregarding any protests from his characteristic modesty, I have to present the author himself, who is only known to the majority of my countrymen as an intrepid traveller. I have had the pleasure of his acquaintance for a number of years, since he was the contemporary and friend of my son at Balliol.

After considerable experience I have come to the conclusion that the experiment of sending students from the East to reside at a Western University is one which should only be tried in exceptional cases and with young men of exceptional character. In the case of Ahmed Hassanein I think all who know him will agree that it has been an unqualified success. He has retained all that is best of his own national and spiritual inheritance, while he has acquired a sympathetic understanding and appreciation of the mentality and feelings of men with very different social antecedents and training. It is possible that the blood of his Beduin forefathers made intimacy with them easier for him since the Briton and the Beduin not infrequently find in one another a certain kinship of instinct which compels their mutual regard. Incidentally it may be mentioned that Ahmed Hassanein represented the University of Oxford as a fencer. In any case, it is possible for him to be a sincere Egyptian patriot and none the less to entertain equally sincere friendship with members of the nation to which justice is not always done by the Younger Egypt.

He began his career at home in the Ministry of the Interior at Cairo. During the War when Martial Law was in force in Egypt he was attached to General Sir John Maxwell, a very old friend of his country. Now he has entered the diplomatic service, for which a wide experience of life, rare in so young a man, as well as his linguistic gifts eminently qualify him. He has occasionally consulted me as an elder friend and as the father of my son on certain matters of personal interests to himself. I may therefore claim to know him intimately and I cannot refrain from recording my testimony that in all such questions, and especially in a very delicate matter which he submitted to me, I have always found him generous in his judgments and, for I know no other way of expressing what I mean, a great gentleman.

The story of his exploration of desert tracts unknown to geography and his discovery of two oases whose existence was only a vague tradition, is the record of a great adventure of endurance. It is told so modestly and with such sober avoidance of overstatement that readers who have no experience of the vicissitudes of desert travel may perhaps hardly realize what courage and perseverance its successful accomplishment demanded. There is also another virtue besides these which is indispensable for penetration into regions where the isolated inhabitants regard every intrusion with profound suspicion, and that is one which Hassanein appears to possess instinctively—the virtue of tact.

English readers are perhaps rather disposed to think of the desert in the terms with which romance has made them familiar, for which the grim reality offers little justification. There is indeed a romance of the desert—the romance of loyalties and sacrifices under the shadow of the inevitable, which is an element in the true romance. And that will not be found lacking in a book which bears upon it the impress of truth, interpreting the beauty which the desert can assume, the spiritual influence and inspiration of the great solitudes, the perpetual consciousness prevailing there of the narrowness of the borderline between life and death.

Apart from its intrinsic interest as a record of discovery and the light which it throws on the origin, teaching and influence of the Senussi fraternity, this volume will be welcome to many because its pages carry the reader away into the atmosphere of a great peace. He will be aware for a while of an ambience where the coarse and the trivial and the competitive do not exist. He will find himself in touch with men who, unconscious of the urge and tumult of a world for which they would have no use, lead strenuous but dignified contemplative lives. And as he perceives how for them privation and danger and even routine are illuminated by the conviction of unalterable faith in the guiding hand of Providence, he will probably formulate the silent hope that these dwellers in the lonely places may be left untouched by the invasion of the modern spirit. Their pleasures are as touchingly simple as their thoughts. These thoughts and these simple pleasures we may for a passing hour share as they are presented to us by a hand which seems to me to have an unerring touch in conveying fidelity of outline and colour.

In conclusion, it is a grateful duty to add that Hassanein Bey has more than once confirmed to me in conversation what is suggested in the dedication of his book, namely that he could not have undertaken his adventurous journey without the assistance and support which he received from his sovereign. The promotion of enterprise is no doubt an inherited impulse in King Fouad, and it is gratifying to feel that his encouragement may confidently be anticipated for that scientific and historical research for which Egypt still offers such an ample field.

The achievement of Hassanein Bey and the spirit in

which his book is written cannot fail to appeal to the sympathies of my countrymen, and he has added another to his services by thus promoting the spirit of good-feeling between the country of his education and the land of his birth which all are anxious to see restored.

RENNELL RODD.

Contents

CHAP.		PAGE
	The Desert	23
I	The Planning of the Journey	31
II	The Blessing of the Baggage	34
III	Supplies and Equipment	37
IV	Plots and Omens	47
V	The Senussis	56
VI	The Peace of Jaghbub	68
VII	Meals—and Medicine	76
VIII	Sandstorms and the Road to Jalo	83
IX	At the Oasis of Jalo	93
X	On the Trek	111
XI	The Road to Zieghen Well	128
XII	The Changing Desert and a Corrected Map	148
XIII	Kufra—Old Friends and a Change of Plan	159
XIV	Kufra—its Place on the Map	171
XV	The "Lost" Oases—Arkenu	185
XVI	The "Lost" Oases—Ouenat	197
XVII	Night Marches to Erdi	210
XVIII	Entering the Sudan	228
XIX	To Furawia on Short Rations	244
XX	Journey's End	257

APPENDICES

PAGE

NOTE ON THE CARTOGRAPHICAL RESULTS OF HASSANEIN BEY'S JOURNEY 271

CONCLUSIONS DERIVED FROM THE GEOLOGICAL DATA COLLECTED BY HASSANEIN BEY DURING HIS KUFRA-OUENAT EXPEDITION 300

NOTES ON THE GEOLOGY OF HASSANEIN BEY'S EXPEDITION, SOLLUM–DARFUR, 1923 303

INDEX 313

List of Illustrations

Between pages 82 and 83:

Ahmed Hassanein

H.M. King Fouad I of Egypt

Siwa

Door to the Tomb of the Grand Senussi

Sayed Idris el Senussi

A Cloister at the Mosque of Jaghbub

The Dome of the Mosque at Jaghbub

Hawaria, a Landmark of Kufra

Remains of a Petrified Forest on the way to Jalo

Jalo

El Taj, the Senussi Headquarters at Kufra

Between pages 158 and 159:

Tuareg (Camel Man) with Hide Shield, Spears and War Kit

A Tebu with his Camel

Camels crossing Sand Dunes

A Senussi Prince at Kufra

The Son of the Governor of Kufra

Sayed Mohammed el Abid

The " King " of Ouenat

Sidi Hussein Wakil

The Council of Kufra

A View of the Desert from the Hills of Arkenu

The Valley of Ouenat
The Caravan arriving at Ouenat

Between pages 196 and 197:
The Caravan approaching the Granite Hills of Ouenat
Rock Carvings discovered by the Explorer at Ouenat
The Hills of Ouenat
The Explorer's Camp at the Foot of the Granite Hills
The Rock Valley Wells found at Ouenat
The Valley of Erdi
The Valley of Arkenu
The First Tree seen approaching Erdi
The Well of Erdi
A Bidiyat Family
A Zaghawa Girl

The Desert

ON my first trip through the Libyan Desert I took a vow.

We had lost our way and we had lost all hope. There was no sign of the oasis we sought, no sign of any well near by. The desert seemed cruel and merciless, and I vowed that if ever we came through alive I would not return again.

Two years later I was back in the same desert, at the same spot where we had lost our way, and landed at the same well that had saved our lives on the previous occasion.

The desert calls, but it is not easy to analyse its attraction and its charm. Perhaps the most wonderful part of desert life is the desert night. You have walked the whole day on blistered feet, because even walking was less painful than riding on a camel ; you have kept up with the caravan with eyes half shut, you follow mechanically the rhythm of the camels' steps. Your throat is parched and there is no well in sight. The men are no more in the humour to sing. Their faces are drawn with exhaustion and with eyes bloodshot they keep a vague, hopeless look on the ever-faint line between the blue of the sky and the dull yellow of the sand. The sheepskin water vessels dangle limply on either side of the camels.

We do not talk very much in the desert. The

desert breeds silence. And when we are in trouble we avoid one another's eyes. There is no need for speech. Everybody knows what is happening and everybody bears it with fortitude and dignity, for to grumble is to throw blame on the Almighty, a thing that no Beduin will do. To the Beduin, this is the life that was intended for him; it is the route that God decreed him to take; maybe it leads to the death that the Almighty has chosen for him. Therefore he must accept it. No man can run away from that which God has decreed, says the Beduin. "*Wherever you may be, Death will reach you . . . even though you take your refuge in fortified towers.*"

But it is at such times as these that you vow, if your life is spared, that you will never come back to the desert again.

Then, the day's work is at an end. Camp is pitched. No tents are erected, for the men are too exhausted, too careless to mind what happens to their bodies. And night falls. It may be a starlit night, or there may be a moon. Gradually, a serenity gets hold of you. Gradually, after a day of silence, conversation starts. Feeble jokes are cracked. One of the men, probably the youngest of the caravan, ventures a joke with more cheerfulness than the rest and his voice is pitched in a higher key. Unconsciously the Beduins attune their voices to that higher, louder pitch and the volume of sound increases. The desert is working her charm.

The gentle night breeze revives the spirits of the caravan. In a few minutes the empty *fantasses* are used as drums and there is song and dance. At the first sound of music men may have been tending the camels, repairing the luggage, or the camels' saddles, but that first note brings all the caravan round the embers of the dying fire. Every one looks at his comrades to make sure that all are alive and happy, and every one tries to be a little more cheerful than his neighbour, to give him more confidence. There is a game of make-believe, a little ghastly in its beginnings. We force ourselves to be cheerful, to make light of our troubles. "The camels are all right—I saw to that wound, and it is not so bad as I thought," says one. "Bu Hassan says he has sighted the landmark of the well not far to our right," says another. We work ourselves up by degrees to a belief that everything is really all right. It is bluff, maybe, from beginning to end, but the charm of the desert has prevailed.

It is as though a man were deeply in love with a very fascinating but cruel woman. She treats him badly, and the world crumples in his hand; at night she smiles on him and the whole world is a paradise. The desert smiles and there is no place on earth worth living in but the desert.

Song and dance take out from the men of the caravan the little vitality that is left after the ravages of the day. Their spirit is exhausted and they fall asleep. They sleep beneath the beautiful dome of the sky and the stars. Few people in civilization know the pleasure of just sitting down and looking at the stars. No wonder the Arabs were masters of the science of astronomy! When the day's work is done the solitary Beduin has nothing left but to sit down and watch the movements of the stars and absorb the uplifting sense of comfort that they give to the spirit.

These stars become like friends that one meets every day. And when they go, it is not abruptly as when men say farewell at a parting, but it is like watching a friend fade gradually from view, with the hope of seeing him again the following night.

"*To prayers, O ye believers—prayers are better than sleep!*" The cry comes from the first man of the caravan to awake. A few stars are still scattered in the sky. The men get up and there is nothing better illustrates the phrase "collect their bodies." Every limb is aching and again their throats are parched. Yet what changed men they are! There is hope in them, confidence, perhaps an inward belief that all will come well.

The world then is a grey void and only the morning fire breaks the cold north breeze. Our eyes instinctively turn to the East where the sun is rising. If there are no clouds, there comes a yellowish tinge in the sky that throws a curious elusive, elongated shadow behind camels and men, so faint that you can scarcely call it a shadow at all. Then comes a reddish tinge that gives warmth. It is just between dawnbreak and sunrise that there is colour in the desert. Once the sun is risen there is nothing but the endless stretch of blue and yellow, and the blue fades and fades until by midday the sky is almost wrung dry of colour.

Morning brings new vitality; night brings peace and serenity. These are the hours wherein one learns the desert's charm.

In the silence of these vast, open spaces human sensitiveness becomes so sharpened that eventually the desert traveller feels the nearness of some inhabited oasis. Likewise his instinct tells him of the few hundred miles that separate him from any breathing thing. In the silent infinity of the desert body, mind and soul are cleansed. Man feels nearer to God, feels the presence of a mighty Power from which nothing any longer diverts his attention. Little by little an inevitable fatalism and an unshakeable belief in the wisdom of God's decree bring resignation even to the extent of offering his life to the desert without grudge. There are times when he feels that it really does not matter. . . .

The desert brings out the best that is in every man. Civilization confronts the crowd with danger, and each one fights for himself and his own safety. In the desert self becomes less and less important. Each tries to do the best he can for his comrades. Let disaster threaten a caravan, there may be one man who can see a chance to save himself, but I do not believe there is a Beduin who would desert his comrades and so save his own life. One of the most appalling things that can happen in the desert is a shortage of water, and you would think that in such a case you would try to keep what water you have for yourself. Instead of that, you find yourself with your favourite water bottle, taking it in your arms, going round the men asking would any of them like a drink, as nonchalantly as though there were plenty of it and to spare. The question of personal safety is eliminated. Whatever happens, let it happen to the whole caravan; you do not want to escape alone. That is the feeling that gets hold of you.

I never cease to marvel at the Beduin serenity and courage, which nothing disturbs. In desert travel there are three elements—camels, water supply, the guide. Camels, the best of them, and for no apparent reason, give in, as it happened when I left Kufra and one of my best camels died on the second night ; while, on the other hand, the weakest camel of the caravan, which left Kufra tottering under its load, went through the whole trip, about 950 miles, and arrived tottering at El Fasher. " God will protect it," said its Beduin owner when rebuked for bringing such a sorry animal, and in truth God did protect it. The death of a camel is a serious matter for it means throwing away most, perhaps the whole, of its load. Water is carried chiefly in sheepskins, and the best of sheepskins, tested for days and weeks beforehand, have suddenly started to leak or the water to evaporate from them ; or, in night trekking two camels may bump together and cause one or two sheepskins to burst. And then, the guide may, for various reasons, say that his head has gone round and round, which means he has lost his head ; if there are clouds that hide the sun for a few hours, or one mistake in a landmark, it may cause the guide to lose his way. But there is one thing still more necessary than these three items—camels, water, guide. It is Faith, profound and illimitable Faith.

The desert can be beautiful and kindly, and the caravan fresh and cheerful, but it can also be cruel and overwhelming, and the wretched caravan, beaten down by misfortune, staggers desperately along. It is when your camels droop their heads from thirst and exhaustion,—when your water supply has run short and there is no sign of the next well,—when your men are listless and without hope,—when the map you carry is a blank, because the desert is uncharted,—when your guide, asked about the route, answers with a shrug of the shoulders that God knows best,—when you scan the horizon, and all around, wherever you look, it is always the same hazy line between the pale blue of the sky and the yellow of the sand,—when there is no landmark, no sign to give the slightest excuse for hope,—when that immense expanse looks like, feels like, a circle drawing tighter and tighter round your parched throat,—it is then that the Beduin feels the need of a Power bigger even than that ruthless desert. It is then that the Beduin, when he has offered his prayers to this Almighty Power for deliverance, when he has offered up his prayers and they have not been granted, it is then that he draws his *jerd* around him, and sinking down upon the sands awaits with astounding equanimity the decreed death. This is the faith in which the journey across the desert must be made.

The desert is terrible and it is merciless, but to the desert all those who once have known it must return.

MAP OF THE LIBYAN DESERT
SHOWING THE AUTHOR'S ROUTES

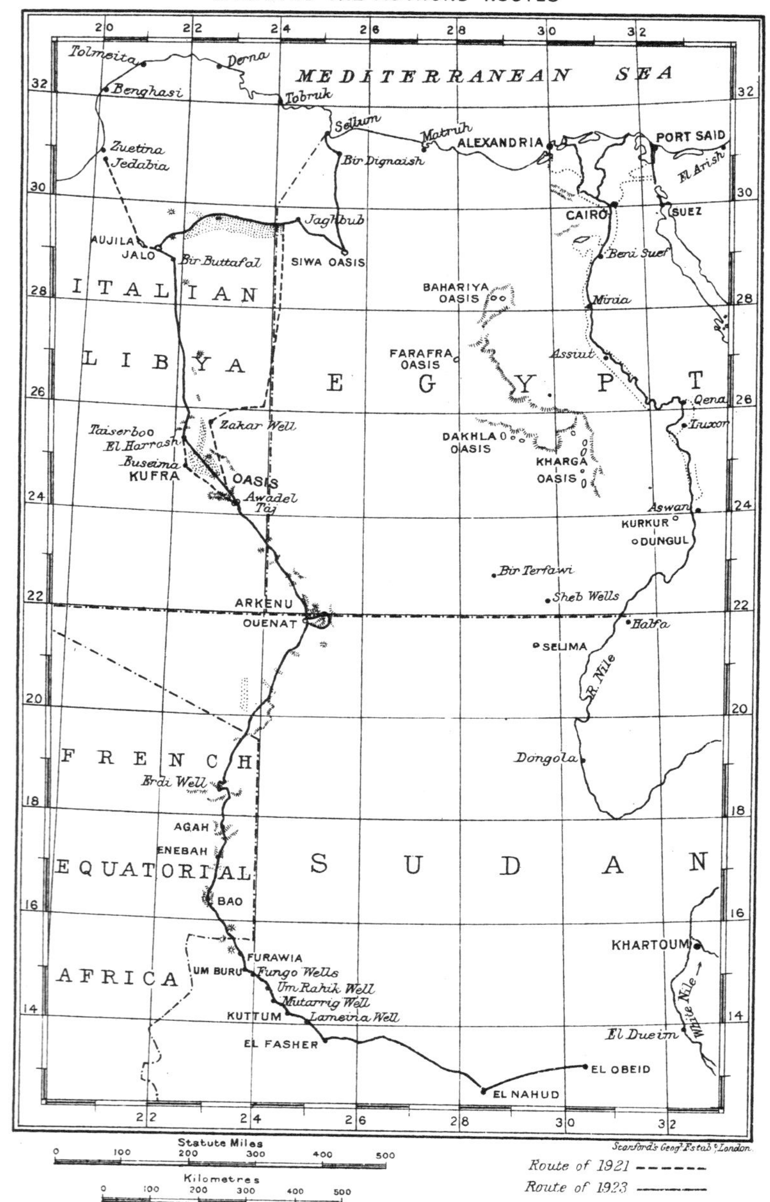

CHAPTER I

The Planning of the Journey

THIS is the story of a journey which I made in 1923 from Sollum on the Mediterranean to El Obeid in the Sudan, some 2,200 miles. In the course of it I was fortunate enough to discover two "lost" oases, Arkenu and Ouenat, which previously had not been known to geographers. My journey was primarily a scientific expedition, but I have tried in this book to avoid wearying the reader with technical matter and to write a straightforward narrative which may be of some interest even to those who are not acquainted with Egypt, the Sudan or the Libyan Desert.

It had always been my greatest ambition to penetrate to Kufra, a group of oases in the Libyan Desert, which had only once been visited by an explorer. In 1879 the intrepid German, Rohlfs, had succeeded, but he had barely escaped with his life and all his notebooks and the results of his scientific observations were destroyed.

In 1915 I had been fortunate enough to meet in Cairo Sayed Idris El Senussi, the famous head of the Senussi Brotherhood, when he was returning from a pilgrimage to Mecca. The capital of the Senussi is Kufra, and when in 1917 I went on a mission to Sayed Idris with Colonel The Honble. Milo Talbot, C.B., R.E., a distinguished officer who had retired from the Egyptian Army, but had returned to the service during the Great War, and renewed my acquaintance with that notable man at Zuetina, a little port near Jedabya in Cyrenaica, I seized the opportunity and told him of my ambition.

Sayed Idris was most sympathetic and asked me to let him know when I proposed to make the expedition, so that he might give me the help and countenance without which a journey to Kufra could not be undertaken. I met him again at Akrama near Tobruk and told him then that I would set out as soon as I was free from my war duties. At Tobruk Mr. Francis Rodd, an old Balliol friend, was with me and we decided that we would go together.

When the War was over Mrs. Rosita Forbes (now Mrs. A. McGrath) brought me a letter of introduction from Mr. Rodd and asked that she might join us. We proceeded to plan an expedition *à trois*, but, when the time came, Mr. Rodd was prevented from making one of the party. Finally in 1920 Mrs. Forbes and I set out by ourselves and with the friendly co-operation of the Italian authorities and the promised countenance and assistance of Sayed Idris—he provided us with our caravan—we reached Kufra in January, 1921.

But this trip to Kufra, interesting as it was, only tempted me to explore the vast unknown desert which lay beyond. There were rumours, too, of "lost" oases which even the people of Kufra knew only by hearsay and tradition, and I returned to Cairo resolved to make another expedition, and instead of coming straight back from Kufra, as Mrs. Forbes and I had done, to strike south across the unknown desert until I came to Wadai and the Sudan.

Again on the first trip our only scientific instruments were an aneroid barometer and a prismatic compass. It was not, therefore, possible for me to make exact scientific observations, and all that I brought back were notes for a simple compass traverse of the route based on the meagre material I had obtained. I was eager to check Rohlfs' observations and to determine once and for all the place of Kufra on the map.

In 1922, then, I submitted my plan for a journey across the desert from the Mediterranean to the Sudan to His Majesty, King Fouad I, who had been gracious enough to display his interest in my first trip by decorating me with the Medal of Merit. He sympathized warmly with my project, directed that I should be given long leave of absence from my official duties, and later caused the expenses of the expedition to be defrayed by the Egyptian Treasury. Indeed, my expedition could not possibly have met with the success that it did, had it not been for His Majesty's invaluable support.

I completed my preparations and in December, 1922, I had collected my baggage in the house of my father so that in accordance with the ancient practice of my race it might be blessed before I set out on my expedition across the Libyan Desert.

CHAPTER II

The Blessing of the Baggage

"ALLAH *yesadded khatak*—May God guide your steps."

The Arabic words fell reverently on the air of the great bare room, where candle light and clouds of drifting incense contended for supremacy. Along the walls bulked a strange collection of baggage —big boxes, little boxes, sheepskin water-bags, tin *fantasses* for carrying water, stuffed food sacks, bales of tents, carrying cases of leather and metal containing scientific instruments, and my own personal kit. After the bustle of getting everything corded and tied and strapped and arranged in order, a hush had come as we took our stand in the middle of the room. Outside the Egyptian night had fallen and across the garden the faint hum of the evening life of Cairo entered our windows.

We were three—myself; Abdullahi, a Nubian from Aswan who was to be one of my most trusted men; and Ahmed, also from Aswan, looking half a wreck after a spell of city life as he stood beside us, but later to prove himself an excellent cook and on the trek "the life of the party."

Before us stood a tall old man with white flowing beard dressed in a deep orange-coloured silk *Kuftan*. His delicately wrinkled features spoke of the peace that comes with saintliness. His long slim fingers clicked softly against each other the amber beads of a rosary. The white smoke from the incense in the wrought silver censer, held by a servant beside him, mounted in a delicate spiral. The saintly man put aside his rosary and lifted his hands, palms upward, towards Heaven. His voice, thin with age but clear with conviction, sounded the prayer for those about to go upon a journey.

"May God guide your steps, may He crown your efforts with success and may He return you to us safe and victorious."

He went round the room, swinging the censer rhythmically before each pile of baggage and uttering little prayers. This was the traditional ceremony of the blessing of the baggage, made sacred by ages of Arab usage at the setting out of a caravan. It has largely fallen into disuse in these latter days, but in the house of my father, who walks through life deeply absorbed in scholarship and the faith of the Prophet, it was the most natural thing in the world, when the only son was going forth into the desert.

As I stood before the saintly man to receive his blessing, I was no longer an Egyptian of to-day, but a Beduin, going back to the desert where his father's fathers had pitched their tents.

Then I turned and went to my father.

For fifteen years, since I had been sent to Europe for my education, our ways had rarely met. Sometimes I wished that I had studied the subjects in which he was interested so that I might profit by his profound learning.

"He is going to live in another generation ; let him

get the education he will need for it," my father had said once of a fellow-scholar of mine. But now when I was returning to the desert from which our forefathers had come we knew what was in each other's minds and understood.

After a moment's silence, he put his hands on my shoulders and prayed: "May safety be your companion, may God guide your steps, may He give you fortitude, and may He give success to your undertakings."

The baggage blessed, Abdullahi and Ahmed took the heavy stuff and set out for Sollum, leaving with me the scientific instruments and the cameras for more careful handling. On the 19th of December I left Alexandria by boat for Sollum.

CHAPTER III

Supplies and Equipment

THE 21st found me disembarking at Sollum, which is a tiny seaport close to the western frontier of Egypt. There we were to take camel and go by way of Jaghbub to Jalo, the important centre of desert trade, where our own caravan would be organized and the great trek southward begun. A journey like this of mine always has several starting points, each with its own variety of emotions and experiences. In the dimly lighted, incense-scented room in my father's house the enterprise was a kind of dream, fascinating in its possibilities but hardly yet real. At Sollum came the practical reality of assembling stores and equipment, packing and repacking to get everything into the smallest compass and most convenient shape for handling, checking it all over to make sure that nothing had been forgotten, and arranging with camel-owners for the first stage of the trip. At Jalo would come the third start, with my own caravan at my back and the road to Kufra, already traversed but still by no means familiar, before me. Then the last setting out of all, as I rode out of Kufra with my face toward the unknown and the unexplored.

Abdullahi and Ahmed were already at Sollum, with the heavy baggage, and the camels were arranged for, the agreement only awaiting my approval. We proceeded to get our outfit and supplies in order.

Some description of the two Egyptians who accompanied me throughout the expedition may be of interest. Abdullahi was a Nubian from Aswan, heavily built, well set up and strong, with a pair of small eyes, deeply set, that could mask a malicious sense of humour with great indifference or dignity. A man of about forty, he was well educated, and knew his Koran well. I met him first in 1914, when he was attached to the Idrissi family in Egypt, and I took an enormous liking to him because of his deeply rooted sense of humour and his loyalty. He was honest too, extremely honest, and therefore I put him in charge of the commissariat. In Abdullahi's kit one could always find anything that was needed, from strips of leather with primitive Beduin needles for mending shoes to elaborate contrivances for propping up a broken tent pole. He was ready, moreover, with "inaccuracies" to suit every situation, whether he wanted me to appear to be a wandering Beduin from Egypt, or a merchant, or an important Government official when we landed in the midst of officialdom in the Sudan. Abdullahi had one peculiarity: between sunset and an hour or two later it was apparently a most difficult task to keep him awake; though he might be sitting down holding a discussion, he would go on dozing as he sat. On one occasion, we had just finished dinner, and it being about the hour, Zerwali, my Beduin loyal companion, who joined our caravan at Jalo, as a joke took a lot of *zatar* (a strong scent used for flavouring tea) and put it in Abdullahi's tea. In between dozes, the latter woke up, tasted his tea, knew what had happened, said nothing, but simply put back his glass. After a while, however, Abdullahi turned round and said to Zerwali: "I believe you are expecting a man to see you—I think I hear him coming." As Zerwali got up to look, Abdullahi quietly changed round the glasses, so that Zerwali drank the highly "flavoured" tea while Abdullahi dozed off peacefully once more.

Abdullahi's business instinct came out at its best when we arrived at inhabited country towards the end of the journey and were short of food. He collected all the odds and ends of the caravan, including empty tins and bottles of medicine, even the few used Gillette blades, and bartered them with the natives for butter, milk, spices and leather.

It was Abdullahi, also, who was greatly upset when I showed my film of the expedition at a lecture given before H.M. King Fouad at the Royal Opera House in Cairo. When Abdullahi found that he appeared in many of the pictures with a tattered shirt, he resented being shown to his King in such an unsuitable garment, and asked if something could not be done so that he should appear in a shirt that was cleaner and less well worn.

Ahmed, too, was a Nubian from Aswan, a slight, wiry fellow who never gave in. He was my valet and cook. Although very well educated, he became a cook because he liked to live a free life; had he become a religious man, as his father wished, he would have been obliged to lead a model life, and that, apparently, did not appeal to him. He was always cheerful, and though no one in the caravan did so much cursing, the Beduins did not mind him. A word that Ahmed said, had it come from any other, there would have been bloodshed, but the Beduins got accustomed to him, and there was only one row. After his cooking was over Ahmed used to sit down with the Beduins and scorn their knowledge of religion ; he would prove his superiority by reciting from memory bits of poetry about religion and the Arabic language and some of the Prophet's sayings. Never once did Ahmed fail to make me a glass of tea even in circumstances of the greatest difficulty. On one occasion after a whole night's trek he was suffering badly from a hurt foot, and as we were pitching camp I told him casually that I did not want any breakfast or tea until I had slept and ordered him to go to bed at once. Nevertheless, just as I was getting my shelter ready, Ahmed arrived with a steaming glass of tea. He cursed all the Beduins, but there was no Beduin in the caravan for whom, if he felt ill, Ahmed would not do everything in his power to give him relief. He had learnt gradually the use of such medicines as I had, and frequently when in doubt would bring me a little bottle to ask whether it was quinine or aspirin.

The requirements for a desert trek are simple, and the list of what one takes with one is almost stereotyped. For food there are, first of all, flour, rice, sugar and tea. All the people of the desert are very fond of meat, but it naturally cannot be carried. One must either shoot it by the way or go without. Tea is the drink in the Libyan Desert, rather than coffee, and for that there are two reasons. The first is religious, the second is practical. Sayed Ibn Ali El Senussi, the founder of that interesting brotherhood that controls the destinies of the country through which I was to travel, forbade his followers all luxuries. His prohibition included tobacco and coffee, but, for some reason, did not extend to tea. His followers, therefore, are tea-drinkers, if you can call by the same name the delicate, aromatic, pale fluid that graces the tea-tables of Europe and America, and the murky, bitter liquid which sustains the Beduin on his marches and revives him at the day's end. The second reason is that tea is a stimulant to work on, while coffee is not. Tea is the thing with which to finish off each meal of the desert day and to refresh the weary traveller at the end of a hard day's trek ; leaving coffee for the less strenuous life of the oasis and the home.

After these staples come dates ; or perhaps they ought to be put first. The camels live on dates, as does the whole caravan, when other foods are exhausted or there is no time to halt and cook a meal. But the dates are not the rich, sweet, sugary things one is accustomed to for dessert or a picnic delicacy in Western lands. The date which one must use for desert travel has little sugar about it. Sugar breeds thirst and where wells are days apart the water supply is not to be prodigally spent.

I took some tinned things with me, bully beef, vegetables and fruits ; but tins are heavy and to carry enough food in tins for a long trek would demand a score of extra camels or more. There was a little coffee in our stores, but we seldom drank it. I used most of it for presents to the friends we made along the way. A few bottles of malted milk tablets proved useful for emergency lunches when food ran low. The Beduins, however, were not keen on them. " They fill us up," they said, " without the pleasure of the taste."

That was our commissary list, except for salt and some spices, especially pepper for the *asida*, a pudding of boiled flour and oil, made pepper hot. There was little variety ; but variety is the one thing one has to give up when one's supplies are to be carried by animals who must themselves live chiefly on what they can carry. There were no luxuries, no matter how pleasant they might have been to relieve the monotony of rice, unleavened bread, dates and tea. If one has experience in desert travel, and the wisdom to learn by it, one takes no foods of which there is not enough to feed everyone in the caravan. On the trek in the desert there is no distinction of rank or class, high or low.

The sole exception to the rule of no luxuries was tobacco. Since only one of the men who were with me at any time on the trip smoked, however, this was no real violation of the rule. A stock of Egyptian cigarettes and tobacco afforded me constant pleasure and comfort throughout the journey.

Next comes water, the one great and unceasing problem of desert travel. Men have lived for an unbelievable number of days without food, whether from necessity or from curiosity. But the man who could go for four days without water would be a miracle. A desert is a desert, just because it lacks water. The desert traveller must think first of his drinking supply.

We carried water in two ways. The regular supply was held in twenty-five *girbas*, the traditional sheep-skin water-carrier of the desert. Each holds from four to six gallons—and is easily burst if two camels carrying *girbas* bump together in the dark on a rocky road ! So the reserve water supply for emergencies is carried in *fantasses*. They are long tin containers, oblong or oval shaped in cross section to hang easily along the camel's side. We had four *fantasses* holding four gallons each and four others holding twelve gallons each. Our full supply, therefore, was something like 200 gallons, enough to last our caravan, when it was finally organized, on the longest trek from well to well that we were likely to encounter. We carried only our reserve supply in *fantasses*, although they were less liable to injury, because the *girbas*, when empty, took up so little space. All twenty-five of them could be carried on one camel, while only two *fantasses* went to a camel, full or empty. We had no camels to spare.

There were also some individual water-bottles, but most of them were soon discarded because the men hated the nuisance of carrying them. A few were kept for cooling water, later on in the journey when the weather became hot. The evaporation of the moisture through the canvas sides of the bottles or bags kept the water within at a pleasant temperature.

Four tents, two bell shaped and two rectangular, and numerous cooking utensils, of which the chief was a huge brass *halla* or bowl for boiling rice, made up the tale of our equipment. For emergencies there was a medicine chest, with quinine, iodine, cotton and bandages, bismuth salicylate for dysentery, morphine tablets and a hypodermic syringe, anti-scorpion serum —which was to plunge me into an apparently serious predicament and rescue me from it—zinc ointment for eczema, indigestion tablets and Epsom salts. I had a primitive surgical kit and a few dental instruments and remedies which a dentist friend had given me. I was equipped to take care of the simple, everyday ills ; if anything more serious befell I should have to say, " Recovery comes from God."

For hunting and possible defence I took three rifles, three automatic pistols, and a shot-gun. By the time of our return the shot-gun had been given as a present, and the rest of the arsenal had been increased by six rifles and one pistol. When the rifles arrived at Sollum in their characteristically shaped boxes, it was immediately rumoured through the town that I was carrying a machine gun, for some mysterious purpose which gossip elaborated to suit itself.

In order to make the report of what I found and saw as vivid and truthful as possible I took five cameras. Three of them were Kodaks, which functioned perfectly to the end ; one a more elaborate instrument with a focal-plane shutter, which was ruined by the penetrating sand ; and the last a cinema machine. For all the cameras I carried Eastman Kodak films, which were packed with elaborate care, first in air-tight tins, then in tin cases, sawdust filled, and finally in wooden boxes. These precautions in packing proved to be none too great, in view of the intense heat of the first part of the route and the rain and dampness which we encountered later on in the Sudan. For the cinema camera I took 9,000 feet of film. Fortune was with me in all the photographic work. The films were not developed until my return eight months later to Egypt, but the percentage of failures was gratifyingly low. For clothing I took the usual Beduin garb of white shirts and long drawers, both made of calico and a woollen *jerd,* the voluminous Beduin wrap ; also silk jackets and waistcoats and cloth drawers like riding breeches, but reaching to the ankles, the latter were used only on ceremonious occasions, such as entering or leaving an oasis ; there were naturally a few changes of each. I did not wish to put on the desert dress until the end of the first stage of the journey, so I left Sollum in old khaki coat and riding breeches, which had already seen their best days. With yellow Beduin slippers on my feet, the only possible wear in desert travel, and a Jaegar woollen night-cap on my head, for the weather was keenly cold, I must have been an amusing figure when we made our start.

When travelling into unknown lands, especially in the East, it is important to be able to make presents to those of prominence whom you meet. I had what seemed to me an enormous supply of silks, copper bowls, and censers inlaid with silver, bottles of scent, silk handkerchiefs, silver teapots and tea glasses, silver call-bells—which the Beduin is delighted to be able to use for summoning his slaves instead of the usual clapping of the hands. When I saw all this array being packed, I felt sure that we should bring half of it back with us. But by the time we had reached Kufra, I discovered that not only those who were of use to me this time but every one who had rendered the slightest service on my previous trip was expectant of reward for services rendered. What with postponed expectations and the opportunities which the present trip afforded for making presents, we had none too many of the goods I have mentioned. In making these gifts, however, I did not feel that it was so much an endeavour to smooth the way of my expedition, as a courtesy from a Beduin of the town to his brother Beduin of the desert.

Most important of all for the ultimate value of the

expedition, if it was to have any, was the scientific apparatus, which is detailed in Dr. Ball's report in the Appendix.

The fortnight at Sollum was filled with busy days. Simple as our equipment was, everything had to be as nearly right as thought and care could achieve. Things carried on camel back, put on each morning and taken off each night and built into barricades against weather and possible attacks, must be snugly and securely packed. At the end of a day's trek, careless or tired camelmen often find it easier to let boxes and bundles drop without ceremony from the camel's sides than to handle them with proper care.

CHAPTER IV

Plots and Omens

MY plans were all made for a trek straight south to Jaghbub, when, two days before the date determined upon for the start, an incident happened which disquieted me.

I was sitting one evening in my room in the little Government rest-house, busy with the figures of my scientific observations. There came a knock at the door. I could not imagine who could want me at that hour, but I went to the door and opened it a little way. A Beduin whom I did not know was standing there, muffled Beduin fashion in his *jerd*. I shut the door quickly and demanded, " Who are you ? "

" A friend," was the answer which somehow did not convince me.

" What is your name and your business ? " I asked.

" I am a friend and I have something to tell you which you ought to know," explained my visitor through the closed door.

I opened the door and demanded what he had to tell. He came in.

" You are going by the straight road to Jaghbub ? " he half queried. I nodded assent.

" Don't go," he continued with vigour.

" Why not ? " I asked.

" The Bey is a rich man," he replied. " He carries

with him great stores of the bounty of God and the Beduins are greedy. The rumour is that you have many boxes of gold."

I could see that he half believed it, though he was pretending not to.

"The camelmen have agreed with friends on the road that you shall be waylaid and robbed. You will lose your money and probably your life."

"One can always fight," I suggested.

"Perhaps," he agreed, "if you had plenty of men of your own."

I hadn't, so I proceeded to question him further about his information. The story seemed straight enough, and when I learned that my visitor was a relative of a man to whom I had done a good turn when on the last mission to the Senussis, I felt that it would be wise to believe him. I thanked him for his warning and he went away into the night. I sat down to consider the unpleasantly melodramatic situation.

The desert people are quick to ferret out your purpose if they can, and if they cannot, to build up imaginary stories to account for what you are and have and intend to do. Much of our paraphernalia was in boxes. Boxes, to the Beduin mind, mean treasure. If three rifles in a case could be translated into a machine gun, why should not cameras and instruments in boxes be translated into gold and bank-notes? It was no wonder that the men whose camels we had hired were convinced that I was going into the desert with vast wealth for some unknown purpose. It was quite possible that they planned to rob me. It was a cheerful outlook for the very beginning of our journey. A fight, no matter how successful, would be a poor start for our undertaking. I decided that it would be better to avoid this first obstacle in our path rather than to encounter it.

Promptly the next day the camel-owners whose pleasant little plan had been revealed to me found themselves discharged. Others with their camels were forthwith hired to take me to Siwa. Instead of the straight line to Jaghbub we would go along the two sides of the triangle, whose apexes were Sollum, Siwa and Jaghbub. It would materially lengthen this first part of our journey, but after all time and distance were less important than safe arrival. The road by way of Siwa had several advantages. It lay in Egyptian territory and not in the country inhabited by the tribes to which the first set of camelmen belonged. In the second place it ran through more frequented territory, where a treacherous waylaying of our caravan would have been more perilous to the waylayers. Lastly, our quick departure after the change of plan gave the conspirators no time to develop any new plot if they had wanted to. It looked safe and it proved to be as safe as it looked.

On January 1st the caravan started and three days later Lieutenant Bather very kindly took me in a motor car to catch it up. We found the caravan at Dignaish, 36 miles out, and saying good-bye to the lieutenant, I took up the journey.

It was then a six days' trek to Siwa. Our spare time was profitably spent in camouflaging the boxes and cases in our luggage to look like the usual Beduin impedimenta. The only event of interest during the six days was the first of three good omens that foretold success to the trip. On the fifth day in the late afternoon I saw a gazelle feeding a little distance off our track. Without other thought than the pleasant anticipation of fresh meat, I set out after it. As I went I heard discouraging shouts and howls from the men behind me. I could not understand their reluctance to have me go after the game, in view of the Beduin's love of meat. I imagined that they were afraid that I would be led away some distance from them and thus hold up the progress of the caravan. The reason did not seem sufficient, so I pursued my quest. After some chase I got a shot at the gazelle and brought it down.

As I approached the caravan with my game, I was surprised again. The men came running toward me with waving arms and shouts of joyful congratulation. I understood their present state of mind no more than I had their former one, until the explanation was forthcoming.

Then I learned that among the Beduins the first shot fired at game after a caravan sets out is the critical one. If it is a miss, disaster is certain to overtake the caravan before the journey's end. If it is a hit, fortune will smile upon the whole undertaking. The men of the caravan had been reluctant to see me put our luck to the test so soon. If I had remembered the Beduin *travel lore,* I should have saved my first shot at game until we reached El Fasher six months later.

We were three days in Siwa, hiring other camels for the trek to Jaghbub and making a few final preparations. Siwa was the last outpost of the world I was leaving behind. There the postal service and the telegraph end. Beyond that point there is nothing to be bought except the products of the desert, or occasionally a little rice or cloth, perhaps at exorbitant prices. In the three days I enjoyed the hospitality and valuable assistance of the Frontier Districts Administration, in the persons of the Mamur Kamel Effendi and town officials and of Lieutenant Lawler, in command of the troops there.

Siwa is the biggest and most charming of oases; springs of wonderful water, excellent fruit, the best dates in the world, picturesque scenery and the quaintest and most interesting of customs. For example, if a woman loses her husband she is kept forty days without washing and nobody sees her. Her food is passed through a crack in the door. When the forty days have expired, she goes to bathe in one of the wells and everybody tries to avoid crossing her path, for she is then called *ghoula* and is supposed to bring very bad luck to anybody who sees her on that day of the first bath.

In the date market, called the *mistah,* all the dates are piled together, the best quality and the most inferior. No one thinks of touching one date that does not belong to him or mixing the dates together with a view to gaining an advantage thereby. On the other hand, anybody can go into a *mistah* and eat as much as he likes from the best quality without paying a *millieme,* but he must not take any away with him.

In Siwa there is a shrine of a saint where people may deposit their belongings for safety. If a man is going away he can take his bags with the most valuable things and put them near this shrine and nobody would dream of touching them. Literally, if any one left a bundle of gold there, no one would touch it, owing to the very simple but unshakeable belief in them that if you touch anything near that shrine and it does not belong to you, you would have bad luck for the rest of your life.

When I was ready to leave Siwa, my little group of personal retainers had doubled in number. At Sollum I had added to Abdullahi and Ahmed a man of the Monafa tribe named Hamad. He was the hardest-working individual in the entire caravan. I never saw him tired. He took charge of my camel and later of the horse which I secured at Kufra. The fourth member of the group was Ismail, a Siwi. He looked like a weakling, but on the trek he was always the last man to give in and ride a camel. Ismail was the one whom I used to take with me when prospecting for geological specimens or making elaborate scientific observations. Coming from an oasis in Egyptian territory where the post and the telegraph made connection with the outside world, he had less of the wild Beduin's suspicion that interprets every simple action of the stranger into something with an ulterior motive. Why should the Bey be chipping off bits of rock, the Beduin might say to himself, unless there were gold in it, or he intended to come and conquer the country? Not so Ismail. If the Bey wanted a bit of rock, that was for the Bey to say.

We left Siwa on the 14th with our new caravan. Our last link with the outside world was broken. At the first stop I took off my faded khaki and put on the Beduin costume and felt myself now a part of the desert life. The effect upon the men was immediate. Till now they had approached me with embarrassment and awkwardness. Now they came up naturally, kissed my hand in Beduin fashion and said: "Now you are one of us."

Our second good omen befell us a few miles out of Siwa. We found dates in our path, where some unfortunate date merchant taking his cargo to market had had an accident. Dates in the way are a promise of good fortune for the journey. Often, when a Beduin is setting out with his caravan, friends will go secretly ahead and drop dates where he will be sure to pass them. With my first shot and the gazelle and the dates in the path we had every reason to be cheerful. But the best omen of all was to come.

I had sent two men ahead with a letter to Sayed Idris at Jaghbub, to inform him of my approach. In the desert one does not rush upon a friend or a dignitary headlong and unannounced. There should be time for both to put on fresh clothing and go with dignity to the meeting as becomes gentlemen of breeding.

Two days out from Siwa I was riding some distance behind the caravan and presently came upon it halted. I asked the reason for the unusual stop and received the reply.

"Messengers have come to say that Sayed Idris will be here within an hour"; the men could scarcely conceal their excitement. To be met by the great head of the Senussis himself at the beginning of our journey was the most auspicious of omens. The rest of the message was indicative of the etiquette of the desert. "He asks the Bey to camp so that he may come to him."

We immediately made camp and before long the vanguard of Sayed Idris's caravan appeared and made camp in their turn a short distance away. A half-hour later Sayed Idris himself, with his retinue, advanced toward my camp and I went to meet him.

Sayed Idris met me with warm cordiality and we renewed the acquaintance made on our previous meetings with deep gratification on my part and apparent pleasure on his. The former trip could never have been successful without the countenance he gave to it and the assistance he rendered; how much more the present one, which was to take me three times as far and into more completely unknown regions.

In his tent we lunched on rice, stuffed chicken and sweet Beduin cakes followed by glasses of tea delicately scented with mint and rose-water. I told him of my plans and gave him news of the outside world. He was interested to know the final issue of the Peace Conference at Versailles.

At his suggestion, I brought all the men of my caravan to his tent to receive his blessing. As I stood with them and heard the familiar words fall from his lips, there came irresistibly to my mind that moment in the incense-shrouded room in Cairo and my father's blessing upon my undertaking. Then my imagination had leaped out to meet the vision of the desert, the camels, the Beduin life. Now the need for imagination was gone. I was in Beduin kit, with the camels of my caravan behind me, and the road to the goal I sought stretching ahead.

To my men the experience of being blessed by Sayed Idris himself was the greatest augury of success that we could have had. Nothing could harm us now.

In the afternoon we said farewell, both camps were

broken and both caravans took up the march, Sayed Idris going east into Egypt and I west to Jaghbub and the long trail into the desert. As we marched, my men insisted on following the track made by the caravan of Sayed Idris, to prolong the great good fortune that had befallen us.

CHAPTER V

The Senussis

ANY story of the Libyan Desert would not be complete without some consideration of the Senussis, the most important influence in that region. The subject is a complicated one. Justice might be done to it if an entire volume were available, but within the limits of a chapter only the important points of Senussi history can be touched.

The Senussis are not a race, nor a country, nor a political entity, nor a religion. They have, however, some of the characteristics of all four. In fact they are almost exclusively Beduins; they inhabit, for the most part, the Libyan Desert; they exert a controlling influence over considerable areas of that region and are recognized by the Governments of surrounding territory as a real power in the affairs of North-eastern Africa, and they are Moslems. Perhaps the best short description of the Senussis would be as a religious order whose leadership is hereditary and which exerts a predominating influence in the lives of the people of the Libyan Desert.

The history of the Brotherhood may be roughly divided into four periods. In each it took its colour from the personality of the leader. These were respectively Sayed Ibn Ali El Senussi, the founder, Sayed El Mahdi, his son, Sayed Ahmed, the nephew of the latter, and Sayed Idris, the son of El Mahdi, the present head of the Brotherhood.

Sayed Mohammed Ibn Ali El Senussi—known as the Grand Senussi—was born in Algeria in the year 1202 after the Hejira, which corresponds to 1787 in the Christian calendar. He was a descendant of the Prophet Mohammed, and had received an unusually scholarly education in the Kairawan University, in Fez and at Mecca, where he became the pupil of the famous theologian Sidi Ahmed Ibn Idris El Fasi. He developed an inclination to asceticism and a conviction that what his religion needed was a return to a pure form of Islam as exemplified in the teachings of the Prophet.

At the age of fifty-one he was compelled to leave Mecca by the opposition of the older *sheikhs*, who challenged his orthodoxy. He returned through Egypt to Cyrenaica and began to establish centres for teaching his doctrines among the Beduins.

At this point an explanation of the meaning of three Arabic words will elucidate the text. They are *zawia*, *ikhwan*, and *wakil*.

A *zawia* is a building of three rooms, its size depending on the importance of the place in which it is situated. One room is a schoolroom in which the Beduin children are taught by the *ikhwan* ; the second serves as the guest house in which travellers receive the usual three days' hospitality of Beduin custom ; in the third the *ikhwan* lives. The *zawia* is generally built near a well where travellers naturally stop. Attached to the *zawia* is often a bit of land which is cultivated by the *ikhwan*.

The *ikhwan* are the active members of the Brotherhood, who teach its principles and precepts. *Ikhwan* in Arabic is really a plural form, which means "brothers." But the singular of the word is never used, *ikhwan* having come to be used for one or more.

A *wakil* is the personal representative or deputy of the head of the Senussis.

The Grand Senussi found the Moslems of Cyrenaica fallen into heresies and in danger of rapid degeneration, not only from a religious but from a moral point of view. Some small examples may serve to illustrate this point.

At Jebel Akhdar, in the north of Cyrenaica, certain influential Beduin chiefs had established a sort of Kaba, an imitation of the true one at Mecca to which every Believer who could possibly do so should make his pilgrimage. These founders of a false Kaba tried to establish the theory that a pilgrimage thither was a worthy substitute for the *Haj*—the authentic pilgrimage to the central shrine of Islam.

The keeping of the month of Ramadan as a time of abstinence and religious contemplation is an important tenet of the Moslem faith. The Beduins used to go before the beginning of Ramadan to a certain valley called Wadi Zaza, noted for the multiple echo given back by its walls. In chorus they would shout a question, "Wadi Zaza, Wadi Zaza, shall we keep Ramadan or no?" The echo of course threw back the last word of the question, "No—no—no!" Those who had appealed thus to the oracle would then go home justified in their own minds in their desire to forgo the keeping of the fast.

There were also prevalent among the Beduins remnants of old barbaric customs—such as the killing of female children "to save them from the evils which life might bring," which stood between them and their development into worthy exponents of Islam.

In such circumstances, what the founder of the Senussi brotherhood had to give, in his teaching and preaching of a return to the pure tenets of Islam, met a poignant need.

Sayed Ibn Ali El Senussi founded his first *zawia* on African soil at Siwa, which is in Egypt close to the western frontier. From that point he moved westward into Cyrenaica, establishing *zawias* at Jalo and Aujila. He travelled westward through Tripoli and Tunis, gradually spreading his teachings among the Beduins. His reputation as a saintly man and a scholar had preceded him, and he was much sought after by the Beduin chiefs who vied with one another to give him hospitality.

On his return to Cyrenaica in the year 1843 he established at Jebel Akhdar near Derna a large *zawia* called El Zawia El Beda, the White Zawia. Until this time he had no headquarters, but led the life of a wandering teacher. He settled down at El Zawia El Beda and received visits from the leading Beduin dignitaries of Cyrenaica.

The Grand Senussi preached a pure form of Islam and strict adherence to the laws of God and His Prophet Mohammed.

His teachings may perhaps be best illustrated by a passage from a letter to the people of Wajanga, in Wadai, the original of which I saw at Kufra and translated. The passage reads as follows:

We wish to ask you in the name of Islam to obey God and His Prophet. In His dear Book He says, praise be to Him, "Oh ye, who are believers, obey God and obey the Prophet!" He also says, "He who obeys the Prophet has also obeyed God." He also says, "He who obeys God and His Prophet has won a great victory." He also says, "Those who obey God and the Prophet, they are with the prophets whom God has rewarded."

We wish to ask you to obey what God and His Prophet have ordered; making the five prayers every day, keeping the month of Ramadan, giving tithes, making the Haj to the sacred home of God (the pilgrimage to Mecca), and avoiding what God has forbidden—telling lies, slandering people behind their backs, taking unlawfully other people's money, drinking wine, killing men unlawfully, bearing false witness, and the other crimes before God.

In following these you will gain everlasting good and endless benefits which can never be taken from you.

The principal concern of the founder of the Senussis was with the religious aspect of life. He did not set out to be a political leader or to grasp temporal power. He counselled austerity of life with the same enthusiasm with which he practised it. He taught no special theological doctrines and demanded acceptance of no particular dogmas. He cared much more for what his followers did than for any technicalities of belief. His only addition to the Moslem ritual was a single prayer, which he wrote and which the Senussis use, called the *Hezb*. It is not opposed to anything taught by the older theologians, nor does it add anything to what is found in the Koran. It is simply expressed in different language. In the letter to the people of Wajanga, which I have quoted, another passage described his mission, which God had laid upon him, as that of "reminding the negligent, teaching the ignorant and guiding him who has gone astray."

He forbade all kinds of luxurious living to those who allied themselves with his Brotherhood. The possession of gold and jewels was prohibited—except for the adornment of women—and the use of tobacco and coffee. He imposed no ritual and only demanded a return to the simplest form of Islam as it was found in the teaching of the Prophet. He was intolerant of any intercourse, not only with Christians and Jews, but with that part of the Moslem world which, in his conviction, had digressed from the original meaning of Islam.

In the year 1854 Sayed Ibn Ali founded at Jaghbub the *zawia* which eventually developed into the centre of education and learning of the Senussi Brotherhood. His choice of Jaghbub was not haphazard or accidental but a demonstration of his wisdom and practical sagacity. He conceived it to be of the first importance to reconcile the different tribes of the desert to each other and to bring peace among them. One more quotation from his letter illustrates this point:

> We intend to make peace between you and the Arabs (the people of Wajanga to whom this letter is addressed are of the black race) who invade your territory and take your sons as slaves and your money. In so doing we shall be carrying out the injunction of God, who has said, "If two parties of believers come into conflict, make peace between them." Also we shall be following His direction, "Fear God, make peace among those about you and obey God and His Prophet if you are believers."

Jaghbub was a strategic point for his purpose. It stood midway between tribes on the east and on the west who had been in constantly recurring conflict. With his headquarters there the Grand Senussi could bring his influence to bear on the warring rivals and carry out the command of the Prophet to "make peace among those about you." From a practical standpoint Jaghbub was an unpromising place in which to set up such a centre of educational and religious activity as the Grand Senussi had in contemplation. It is not much of an oasis, if indeed it can be called an oasis at all. Date trees are scarce there, the water is brackish and the soil very difficult to cultivate. Its strategic importance, however, was clear and without hesitation he selected it as the site of his headquarters. The raids made upon each other by the tribes to the east and the west were brought to an end through his influence. He settled many old feuds not only between those tribes but among the other tribes in Cyrenaica.

Sayed Ibn Ali lived for six years after establishing himself at Jaghbub and extended his influence far and wide. The Zwaya tribe, who had been known as the brigands of Cyrenaica, " fearing neither God nor man," invited him to come to Kufra, the chief community of their people, and establish a *zawia* there. They agreed to give up raiding and thieving and attacking other tribes and offered him one-third of all their property in Kufra if he would come to them. He could not go in person but sent a famous *ikhwan*, Sidi Omar Bu Hawa, who established the first Senussi *zawia* at Jof in Jufra, and began the dissemination of the teachings of the Grand Senussi among the Zwayas. He also commissioned *ikhwan* to go into many other parts of the Libyan Desert, and before his death all the Beduins on the western frontier of Egypt and all over Cyrenaica had become his disciples.

He died in the year 1859, and was buried in the tomb over which rises the Kubba of Jaghbub.

The Grand Senussi was succeeded by his son Sidi Mohammed El Mahdi, who was sixteen years old when his father died. In spite of his youth his succession as head of the Order was strengthened by two circumstances. It was remembered that on one occasion at the end of an interview with his father, El Mahdi was about to leave the room, when the Grand Senussi rose and performed for him the menial service of arranging his slippers, which had been taken off on entering. The founder of the Order then addressed those present in these words: "Witness, O ye men here present, how Ibn Ali El Senussi arranges the slippers of his son, El Mahdi." It was realized that he meant to indicate that the son not only would succeed the father but would surpass him in holiness and sanctity.

Then, too, there was an ancient prophecy that the Mahdi who would reconquer the world for Islam would attain his majority on the first day of Moharram in the year 1300 after the Hejira, having been born of parents named Mohammed and Fatma and having spent several years in seclusion. Each part of this prophecy was fulfilled in the person of El Mahdi. The choice as successor to the Grand Senussi fell upon him.

When Sayed El Mahdi reached his majority there were thirty-eight *zawias* in Cyrenaica and eighteen in Tripolitania. Others were scattered over other parts of north Africa; and there were nearly a score in Egypt. It has been estimated that between a million and a half and three million people owed spiritual allegiance to the head of the Brotherhood when El Mahdi became its active head. He was the most illustrious of the Senussi family.

He saw from the first that there was more scope

for the influence of the Brotherhood in the direction of Kufra and the regions to the southward than in the north. In the year 1894 he removed his headquarters from Jaghbub to Kufra. Before his departure he freed all his slaves, and some of them and their children are still to be found living at Jaghbub.

His going to Kufra marked the beginning of an important era in the history of the Senussis and also in the development of trade between the Sudan and the Mediterranean coast by way of Kufra. The difficult and waterless trek between Buttafal Well near Jalo and Zieghen Well just north of Kufra became in El Mahdi's time a beaten route continually frequented by trade caravans and by travellers going to visit the centre of the Senussi Brotherhood. "A man could walk for half a day from one end of the caravan to the other," a Beduin told me.

The route from Kufra south to Wadai was also a hard and dangerous journey in those days, and El Mahdi caused the two wells of Bishra and Sara to be dug on the road from Kufra to Tekro.

Under the rule of the Zwaya tribe of Beduins, who had conquered Kufra from the black Tebus, that group of oases was the chief centre of brigandage in the Libyan Desert. The Zwayas are a warlike tribe and in the days before the coming of the Senussis they were a law unto themselves and a menace to all those who passed through their territory. Each caravan going through Kufra north or south was either pillaged or, if lucky, was compelled to pay a route tax to the Zwayas. These masters of Kufra were induced by El Mahdi to give up this exacting of tribute. He realized the importance of developing the trade of the oases and of the routes across the Libyan Desert from the north to the south. He strove to make desert travel safe, and in his day, Bu Matari, a Zwaya chieftain, told me at Kufra, a woman might travel from Barka (Cyrenaica) to Wadai unmolested.

El Mahdi also extended the circle of influence of the Senussis in many directions. *Ikhwan* were sent out to establish *zawias* from Morocco as far east as Persia. But his greatest work was in the desert, among the Beduins and the black tribes south of Kufra. He made the Senussis not only a spiritual power in those regions, and a powerful influence for peace and amity among the tribes, but a strong mercantile organization under whose stimulus trade developed and flourished. In the last years of his life he undertook to extend the influence of the Brotherhood to the southward in person. He had gone to Geru, south of Kufra, when his death came suddenly in the year 1900.

The sons of El Mahdi were then minors, and his nephew Sayed Ahmed was made the head of the Brotherhood. He was the guardian of Sayed Idris, who, as the eldest son of El Mahdi, was his legitimate successor.

The new head of the Senussis made an abrupt departure from the policies of his predecessors. He sought to combine temporal and spiritual power. When the Italians took over Cyrenaica and Tripoli from the Turks, Sayed Ahmed attempted to unite his spiritual power as head of the Brotherhood with the remnants of temporal and military power left by the Turks. Then the Great War broke out and he allowed himself to be persuaded by Turkish and German emissaries to attack the western frontier of Egypt.

The effort was a complete failure and Sayed Ahmed was compelled to go to Constantinople in a German submarine.

The third of the Senussi leaders saw things differently from the Grand Senussi and his great son. They had realized that a spiritual leader cannot be beaten on his own ground, whereas if he takes the field in quest of temporal supremacy it requires only a few military reverses to destroy his prestige. The power of Sayed Ibn Ali El Senussi and Sayed El Mahdi lay in themselves and in the spiritual influence that radiated from them. Sayed Ahmed surrendered this influence to rely upon arms, ammunition and circumstances. When these failed, there was nothing left.

From the hands of Sayed Ahmed the Senussi leadership fell to the lineal successor, Sayed Idris. He derives a considerable part of the prestige which he undoubtedly possesses from the fact that he is the son of El Mahdi. But even without that advantage his own personal qualities would be an adequate foundation for success in the important position to which he has been called. He combines gentleness of disposition with firmness of character to a high degree. He has the loyal allegiance and support not only of the Senussi *ikhwan* but of the people of the Libyan Desert.

In 1917 an agreement was entered into by the Italian Government with Sayed Idris, as head of the Senussi Brotherhood, by which his right to administer the affairs of the oases of Jalo, Aujila, Jedabia and Kufra was expressly recognized. This agreement was again ratified two years later at Regima. Unfortunately in 1923 a misunderstanding between the parties to this agreement caused it to lapse. It is to be hoped, however, that a new arrangement will be entered into between Sayed Idris and the Italian authorities which will restore to these oases of the Libyan Desert their peace and prosperity.

There can be no question that the influence of the Senussi Brotherhood upon the lives of the people of that region is good. The *ikhwan* of the Senussis are not only the teachers of the people, both in the field of religion and of general knowledge, but judges and intermediaries both between man and man and between tribe and tribe. The letter to the people of Wajanga already quoted clearly illustrates how the Grand Senussi laid down this office of peace-making as the duty of the Senussi brothers. It was developed and made even more important by his great son, El Mahdi.

The importance of these aspects of the Senussi rule in maintaining the tranquillity and well-being of the people of the Libyan Desert can scarcely be over-estimated.

CHAPTER VI

The Peace of Jaghbub

ON the afternoon of the second day after the meeting with Sayed Idris we saw the snow-white *kubba* (dome) of the Mosque at Jaghbub rising before us. In proper Beduin fashion we camped a short distance from the town and sent a messenger ahead to announce our arrival. Two hours later he returned to say that they were ready to receive us. The caravan went forward, and as it approached the walls we fired our rifles in the air. We were met at the gate by Sidi Hussein, the *wakil* or representative of Sayed Idris in the town, accompanied by a group of *ikhwan*, who are teachers in the school. The students lined up along the way and gave a cheer as we went through. The warmth of the welcome aroused an echo in our hearts.

Entering Jaghbub was to me like coming home. Two years before it had been close to the finish of our journey; now it stood as a starting-point, one of several, it is true, but still a starting-point, on the greater journey that was to come. The first time at Jaghbub had been marked by the reaction that comes when the long trek is over. Now I was expectant and excited. Journey's end and trek's beginning are both great moments, but the emotions they arouse are not the same.

I was impatient to start again. But one month and four days were to pass before I took the road, for there were no camels waiting for me. Before leaving Sollum I had sent a man, Sayed Ali El Seati, by the direct route to Jaghbub to hire camels and have them waiting when I should arrive over the longer route by way of Siwa. But Ali had apparently vanished into thin air. He had gone as far as Jedabia, I learned, without success, for none of the Beduins on the way from Sollum would let him have the beasts I wanted. At Jedabia, too, he had found no camels available. I waited two weeks with no sign of Ali. Then I discovered that the reason he could get no camels was because the road from Jaghbub to Jalo was used exclusively by Beduins of the Zwaya and Majabra tribes, and no other Beduins dared to venture upon it.

Though I was eager to get going again, I could not resist the charm and peace of the place in which I found myself immured. Jaghbub is a centre of education and religion. There is no trade there and no cultivation of the soil, except for some small bits of oases where former slaves, who had been freed by Sayed El Mahdi when he moved to Kufra, grow vegetables and a few dates. The life of the town centres about the Mosque, which is large enough to hold five or six hundred persons, and the school, which is the centre of religious education for the Senussis. Near the Mosque are a few houses belonging to the Senussi family and the *ikhwan* ; and scattered about both within and without the walls are a number of private houses. Buildings with rooms for some two or three hundred students are also grouped near the Mosque.

Jaghbub had reached the height of its importance when Sayed Ibn Ali, the Grand Senussi, had made it the centre of the Brotherhood. When his son, Sayed El Mahdi, succeeded him, the importance of the town continued for some dozen years until he transferred the centre of the Brotherhood's activities to Kufra. Then, when Sayed Ahmed el Sherif, as guardian of young Sayed Idris, was in control, Jaghbub again flourished as the capital. Its importance has fluctuated through the years with the presence or absence of the heads of the family within its walls. If Sayed Idris were to make it again the seat of the Senussi rule, in two months the school and the town would be overflowing with members of the Brotherhood, with students, and with pious visitors to the shrine of the Grand Senussi.

But at the time of my visit, there were only eighty young Beduins—from eight to fifteen years of age—studying under the *ikhwan*. If there had been more teachers there would have been more students. But at the time of our visit the head of the Senussi family, whom we had met on his way to Egypt, had his headquarters in Jedabia, far to the westward.

In an inner room of the Mosque a beautifully wrought cage of brass encloses the tomb where lies the body of that great man, who sought for his people a pure, austere and rigidly simple form of Islam, untainted by contact with the outside world. To this shrine every adherent of the Brotherhood who can accomplish the journey comes to pay homage and to renew his vows. The students of the school come to Jaghbub with one of two purposes—either to fit themselves to become *ikhwan*, the brothers of the fraternity, or simply to go back to their homes in the oases educated men with a right to spiritual leadership in their communities.

Except for the annoying problem of getting camels to take my expedition to Jalo, about 350 kilometres away to the westward, my life in Jaghbub was one of peaceful reflection and preparation for the undertaking before me.

The desert demands and induces a quite different attitude of mind and of spirit from the bustling life of the city. As I wandered about the little town and out into the oasis around it, or stood in the cool, shadowed spaces of the Mosque, or sat at times in the tower above it in conversation with learned Beduins, watching the night fall over the milk-white *kubba* and the brown mass of buildings it dominates, there dropped away from me all the worries and perplexities and problems that the sophisticated life of crowded places brings in its train. Day after day passed, with a morning's walk, midday prayers in the Mosque, a quiet meal, a little work with my instruments or cameras, afternoon prayers, another walk, a meal, followed by the distribution to my men of friendly glasses of tea according to the Beduin custom, again prayers, and after quiet contemplation of the evening sky with its peaceful stars, retirement to sleep such as the harassed city dweller does not know.

Among all the *ikhwan* whom I met and talked with at Jaghbub, there was one who particularly interested me, for he would neither sit and talk with me himself nor could I learn from his brother *ikhwan* the reason for his strange aloofness. At length, by chance, I learnt the story of Sidi Adam Bu Gmaira.

Sidi Adam is a withered old man with a refined proud face and a bitter twist to his mouth. Life has not been kind to him in his old age. On my first visit to Jaghbub I stayed at his empty house for three days. I had no chance then of a long conversation with him. This time he came to see me on the evening of my arrival to welcome me back to Jaghbub. I felt that a tragedy lay behind this old man. He is one of the Barassa tribe, one of the élite among the Beduins, and he is as proud as any of them; yet he does not accept his fate, and for some time I wondered how it was that he, a Beduin, had not learnt to do so. All around me at Jaghbub were types of benevolent humanity. Sidi Adam alone stood out distinct from his brethren, a tragic picture of beaten pride.

Late one evening as I was coming back from the Mosque after prayers, I found Mabrouk, an old slave of Sidi El Mahdi's. "Peace be on you and the blessing of God," I greeted him.

"And on you, my master, and God's mercy and blessing," he replied.

I sat down with him and we started talking about the little patch of cultivation to which he was attending. "Ei!" he exclaimed, "we have not much food, but by the blessing of Sidi El Mahdi the little we have is as great as abundance anywhere else."

Just then a frail, tall figure in a white robe flitted like a ghost across the courtyard. It was Adam Bu Gmaira. "There goes Sidi Adam," I said, pointing after him. "He was not looking well when he came to see me to-day. What ails him, I wonder?"

" Nay, it is not his health, my master. It is an unlucky man who incurs the displeasure of our masters [meaning the Senussi chiefs]. The poor man is suffering for his brother's bad faith."

It was then that the story of Bu Gmaira was unfolded to me by Mabrouk.

" Sidi Bu Seif Bu Gmaira, Adam's brother, was at one time the trusted and all-powerful *wakil* of Sidi El Mahdi at Jaghbub. When he was quite a child a wall fell on him and smashed in his head. The great Sidi El Senussi, founder of the sect, was fortunately near by. He took the child's head and bandaged it together, saying, ' This head will one day be a fountain of knowledge and enlightenment.' His prophecy came true. Bu Seif's father sent the child to Jaghbub when the Grand Senussi settled there and left him to study at the Mosque of Jaghbub. He became the leading *ikhwan* and great professor of Jaghbub. He was also a poet of no small merit. After the death of the Grand Senussi, Sidi El Mahdi took him up and made him his sole *wakil* at Jaghbub when he left for Kufra, entrusting him with all his property and the management thereof. But God willed that he should become an example to the other *ikhwan* of one who betrays the *asyad's* (master's) trust. He ran with the world and was seduced by her. He squandered much of Sidi El Mahdi's property and sold many of his slaves, putting the money in his own pocket. It was decreed that he should be punished. He wrote a letter to a big governor in Egypt, telling him that Sidi El Mahdi was away at Kufra, that there was no one at Jaghbub to defend it, and that it was an opportune moment to occupy the place." (Why he did this is inconceivable, as nobody then had any desire to occupy Jaghbub, but doubtless Bu Seif thought he might get something out of it.)

" At that time Sidi Mohammed El Abid El Senussi, a nephew of El Mahdi, was staying at Jaghbub. He heard that Bu Seif had written a letter and was sending it to Egypt and that he had arranged for a messenger to take it across the frontier after nightfall. El Abid at once dispatched two *ikhwan* to waylay the messenger and bring him back the letter. Two days later the messenger was brought. El Abid saw the letter but said nothing to Bu Seif. He simply ordered a caravan to be prepared for Kufra and asked Bu Seif to accompany him. The latter tried to excuse himself on account of old age and health, but El Abid insisted. He had no alternative but to go. So they set out on the silent journey across the desert and on arrival at Kufra the letter was shown by El Abid to Sidi El Mahdi.

" On the Friday following their arrival, after the midday prayers at the Mosque of Taj in Kufra, Sidi El Mahdi called together all the *ikhwan*, including Bu Seif. ' Sidi Bu Seif, thou knowest what thou hast done.' There was a hush. Everybody in the Mosque tingled with excitement, knowing there was something to come. ' But we shall not punish thee. Thou shalt live, thou shalt draw thy pay and thy rations according to custom. God alone will punish those who have betrayed our trust. But thou shalt read aloud to this gathering of *ikhwan* the letter which thou hast written with thine own hand.'

" Bu Seif had no alternative but to read the letter. The *ikhwan* were silent, though there was much surprise, for this was thought to be the most trusted man of Sayed El Mahdi.

" 'Henceforward thou shalt be relieved of the trouble of looking after our affairs,' said Sidi El Mahdi, dismissing him. Bu Seif was then led to his house, a sick man. He died a few days later. His two sons died in the following few months. His remaining two daughters were taken in marriage by members of the Senussi family. All his books—and it is said he possessed the best library in the Senussi circle—and his property were taken by the Senussi family. The only remaining man of his family is Adam, his brother, who has inherited the empty house at Jaghbub and the stigma attaching thereto. With the death of Adam the family will be extinct."

CHAPTER VII

Meals—and Medicine

AT intervals there were pleasant marks of hospitality from the Senussi leaders at Jaghbub. There are various forms of hospitality among the Beduins, depending upon the rank both of the host and of the guest and upon the circumstances of the given case. When a traveller comes to an oasis or a town in the desert he has with him his own caravan, provided with all the necessities of living. He does not put up at an hotel or go to a friend's house to live, but sets up his own establishment, either pitching his tents and making a camp, or perhaps, as happened to me at Jaghbub, at Jalo, and again at Kufra, occupying a house put at his disposal by some one in the place. Then comes the question of entertainment and honour from the dignitaries of the community. They may either invite one to luncheon or to dinner in their own houses or send a meal to the guest at his own house or camp. The first form of hospitality I shall describe when we reach Jalo, where I was entertained by twelve or fifteen notables in turn. The second form was that which I received at Jaghbub. This variety of hospitality may be extended for one, from three to seven days, depending upon the respective ranks of host and guest.

Several days after my arrival Sidi Ibrahim and Sidi

Mohi Eddin, young sons of Sayed Ahmed, the former guardian of Sayed Idris, who is now in Angora, boys of thirteen and fifteen years of age, made the *beau geste* of showing me hospitality. There arrived at my house a Beduin of the Barassa tribe, with two slaves laden with food. They set before me a feast of at least a score of dishes, and I was bidden to eat. The representative of my hosts sat courteously by, himself not touching a morsel, while I tasted the dishes in turn—no mortal man could eat them all and live. It was his function as deputy host to see that I lacked nothing to make the meal a satisfying and pleasant one, and to entertain me with conversation while I ate. The men of his tribe are the aristocrats of the desert, tall, erect, handsome, proud and with the spirit and courage of lions. A Barassa, if he were alone in the midst of an alien tribe, would not hesitate to meet an insult or a discourtesy with instant challenge and to fight the whole lot single-handed if it came to that.

Under his solicitously attentive eye, and waited on by the slaves who accompanied him, I ate my meal. I am not sure that I can remember the full tale of the dishes that were set before me, but they ran something like this. A rich meat soup, made with butter and rice ; a great dish of boiled meat ; a big bowl of rice with bits of meat in it ; eggs, hard-boiled, fried, and made into an omelette with onions and herbs ; tripe ; meat in tomato sauce ; meat croquettes ; sausages ; vegetable marrows ; *bamia* or *okra* ; *mulukhia*, an Egyptian vegetable with a peculiar flavour of its own ; marrows stuffed with rice and bits of meat ; *kus-kus*, a distinctively Arab dish made of flour and steamed ; a salad ; a kind of blancmange or pudding of cornflour and milk ; Beduin pancakes with honey ; a sweet pudding of rice ; a delicate kind of pastry made of flour with raisins and almonds. This last is an Egyptian dish rather than one native to the desert. The slave who had cooked my meal, knowing me to be an Egyptian, had put forth her best energies to please me, and as a climax had provided this Egyptian delicacy. At home we call it *sadd-el-hanak,* " that which fills the mouth." It fills the soul of the epicure with joy as well.

In the Beduin cuisine meat predominates, generally lamb or mutton. True hospitality without meat is impossible for the desert dweller to imagine. It is the keystone of the structure not only of Beduin hospitality but of Beduin living, except of course when one is on the trek and cannot get it. A guest must be given meat, and it must be meat specially provided for him. When a Beduin invites one to dine with him, he slaughters a sheep expressly for his visitor. As a rule he will neither prepare the meal nor even kill the animal until one has arrived, in order that there may be no doubt that the preparations were made expressly for the guest. He carries his courtesy to the point of asking a guest, on his arrival, to partake of a meal, to lend him a knife with which to slaughter a sheep, for hospitality demands that the guest shall be convinced that full honour is being done him.

The great variety of dishes on the Beduin menu, when a friend or a stranger is being formally entertained, is the essence of the ceremony. The greater the number the better the host and the higher the honour he is able to pay the partaker of the meal.

Beduin entertaining concentrates itself upon food, for in the desert there is nothing to be had in the way of pleasure except eating. In the primitive surroundings of an oasis to eat is the whole story.

Two incidents of that month in Jaghbub interested me as illustrating how, with all their differences, the East and the West are often humorously alike. The one incident was comic, but the other had pathos in it as well as humour.

I had given instructions that no one who came to my house in quest of medicine should ever be turned away. Sidi Zwela, an *ikhwan,* had appealed for help for his cough, and I had given him a bottle of cough syrup. Two days later he appeared again. He said that the first few doses had done him so much good that he had quickly finished the bottle. Might he have another bottle ? Abdullahi, who was present at the interview, after his departure growled out a cynical comment : " Yes, he found it sweet and pleasant to the taste. He takes it as a delicacy and not as a medicine." The comment was probably accurate. More than one child I had heard of during my years in England whose cough persisted strangely so long as the cough medicine was sweet and tasty.

I am afraid that my men used to boast about the things that could be done with what we had among our stores. The Baskari, after Ahmed had been pulling his leg about my having medicine for everything, came to me to ask for something to cure a slave-girl of absent-mindedness. I could only reply that from my experience in various lands to keep a servant from forgetting was as easy as to prevent water from sinking into the sand.

The second incident involved two men as different as day and night. There came to my house one day a slave of the *wakil,* sent by his master to consult me. It was a matter about which Sidi Hussein could not approach me in person. Beduin etiquette forbids a man to talk to another about his wife, or even about any particular woman who is not known to both of them. But a slave could say for him what his dignity forbade him to speak in person. The slave's message was that the wife of the *wakil* had borne no children, which was a keen disappointment to the husband. Surely, his master thought, I must have in my medicine chest filled with the wonders of the science of the West, some remedy for the poor woman's childless state.

My thoughts went straight back to my last days at Oxford. An old college servant was an excellent fellow, but most inordinately shy. He came to me one day as I was preparing for the journey home, and with a tremendous summoning of his courage proffered a request.

" If you would allow me, sir," he said, " to ask a favour. My wife and I have no children. The doctor can't help us ; he has nothing to suggest. Now, sir, back in that country of yours, I've heard it said, they have wonderful talismans that will do all kinds of things. I'm not one who has believed much in having to do with magic, but this is a very special case. Do you think you might find me a talisman and send it on ? If it's not asking too much, sir ? "

In the face of his anxiety and the courageous breaking down of the barriers of his shyness, I could only answer gravely but sympathetically, that I would do what I could. But the necessity did not arise. He had died, remembered by Balliol men past and present, before I came to Oxford again.

In the case of Sidi Hussein, however, I could not put the matter off. The slave was waiting for an answer, and doubtless his master was waiting for him. I thought quickly. I gave the slave half a bottle of Horlick's malted milk tablets, with solemn instructions that three were to be taken by the lady each day until all were gone.

When the slave had left, I reflected on the amusing parallel between the two cases. There in Oxford the West, having exhausted all that its science had to offer on behalf of the universal desire for offspring, had tried to draw upon the spiritual resources of the East. Here in Jaghbub, the East, finding all its spiritual appeals of no avail, had turned to the science of the West for aid. East or West, we alike believe in the miraculous power of the unknown.

But all this pleasant peaceful life and courteous hospitality did not produce camels. I sent messengers out into the surrounding country in quest of the beasts, making my offers of money for their hire larger and larger as time went on, but I could get no favourable responses. I invoked the aid of Sidi Hussein, but he professed himself powerless. I sent a messenger back to Siwa with a telegram to Sayed Idris in Egypt, informing him of my predicament and asking his aid. As soon as could be expected, a reply came directing Sidi Hussein to give me all the assistance in his power. Still the *wakil* seemed to be unable to help me.

At last, when things began to seem hopeless, a Zwaya caravan arrived from Jalo on its way to Siwa for dates. I wanted those camels, but of course their owners had no desire to turn back without the dates they had come for. However, a way was found to persuade them, for I communicated to them, through Sidi Hussein, the news that an order had been issued by the Egyptian Government forbidding Zwayas to enter Egyptian territory until they had composed their differences with the Awlad Ali, who live in Egypt, and with whom they had a feud. Since they could not go to Siwa, which is in Egypt, without fear of punishment, there they were stranded at Jaghbub, with nothing to do but go back the way they came. That was precisely the way I wanted them to go. The combined effect of the order of the Egyptian Government, of the message from Sayed Idris, of the persuasions of Sidi Hussein and of the promise of exorbitant prices for hire of their camels, which they succeeded in dragging out of me because of my necessity—finally made them agree to take me to Jalo.

The quiet days of contemplation under the shadows of the white *kubba* and the anxious days of striving for the means of continuing my journey came at last to an end. On February 22nd, thirty-four days after I had entered Jaghbub, I turned my face to the westward and set out for Jalo.

Ahmed M. Hassanein.

HIS MAJESTY KING FOUAD I OF EGYPT.

SAYED IDRIS EL SENUSSI, HEAD OF THE SENUSSI SECT.

A CLOISTER AT THE MOSQUE OF JAGHBUB.

THE DOME OF THE MOSQUE AT JAGHBUB.

HAWARIA, A LANDMARK OF KUFRA.

It can be seen for hours before arriving at Kufra, and once it is sighted the caravan is safe.

REMAINS OF A PETRIFIED FOREST WHICH THE EXPLORER CAME ACROSS ON THE WAY TO JALO.

The small bits of petrified trees have been covered by the sand. Only the bigger trunks remain, because of the etiquette of the desert, which asks of every traveller to put up any lying stones as a landmark to show those coming behind them that some one has passed by that route.

JALO.

EL TAJ, THE SENUSSI HEADQUARTERS AT KUFRA.
Built on the crest of the hill overlooking the valley.

CHAPTER VIII

Sandstorms and the Road to Jalo

I LEFT Jaghbub in accordance with the best tradition. It was a day of sandstorm. The Beduins say that to start a journey in a sandstorm is good luck. I am not sure, though, that they are not making a virtue of necessity. It is as though an Italian were to say that it is good luck to set out when the sun is shining or a Scotsman when it is raining ! Sandstorms are a commonplace in the desert, but as an experience there is nothing commonplace about them.

The day dawns with a clear sky and no hint of storm or wind. The desert smiles upon our setting out and the caravan moves forward cheerfully. Before long a refreshing breeze comes up from nowhere and goes whispering over the sands. Almost imperceptibly it strengthens, but still there is nothing unpleasant in its blowing. Then one looks down at one's feet and the surface of the desert is curiously changed. It is as though the surface were underlaid with steam pipes with thousands of orifices through which tiny jets of steam are puffing out. The sand leaps in little spurts and whirls. Inch by inch the disturbance rises as the wind increases its force. It seems as though the whole surface of the desert were rising in obedience to some upthrusting force beneath. Larger pebbles strike against the shins, the knees, the thighs. The spray of dancing sand grains climbs the body till it strikes the face and goes over the head. The sky is shut out, all but the nearest camels fade from view, the universe is filled with hurtling, pelting, stinging, biting legions of torment. Well for the traveller then if the wind is blowing at his back ! The torture of the driving sand against his face is bitter. He can scarcely keep his eyes open and yet he dare not let them close, for one thing worse than the stinging of the sand grains is to lose one's way.

Fortunately the wind comes in driving gusts, spaced in groups of three or four, with a few seconds of blessed lull after each group. While the gusts are making their assault, one turns one's face away, pulls one side of one's *kufia* forward like a screen, and almost holds one's breath. When the lull comes, one puts the *kufia* back, takes a quick look about to see that one has kept one's bearings, then swiftly prepares for the next attack.

It is as though some great monster of fabled size and unearthly power were puffing out these hurtling blasts of sand upon the traveller's head. The sound is that of a giant hand drawing rough fingers in regular rhythm across tightly stretched silk.

When the sandstorm comes there is nothing to do but to push doggedly on. Around any stationary object, whether it might be a post, a camel or a man, the eager sands swiftly gather, piling up and up until there remains only a smoothly rounded heap. If it is torture to go on, it is death itself to halt.

A sandstorm is likely to be at its worst for five or six hours. While it persists, a caravan can only keep going, with careful vigilance that the direction be not missed. When the storm is at its fiercest, the camels will be scarcely moving, but their instinct tells them that it is death to halt. How instinctively wise they are, is shown by the fact that when it begins to rain, they sense no such danger and will immediately stand still and even lie down.

The storm drives the sand into everything one possesses. It fills clothes, food, baggage, instruments, everything. It searches out every weak spot in one's armour. One feels it, breathes it, eats it, drinks it—and hates it. The finest particles even penetrate the pores of the skin, setting up a distressing irritation.

There are certain rules about the behaviour of sandstorms which every Beduin knows and is quite ready to tell the stranger to the desert. The wind that makes the storm will rise with the day or go to sleep with the sun. There will be no sandstorm at night when there is a moon. A sandstorm never joins the afternoon and evening. These are excellent rules; but on our trek to Jalo every one of them was broken! We had storms when the moon was shining and storms when the night was dark. We had storms that begun before dawn and storms that did not pause till long after the sun was set. We had storms that not only joined afternoon and evening, but wiped out the line of demarcation between them. We had little storms and great storms—the worst I had yet seen—storms that were short and storms that were long; storms by day and storms by night. But even under this interminable bombardment, I did not lose the spell of the desert's charm. Sometimes at evening, when we had been battling doggedly against the flying squadrons of the sand for hours, the wind would stop dead as if a master had put up a peremptory finger. Then for an hour or so the fine dust would settle slowly down like a falling mist. But afterwards the moon would rise and under the pale magic of its flooding light, the desert would put on a new personality. Had there been a sandstorm? Who could remember? Could this peaceful expanse of loveliness ever be cruel? Who could believe it?

The trek to Jalo was therefore not an easy one. The sandstorms were a constant annoyance and sometimes a menace. The latter part of the way led through a country of sand dunes, and the caravan had to go winding about among them. To keep one's course straight to the proper point of the compass in spite of those wrigglings and twistings takes all one's skill and attention at the best of times. When a sandstorm is torturing and blinding the whole caravan, the task becomes a staggering one. Nevertheless we pushed steadily on, making on the whole good time of it.

In spite of the viciousness of the attacking sands there were hours of pleasure on this trek.

Memorable were the genial evenings when we were all gathered around the fire of *hatab* for our after-dinner glasses of tea. Then stories would begin to go around. Old Moghaib, with the firelight playing on the grey hairs of his shaggy beard, would begin by telling bits of Zwaya history when his grandfather used to go to Wadai to fight the black tribes and bring back camels and slaves. Saleh would follow with a tale of the great profits that his cousin had made on his last trip to Wadai, when he did not have to fight anybody but brought back leather, ostrich feathers and ivory to sell in Barka, which is the Arabic name for Cyrenaica.

Then I would turn to Ali and demand a love song. He was a poet of sorts and betrothed to Hussein's sister. If the girl is anything like her brother, the boy is not doing badly for himself. Ali would look to his uncle for permission to comply with my request and find the old man busy with his rosary and pretending to be oblivious of the turn that matters had taken. It does not befit the dignity of a grey-haired Beduin to sit and hear love songs from the younger generation. But his respect for me keeps him from leaving the gathering.

Finally he mutters in his beard, " Sing to the Bey, since he likes to hear our Beduin songs." Ali's pleasant voice rises on the evening air and the beads of old Moghaib's rosary fall through his fingers with the deliberate regularity characteristic of a man who is conscious of nothing but his devotions.

So Ali sings :

I went singing
And all men turned to hear me.
It is Khadra
Who draws the song from my soul.
Red is her cheek like spilt blood,
Slim and round she is like a reed.
None so young, none so old
Not to know her.
If I meet her in the way,
I will flaunt her—
Like a scarf upon my spear.

As his voice dies away, Is it my imagination or are

the rosary beads in Moghaib's fingers moving a little faster? After a pause Ali sings again:

> Thou slim narcissus of the gardener's pride,
> Thy mouth flows honey
> Over teeth of ivory.
> Thy waist is slender
> Like the lions running in the chase.
> Wilt thou have me?
> Or thinkest thou of another?
> Thy form is rounded like a whip—
> To lie on thy breast
> Were to be in Paradise.
> Love cannot be hidden,
> But Fate is in the hands of God.

There is silence in the camp, except for the murmur of the dying fire and the clicking of the rosary. But the rhythm of the beads is significantly changed now. Toward the end of Ali's song Moghaib's fingers had stopped dead for a moment and then hurried nervously on as though to deny that they had halted. The old man had been a great lover in his time and the boy's song had stirred his blood with memories. Perhaps it was fortunate for others around that fire that they had no clicking rosary beads to betray them.

After Busalama Well, which is a day's trek from Jaghbub, we were going through a region where there were remains of a petrified forest. At intervals we passed great blocks of stone erect like guide-posts along the way. Ages ago they had been living trees, but now the forces of Nature had transferred them from the vegetable kingdom to the mineral. A few smaller bits of petrified wood were scattered about, but most of those were hidden beneath the sand. The larger tree sections had remained visible because the etiquette of the desert demands that anyone passing such a fallen landmark shall set it erect again. It is also good form, on a newly travelled track, to build little piles of stones at intervals as notice to later comers that here lies the way. Sometimes one comes upon a tree or a shrub on which hang shreds and patches of clothing, and there one is under obligation to add a thread or a fragment from his own outfit. These accumulating tokens confirm the tree as a landmark to later comers and afford the encouragement of the thought that others have been this way before. In the dead waste and monotony of the desert any evidence of the passing of one's fellow-man is a cheering incident. The sign of camel dung, of the bleached bones of a camel, or even the skeleton of an unfortunate traveller are welcome to the eye, for at least they show that a caravan had passed that way.

Shortly after leaving Jaghbub we came upon a different kind of landmark. It consisted of a row of small sand hillocks like ant-hills stretching across the track. It is called Alam Bu-Zafar, the "Bu-Zafar" landmark, and it is the sign and symbol of a pleasant Beduin custom. On any trek, the new-comers to that particular route are expected to slaughter a sheep for those in the caravan who have come that way before. The custom is called "Bu-Zafar." If the novices do not awaken promptly to their responsibilities, the veterans give them a hint. One or two of them dash ahead of the caravan and build a row of sand-piles across the way. When the caravan reaches the significant landmark, they call out suggestively, "Bu-Zafar, Bu-Zafar." Invariably the hint is taken, a sheep is slaughtered, and the ceremonial feast is held.

In our caravan there were several who had not gone over this route before, including myself. I bought a sheep before leaving Jaghbub so that we who were new to this route might give " Bu-Zafar " to the old-timers. The Alam Bu-Zafar that we came upon, therefore, were not of our making, but left by some other caravan.

We were fortunate in finding grazing for our camels almost every day until we reached Jalo. Sometimes, it is true, we had to go out of our way to reach the patches of green among the sand dunes, but we always found them. Three kinds of vegetation grow sparsely and in infrequent spots in this part of the desert. *Belbal* is a greyish-green bush, whose foliage is not good eating for the camels. It grows only in the vicinity of a well. Ordinarily the camels will not touch it, but if very hungry they will. Then unceasing vigilance is necessary to save oneself from the annoyance of having a sick camel on one's hands.

Damran is a similar bush, but with darker foliage and with brown stems which make good fuel when dried. This is excellent food for the camels and they eat it eagerly. The third variety of vegetation is *nisha*, which grows in tufts of thin leaves up to a foot high. This too makes good grazing. It is only in the winter months, however, when the scanty rains come, that these plants are available. No Beduin would think of making a journey between Jalo and Jaghbub in summer without carrying a supply of fodder for his camels.

On the tenth day from Jaghbub we reached the Well of Hesaila, the first water after Busalama. It was marked by a few trees and small green bush, and after we had scooped out the drifted sand with our hands, the water seemed good. But the after-effects were not so pleasant.

Two days later we found ourselves on the outskirts of the Oasis of Jalo. Before we could enter a messenger came rushing to meet us. He carried a letter from Sidi Mohammed El Zerwali, the *ikhwan*, who had been directed by Sayed Idris to accompany us to Kufra, asking me to camp outside until they could prepare to receive us properly. Sayed Idris, before he had left Jalo two months before, had told them that I was on the way and directed that I should be shown all possible courtesy. They had expected us long before this, and when we did not come, they decided that I had changed my plans.

We withdrew a short distance from the town and camped. A few hours later an impressive group of a score or more of Beduins came out and drew themselves up in a long line before the village of Lebba, one of the two villages that make up Jalo. Dressed in our cleanest and most ceremonial clothes, and my men provided with ammunition for the complimentary salute, we went forward. I approached and shook hands with Sidi Senussi Gader Bouh, the Kaimakam or Governor of the District, the members of the Council of Jalo and other prominent citizens. The Kaimakam made a speech of welcome, to which I replied. My men fired their guns in salute, and we passed into the town.

I went to the house which was put at my disposal,

and received a visit of ceremony from the Council of Jalo and from Sidi El Fadeel, the uncle of Sayed Idris. After dinner with Senussi Gader Bouh, I spent the evening in discussing plans for the trip with Sidi Zerwali.

CHAPTER IX

At the Oasis of Jalo

JALO is one of the most important oases in Cyrenaica. It lies 240 kilometres from the Mediterranean at its nearest point, beyond Jedabia, and about 600 kilometres from Kufra, which is directly south. The oasis is not only the largest producer of dates in all the province, but it is the trade outlet for the products of Wadai and Darfur which come through Kufra. Everything from the outside world that goes to Kufra passes through Jalo.

" The desert is a sea," said El Bishari, a prominent chieftain of the Majabra Tribe, " and Jalo is its port."

It was at the height of its importance something like thirty years ago, when El Mahdi maintained the Senussi capital at Kufra. In those days caravans of two or three hundred camels came and went between Jalo and the south each week, but when I was there the traffic had shrunk to less than a tenth of that. In summer, however, it is swollen by the demands of the date harvest.

There are two villages at Jalo, over a mile apart, El Erg and Lebba. Between and around them are scattered the date palms in picturesque profusion to the number of nearly a hundred thousand.

Twelve miles to the west lies Aujila, which is the ancient oasis mentioned by Herodotus as famous for its dates. In Aujila is the tomb of Abdullahi El Sahabi, who is reputed to have been a clerk of the Prophet Mohammed. Whether such is actually the case is somewhat problematical; but at least the prophet did have a clerk named Abdullahi El Sahabi. Abdullahi did come to North Africa, and the tomb of a man of that name is found at Aujila. Many a tradition has been based on flimsier evidence. The story is told that the Grand Senussi found the body of Sahabi buried in a remote spot, and forthwith saw in a vision the spirit which had once inhabited the body.

"Dig up my body," said the ghostly visitor, "put it on a camel and go forth. Where the camel halts there you shall build my tomb."

The Grand Senussi obeyed the injunction and journeyed till he came to Aujila. There the camel stopped dead and refused to go on, and on the spot the tomb was built.

The founder of the Senussi sect and all the members of the Senussi family and even their prominent *ikhwan* are believed to possess occult powers and second sight. Sayed El Mahdi is credited with having particularly strong occult powers which the Beduins call "miracles." One of the *ikhwan* at Jaghbub told me the following story about Sayed El Mahdi. An ignorant Beduin came to him intending to study under him at Jaghbub. Suddenly the man realized that it was the sowing season, and that he had nobody to look after the sowing of his land. So he thought it best to go away till after the crop season and then return to his studies. He went to say good-bye to Sayed El Mahdi. He entered the room, sat down, and, as is the custom, waited until he was spoken to. Sayed El Mahdi appeared to ignore him for a few minutes. The man felt sleepy and just dozed off for a minute or two, awaking to Sayed El Mahdi's gentle voice saying, "Now you feel at rest and you know that matters have been arranged for you." In that short time the man had seen in a dream his brother ploughing his land and sowing the barley crop. "Now you shall be our guest," continued the Sayed, "and study and pray that God may guide you to the right path. All will be provided for, as you have seen, and you will have no reason to worry. God is merciful and He looks after us all." The man remained at Jaghbub and afterwards went home just in time for the harvest. On his return to Jaghbub he told one of the *ikhwan* that not only had his crop been sown as he saw in the dream, but the place seen and the time of the dream were exactly corroborated by the facts.

Another incident was told me by the Kaimakam of Jalo. He was travelling with a party from Benghasi to Jaghbub to visit Sayed El Mahdi. They missed a well and were in dire straits. At night a man, the least enthusiastic of the pilgrims, turned to him and said, "Now that you have brought us to visit that wonderful man Sayed El Mahdi, will you ask him to send us some water, if he be as saintly as you say he is." That same night at Jaghbub, Sayed El Mahdi, so the story goes, ordered two of his slaves to take five camels loaded with water and food, and going out into the open he pointed out the direction they should take, adding that until they met a caravan they must not stop by the way. In due course they came across the caravan in distress and rescued it.

There are some of the old *ikhwan* still living whom even members of the Senussi family themselves avoid displeasing because they fear their occult powers. One of these who lives at Kufra was the *ikhwan* of a *zawia* in Cyrenaica. A Beduin once brought some sheep to water at the well and some of them strayed into the patch of ground attached to the *zawia* and ate the young barley. The *ikhwan* warned the Beduin to stop his sheep from doing this and the man pretended to pay attention, but was really determined that not only these sheep but the whole flock should go in and help themselves to the crop. And when the *ikhwan* came out again it was to see all the flock feeding on his barley. "May God curse them," he cried, "the sheep that eat the crop of the *zawia*." The story goes that not a single sheep emerged alive from the *zawia* garden.

Until this day the Beduins fear the Senussi family not so much because of any temporal power, but on account of the spiritual powers with which they credit them. A Beduin cursed by one of the Senussi family lives the whole time in fear of something awful about to happen to him. His friends, even his own people, try to avoid his presence lest the curse upon him should account for a harm to them also.

There is the famous case of the chief clerk of Sayed El Mahdi, who lies in Kufra now half paralysed. I went to see him. He was quite happy and very content in spite of the fact that he could not move his body. On my second visit he was getting confidential and—half believing, half disbelieving—asked if I had any medicine for his malady. I hesitated, for I did not want the man to lose hope entirely. He saw this, and without even giving me the chance of answering him, said : " No, it is decreed that it should be thus. It was my fault. Sayed El Mahdi wanted me to journey north. I could not disobey him, but I tried to avoid the journey. I went as far as Hawari, and there wrote to him pretending to be ill. The answer came with a messenger that if I were ill I should certainly be relieved of the journey. The next day I was struck with paralysis and brought back to Kufra and have been here ever since. That was twenty-five years ago."

The Kaimakam at Jalo told me a story when we were discussing miracles. He said that on one occasion there was a very severe sandstorm which nearly covered the whole of the tomb at Aujila. So they brought the slaves to dig it out again. As it was being dug out the Kaimakam came into the chamber which contained the shrine and noticed a very strong smell of incense. He called one of the slaves and asked whether he had burned any incense. The man denied it, yet till now, upon occasion, a visitor to the tomb will smell this incense, though it is known that none has been burned.

Jalo is the headquarters of the Majabra tribe of Beduins, the merchant princes of the Libyan Desert. A few Zwayas are also found there, but the Majabras make up the great majority of the two thousand inhabitants of the two villages. The Majabras have wonderful business instinct. The Majabra boasts of his father having died in the *basur*—the camel saddle—as the son of a soldier might boast that his father died on the field of battle. When I was in Jalo, the Italian authorities, who were then on unfriendly terms with Sayed Idris, had prohibited the sending of goods from Benghasi and the other ports of Cyrenaica into the interior. Consequently prices of commodities at such inland places as Jedabia went up with a leap. Majabra merchants, arriving at Jalo with caravans of goods from Egypt, heard of this abnormal situation in the north. Without a moment's hesitation they changed their plans, trekked north instead of south and sold their goods to splendid advantage in Jedabia. Then back they dashed—if the camel's pace of less than 3 miles an hour can be so described—to Egypt or the south for another caravan load. Arrived again at Jalo with their merchandise, they inquired carefully as to comparative conditions in the markets of Jedabia and Kufra, and directed their further journey accordingly. Considering the remoteness of the desert places—Jalo five days from Jedabia, Kufra from twelve to eighteen days from Jalo—and the snail-like speed of a caravan, news travels across the desert with surprising swiftness. At least it seems so. I suppose the true explanation is that all things are relative, and while news moves at the camel's pace, so does everything else.

While the Majabras are the great traders of the Libyan Desert, the Zwayas have also their claims to prominence. The rivalry between the two tribes is always present under the surface and occasionally it flashes forth into the light.

There is some envy of the Zwayas by all the other tribes of Cyrenaica because the man second in importance to Sayed Idris among the Senussis is Ali Pasha El Abdia, who is a Zwayi. Abdia is a splendid soldier, a powerful support to Sayed Idris and a man much trusted by the Senussi leader.

One evening after dinner at Jalo some expression of this rivalry was given by Sidi Saleh, who belonged to no tribe in Cyrenaica and was in fact a Sherif or descendant of the Prophet, in an argument with Moghaib and Zerwali, who were both Zwayas. Moghaib launched into a little history of the achievements of the Zwayas. Sidi Saleh listened to the Zwayi's eulogy of his tribe, shook his head and remarked, " Their history may be as glorious as Sidi Moghaib tells you, but they do not fear God."

At this Moghaib burst forth, " By God, Sidi Saleh, they may not fear God, but neither do they fear man. Woe to him who dares molest their caravan or attack their camp."

Then he came quickly over to me and continued, " We have the blessing of El Mahdi upon us, for it was to our headquarters in Kufra that Sidi El Mahdi came and from which he disappeared."

The Senussis will never say that El Mahdi died, but always that he " disappeared " or some equivalent expression. In fact there is a legend among them that he is not dead, but wandering over the earth until such time as he shall come again to his desert people. To the Zwayas, El Mahdi is the most beloved of the Senussi leaders because it was he who moved the centre of activity of the Brotherhood to Kufra, their headquarters. The *kubba* of the mosque that he built is the glory of Kufra.

In my own experience the Zwayas at times showed hostility and made it clear that, although I was a Moslem, the son of a religious man and a confidant of Sayed Idris, they did not want me in Kufra. Some of them even expressed the hope that they would have seen the last of me when I left Kufra. In spite of this scarcely veiled antagonism to me, however, I never expect to find better men for a desert journey than the Zwayas who formed part of my caravan. Zerwali in particular, a typical Zwayi Beduin, was the best of companions and the most reliable of associates.

The Beduin of Cyrenaica has in him the blood of the Arabs who passed through the north of Africa on their way to Spain. Although he has mixed with other native tribes of North Africa, he still preserves the old Arab tradition. In the case of murder, amongst the Senussis, the Beduins have their own law. As a rule the Senussi *ikhwan* intervenes as a peaceful intermediary. He takes the murderer and an old member of his tribe and goes to the murdered man's camp, pitching camp near by. The *ikhwan* then approaches the family of the murdered man, saying: "He who murdered your man is here," and taking him by the hand, he adds, "This is he who murdered your son, I hand him over to you that you may do as you will with him." Usually the answer is: "May God forgive him and may God's justice and mercy fall upon him." Thereupon the *ikhwan* starts arranging for the blood money, which is generally three thousand dollars and a slave, the market value of the latter being known. The injured party may choose between accepting the money or having its equivalent in camels, sheep or other commodities. The money may be paid in instalments extending over from one to three years and the arrangement is generally carried through. In very rare cases or a deep-rooted feud the family of the deceased refuse to accept blood money, which means that they intend to kill the murderer himself, or else one of his relations or a leading member of his tribe.

Beduin boys and girls mix freely; it is only in the higher families that the women are kept in seclusion. As a rule a boy knows his sweetheart, and he goes to her camp and sings to her, generally in verse of his own making. If she likes him, she comes out and answers his song, not rarely in words of her own composition also. The boy then goes and asks for the girl from her people, paying a dowry if an agreement is reached. Then with ceremonial he goes with his friends and takes the girl home to his camp amid displays of horsemanship and much firing of guns. Cases have been known of elopements which usually end in feuds between tribes, for the Beduins look upon the man as having stolen the girl from them. There is a marriage contract, in many cases drawn up by the *ikhwan*, and the marriage takes place according to the Moslem religion. Marriages take place at a very early age, according to the development of the girl, who may be thirteen or fourteen, while the boy is between seventeen and twenty. Beduins who can afford it marry more than one wife, but in that case the first wife remains the mistress of the house and takes precedence even over the favourite wife in anything that has to do with household management.

I have heard of many cases of lads going off their heads through falling in love with a girl they could not marry. A Beduin boy once came to me to ask for medicine. He looked very frail. He was slim, with a rather refined face, and spoke very little. "I have come to ask you for medicine to give me health," he said. He shook his head when I asked what was his ailment and answered, " God knows best." There was something queer about the boy, something that puzzled me, but as usual in these cases a few malted milk tablets were wrapped up carefully in paper and given to him with strict orders not to take more than three each day. When the boy had gone, an elderly man came to my tent. He squatted on the floor. " May God give you health and make your hand give recovery. My son came to you just now and you gave him medicine. I have come to explain his ailment. He is always weak and afflicted by headaches. When night falls he shuns everybody and seeks solitude; often he goes out to spend the night in the open."

I told the old man that the medicine I had given the boy was the only one I had that might give some relief. " Recovery comes from God," replied the man in a sad voice. " We know his remedy, but it is decreed that he should not have it. The boy is in love with a girl whose parents refused to give her to him in marriage."

" Why don't you make an effort, if you know this is the reason of your son's illness, and try to get the girl in marriage for your son ? "

" It is too late, now," replied the father, " she is already married. But God knows best . . . she may be many days' journey away from here, but she is suffering from the same ailment." With that he rose and left my tent, a resigned, pathetic figure.

At Jalo, as at Jaghbub, there were no camels waiting for me when I arrived. But the reason was not the same, nor the uncertainty so disturbing. The hire of the necessary camels had been arranged for, and Omar Bu Helega, their owner, was ready to start just as soon as the beasts returned from grazing. No good Beduin starts out on a long trek until his camels have been fattened, and especially have had their fill of green fodder. A long stretch like that to Kufra, with no grazing on the way, means feeding the camels on dried dates exclusively. Dates, say the camelmen, are hot on the liver. Therefore they prepare their animals for the ordeal by a course of green feeding before they start.

Bu Helega's camels had been taken to nearby grazing grounds for this course of preparation, and on the appointed day for their return they did not appear. The next day I wondered about them, the second day I was concerned, and the day after worried, lest when taken from grazing, the beasts might have run away. However, they had not done so. They put in their appearance on the fourth day, and when they came they were in excellent condition.

I hired thirty-five camels, paying a high price for them. I could have bought the beasts outright for from £12 to £18, while Bu Helega demanded £13½ for their hire for the two or three months' journey to Abeshe in Wadai. But it was better so. If I had owned the camels myself the responsibility for their welfare would have been all mine. It would have been my men who had them in charge, with no motive beyond the general one of loyalty to the leader and the job for carrying the camels through in good condition. But when Bu Helega's men went along with his own animals they were sure to have the best of care. During the trek to Kufra he kept his eye expertly on each one of them. If a camel weakened or seemed ill, he shifted loads to meet the emergency. He did everything to keep them fit to the journey's end, and his care of them was worth to me all that it cost.

In addition to camels I needed more men. The four who had been hired in Cairo, Sollum and Siwa were still with me—Abdullahi, Ahmed, Hamad and Ismail. I now added five more—Zerwali, Senussi Bu Hassan the guide, Sad, who came from Aujila, Hamid, and Faraj, a slave. Bu Helega had with him his son and two camelmen. The list was supplemented at the least by five Tebus, nomadic blacks from Tibesti, a region north-west of Wadai. Abdullahi and Zerwali were the two headmen of the caravan. The former was in command of the luggage and the commissariat, while Zerwali was in charge of the camels and the men. They were the best companions that any man could have on a desert trek.

We needed clothing, certain articles of food and shoes, especially the last. The heelless Beduin slipper is the only possible wear for the desert, but it will wear out, and it often has to be repaired on the way. It was necessary to be sure that each of us had not only shoes, but the leather that we should need for patching them until we reached Kufra.

At Jalo I found a famous shoemaker, Hemaida, whom I had met at Kufra two years before. I had with me the very shoes that he had made for me then, with soles badly in need of patching. Great was his delight when I took them to him for his ministrations. He was a venerable-looking personage, whom it would have been easy to take for a judge or a member of the council at least. He came to my house day after day to work on the five pairs of shoes he made for me, on the making of shoes for my men and the repairing of our saddles and other leather accoutrement. It was a pleasure to give him a meal and then to invite him to a friendly glass of tea. One day he was coughing as the tea was brought and I expressed sympathy for his ailment. He looked at me across his glass of tea and answered in his quiet voice, "But your tea always stops my cough, Sidi El Bey. Not other tea, but yours always does." I did not ignore the hint so gracefully given. Hemaida received his little packet of the miraculous tea as a present before we left Jalo.

Besides my shoes and the leather, I bought cloth for clothing for my men, butter, oil, barley, firewood and eight *girbas*. Ali Kaja, who was the favourite slave of Sayed Idris and had been made by him his trusted person, a *wakil* in Jalo, told me that his master had directed him to put all his store of supplies of every kind at my disposal. I thanked him, but did not avail myself of the offer. I had just come from Egypt, well equipped, and I knew how much these stores meant to those who lived in this isolated spot.

Besides the making of preparations, my ten days in Jalo were spent in receiving and giving entertainment and in scientific work. The entertainment was up to the best Beduin standards. The first day I dined with Senussi Gader Bouh, the Kaimakam or Governor of Jalo. The second day I lunched at the house of El Bishari, the most important of the Majabra merchant chiefs, waited on by my host and his sons. The third day luncheon was sent to me by the members of the Council, and I was joined in the repast by Zerwali, the *kadi* or judge, Ali Kaja and Moghaib. After the meal I had a talk with the *kadi* on Senussi history and was shown letters from the Grand Senussi, and from El Mahdi, his son. Dinner that day came from Haj Farahat, another Majbari merchant, with the Kaimakam, Zerwali, Ali Kaja, Moghaib and Abdullahi as sharers of the feast. We discussed the custom of "Bu-Zafar," which all agreed must not be a meal but the slaughtering and eating of a sheep.

On the fourth day I lunched at the house of Haj Ali Bilal, a Majbari. My diary records the fact that there was the "usual crowd" and a "very good lunch." Dinner was sent to me by Haj Seid, also one of the Majabra merchants, and the Kaimakam, Zerwali and the *kadi* joined me in it. On the next day I lunched at the house of Haj Ghraibil, and that evening my most interesting experience in the way of hospitality took place. There were living at Jalo several ladies of the Senussi family, including the wife of Sayed Idris and his sister. Shortly after my arrival at Jalo they sent me an invitation to dinner. This was an unusual occurrence, for Beduin women of high class do not offer entertainment to men as women of the Western world may do with perfect propriety. I realized, of course, that I would not actually dine with my hostesses in person, but I was appreciative of the unprecedented honour nevertheless.

At the appointed hour Zerwali and the Kaimakam came to escort me to dinner. The house which the ladies occupied was the former Government house of the days of Turkish rule. We were ushered into a spacious room where the soft light from a magnificent brass lantern and innumerable candles served to deepen the mellow tones and the rich combinations of colour of priceless rugs and silken cushions. Sidi Saleh, who was the husband of one of the Senussi ladies, acted as host on their behalf. Under his hospitable direction, a splendid banquet was served to us by half a dozen slaves. When we had eaten all that was demanded by courtesy, and, I am afraid, much more than was required by nature, the banquet was completed with the washing of our hands in basins brought by the slaves, the ceremonial three glasses of tea, the sprinkling over us of rose-water and the burning of incense before us. Then the chief slave came and deferentially whispered in my ear. Would the Bey care to hear some music? There was a gramophone, with records made by the famous singers of Egypt. The Bey had only to command.

Perhaps to the disappointment of my companions—I do not know—but quite to my own satisfaction, I courteously declined the offered entertainment. There was something rare and precious in the perfumed atmosphere of that softly-lighted room which the coming of voices from beyond the desert would have profaned. Partly the beauty of the place, the remoteness from the world, but especially the sense that I was the guest of noble Beduin women, who were hidden from me by the customs of our Eastern lands, but were in a real sense present through their gracious hospitality and kindly thoughtfulness, made of that evening a unique memory. I told the slave to convey my respectful *salaams* to the ladies and to tell them how much I had been touched by their courtesy. Then I went out into the clear desert night with the soft breeze stirring little breaths of incense from the folds of my *jerd* to remind me vividly of the peace and mystic calm of the room from which I had come.

The next day I returned the hospitality of those

who had entertained me so generously. My room with its dry mud floor and travel-stained luggage, ranged about the walls, could not bear comparison with the charming apartment in which I had dined the night before. But Ali Kaja took it upon himself to see that we were made as presentable as circumstances would permit. With a pair of beautiful brass lanterns and a few rugs borrowed from Sayed Idris's house and some other accessories he created a very decent imitation of a banquet hall. My guests included the Kaimakam, the members of the Council, the two *ikhwan*, the Judge, Ali Kaja, Musa the captain of the Senussi artillery, and Zerwali. Dressed in my best Beduin robes, I waited on them as a Beduin host should, and when some of them, who had been out into the world, asked me to sit with them and eat, I assured them that I would—when they were my guests in Cairo. Ahmed, my cook, had laid himself out to provide several distinctively European dishes to give a note of novelty to our entertaining, and the delight of my guests was great at his achievements.

My banquet ended the round of entertaining and for a day or two I was permitted to lunch and dine in peaceful solitude. It was a relief, grateful though I had been to my generous hosts for their hospitality.

An important part of my activities at Jalo was the making of scientific observations. I observed the sun and the stars to determine the latitude and longitude and took regular readings of the aneroid barometer and thermometer for the determination of the altitude. My observations on the latter point, when finally worked out in relation to barometric records made on the same days at Siwa, disclosed the interesting fact that the level of Jalo is 60 metres higher to-day than it was when Rohlfs ascertained it in 1879. He found Jalo almost exactly at sea level ; I found it 60 metres higher. I saw the explanation of it going on before my eyes. The drifting sands were climbing slowly up the trunks of the palm trees and against the walls of the houses, threatening to engulf them. Some of the inhabitants had already moved their houses and rebuilt them on higher levels. It is the steadily accumulating sand driven by sandstorms and gathering wherever trees and houses stop its progress, that has raised Jalo nearly 200 feet above sea level in forty-four years. The house I was living in, and at which the barometric readings were recorded, was from 15 to 20 metres higher than the rest of the houses at Jalo.

In the taking of my observations I had to be cautious, for the Beduins are suspicious of anything so elaborately scientific looking as a theodolite. They were sure to say that I was making a map with a view to coming back and conquering their land. The first time that a Beduin chief and the man who was to guide us to Kufra caught me at my theodolite, I had to explain hastily and persuasively that I was getting data for the making of a calendar for the month of Ramadan.

Abdullahi, who was of course not a Beduin, was invaluable to me in the camouflaging of my scientific activities. In fact he was rather a specialist in the manufacture of those little inaccuracies that smooth the path of life and preserve the social amenities. One day we were using the theodolite some distance from the town. A native demanded what we were doing and Abdullahi said we were taking a picture of Jalo.

" How can that be, at such a distance ? " demanded the Beduin.

Abdullahi had his explanation ready.

" The machine attracts the picture, so that it comes right out and flies into it," he asserted glibly.

" But how can a box attract a picture ? " demanded the incredulous Beduin.

Abdullahi struck an attitude.

" Ask the magnet how it attracts the iron," he commanded rhetorically, and the debate was closed.

CHAPTER X

On the Trek

ON Thursday, March 15th, we were ready to trek. I got up at 6 to pack and get my baggage ready. As is usual on the first day of a journey, when the caravan is not yet shaken down and accustomed to the routine, it took us three hours to load. We were to follow the Beduin custom of *tag-heez,* which means going to a near-by well before beginning a journey and spending several days, sometimes a week, in final preparations away from the distractions of town life. Buttafal Well, 30 kilometres from Jalo, was the point where we were to make our *tag-heez,* or preparation.

When the packing was well under way the Kaimakam, notables and *ikhwan* came to give us the ceremonial *mowad-a* or farewell. We squatted down together and discussed the prospects for the journey. I had made this same trip to Kufra two years before under somewhat more favourable conditions, and nevertheless we had lost our way before getting to Kufra. It had been cooler then, two months earlier in the year, the winds and sandstorms had not been so incessant, and the caravan had been smaller.

The problem of providing camels, their fodder, men, and food and equipment for the men, did not arise then as the whole caravan was produced complete and provided for by the generosity of Sayed Idris, a fact which had a considerable effect in lulling the suspicions of the Beduins and subduing their hostility to strangers. On this occasion, I had to arrange for the camels and personnel, and so big a caravan journeying with the quantity of unusual luggage necessary for a long journey naturally aroused curiosity.

On these long waterless treks Nature is often the only enemy—and she can be one if she chooses. The men of my caravan worked well together. The four whom I had brought from Cairo, Sollum and Siwa got on excellently with all the people we met. Zerwali, the Senussi *ikhwan* delegated by Sayed Idris to accompany us, was kindness itself and did everything in his power to make the journey as comfortable as possible. I felt no real concern over the outcome, no matter what Nature might choose to do.

When the camels were all loaded, we went through the dignified ceremony of the farewell. We took our stand in two half-circles facing each other, the men of my caravan and myself in one and the chiefs of Jalo and the *ikhwan* in the other. Solemnly and reverently we raised our hands, palm upward, for prayers that the journey would be a blessed one, that God would guide us and return us safe to our homes. We read the " Fat-ha," the first chapter of the Koran, the eldest of the *ikhwan* saying the " Amen." Then we shook hands and parted. The shouts of the men urging on the camels were echoed by " lu lias " from the women, and we were on our way.

As we passed El Lebba, the second village of Jalo, a pleasant incident occurred to send us cheerfully on our way. The solitary graceful figure of a girl appeared beside our path, her face hidden from us by the Beduin veil. With one voice the men nearest her called out the traditional greeting:

"Wajhik! wajhik! Your face! Your face!"

The girl turned and demurely drew aside her veil to disclose the finely chiselled features, the clear olive skin, and the shy yet dignified expression of a Beduin maiden. The men shouted with delight at her beauty and her courtesy. To complete the tradition I ordered them to "empty gunpowder" at her feet. Hamid and Sad performed the graceful ceremony, first one and then the other. The man danced lightly toward her as if to the imaginary rhythm of a Beduin drum, his rifle held in both hands over his head, the muzzle pointing forward, shouting a desert love song as he went. Just in front of her he dropped lightly on one knee, brought his gun to the vertical position butt upward, and fired, a hair's breadth from her feet.

So close was the shot and so accurate his aim, that the girl's slippers were singed by the powder flash. She did not flinch at the explosion, but stood gracefully erect in her pride at the honour done her. Singed slippers are a mark of distinction in the desert that any Beduin girl cherishes.

When Sad had followed Hamid's example, another shout rose from the men of the caravan and we moved on.

The girl smiled after us, as flattered by the homage that had been paid her as we were by the good omen of a pretty face crossing our path at the outset of our journey. Within an hour we were in the open desert again.

Eight hours' trekking brought us to Buttafal Well, where we were to stop a day. We took matters easily that first night, with singing and conversation about the camp fire till after midnight.

When the camp had settled down for the night, I took my pipe and went for a stroll. This was always one of the pleasures of my life in the desert—that last pipe of peace before turning in—and of peace it always was. If the day had been good, there was contentment; if bad, there was hope for the next day and faith that all would be well. During the whole journey, I never went to sleep with anything really worrying me—worrying, that is, my mind itself, no matter how I might have been tried by occurrences or by conditions.

The next day was spent in final preparations. Bu Helega, the owner of the camels, arrived with his own little caravan of three camels. During the day another man had come from Jalo to catch us up. We had been in need of rope and twine, but the price asked by the dealers had been too high. So Abdullahi chattered with them, and left the actual closing of the bargain to the last minute. Then he had arranged with a man named Senussi Bu Jabir to bring the rope after us to Buttafal.

When this man arrived, he came to my tent to tell me that his brother was in Wadai and to ask me to take him with us. He would work to pay for his passage. I looked him over and quickly decided that he would do. I discovered particularly that he had a sense of humour, almost if not quite the most valuable asset in desert travel. Ability may fail, but a keen sense of humour enables one to get the last ounce out of a man in possession of it. I was ready to take him, but it did not seem possible.

"We are leaving at once," I said. "There is no time for you to make the day's journey to Jalo and back for your luggage."

"I have it," he said.

"Where is it ?" I demanded, looking about in bewilderment.

"Here," he answered, pointing to the shirt he wore and the stick he carried.

I burst into a hearty laugh at the idea of such an outfit for a hard desert trek, and he joined me cheerfully. I assured him that he might go, and never regretted my decision. He proved to be one of the best men I had.

The next morning we watered the camels, a process which must not be hurried. Nothing is more important in trekking than the condition of your camels. Not only must they be fat and well nourished at the start, but they must be allowed to drink their fill with deliberation and permitted to rest after the drinking.

When the camels were ready they were loaded with the greatest care, for good packing and loading at the beginning means time and trouble saved all through the journey. The rapidity with which the loading and unloading can be accomplished day after day sometimes means a gain of a day or two in time before the trip is over.

At 2.30 we were ready to start. As the camels moved slowly off, the sonorous voice of Bu Helega rose in the *azan*, the "Calling to Prayers," according to the Beduin custom at the beginning of a long trek. It is the Beduin tradition that those who begin the journey with the *azan* will end it with the *azan*—they will, that is, meet with no disaster by the way.

Our caravan had gradually become enlarged until it consisted of thirty-nine camels, twenty-one men, a horse and a dog. Our personnel was as follows: Myself and my four men, Abdullahi, Ahmed, Hamad and Ismail; Zerwali, Bu Helega the owner of the camels, with his son, his nephew and his slave. There was also Dawood, Zerwali's uncle, who was going with a single camel to Ṭaiserbo to bring back his wife and daughter; Senussi Bu Hassan, our guide; Senussi Bu Jabir, the boy with the shirt and staff; Hamad Zwayi, another boy who was a pleasant singer; Sad the Aujili; Faraj the slave; two Tebus, with their three camels. In addition there were three other Tebus with three camels loaded with merchandise which they were taking to deliver to merchants in Kufra.

We set our faces southward and journeyed toward Kufra. It was hot and windy and the desert lay about us like an interminable pancake. The ground was *serira*, which is flat hard sand, with a little gravel scattered over it. Our first objective was the Zieghen well, which we ought to make in eight or nine days. In the old days, before the times of the Senussis, it had been the custom to make the trek from Jalo to Zieghen in three days and five nights, marching continuously without a stop for food or rest. But the Senussis changed all that. They inaugurated the custom of taking enough water and food to permit the journey to be made in twice the time, with adequate rest for camels and men each day.

At first our camels moved reluctantly, for they had just left good grazing and would much rather have gone back to it. Bu Helega tried his best to persuade the trading Tebus to lead the caravan with their camels, but they cleverly refused. The place of honour at the head of the line is an arduous one. Camels are quite ready to follow others ahead of them, but dislike to go forward independently. So the first camel in the caravan has to be driven and often beaten with a stick to keep him going. The Tebus preferred to bring up the tail of the procession, where their camels needed no urging. Bu Helega got even with them later, however, because of their choice of position.

It was hot and windy all the afternoon, but in the evening the wind dropped to a gentle breeze and the desert put forth its full charm. I find recorded in my diary some of the thoughts and feelings on getting back into this old familiar desert, where I was approaching the point at which we lost our way two years before.

> The same old flat desert and feelings of old memories;
>
> How one forgives the Desert her scorching sun and her torturing wind for the calm of the evening, the sunset, the moon rising and then that gentle and serene breeze. How easily one forgets the presence of her dangers. It is the full appreciation of simple pleasures that endear the Desert to one, in spite of all her harshnesses and crudities;
>
> A glass of tea;
>
> A cigarette;
>
> A pipe when all the caravan is asleep and the fragrance of the tobacco is wafted by the gently stirring air;
>
> A glimpse of the playing of the firelight on the faces of the men of the caravan, some old and rugged, some smooth and youthful;
>
> To see men toil, succeed and fail, and suffer in another sphere of life;
>
> Above all, to be near to God and to feel His Presence.

On the 18th we got up at 6, and the camels were

briskly loaded in thirty-five minutes. The careful first loading at Jalo and Buttafal made speed possible now. Nevertheless it was 9 o'clock before we were ready for the start. The morning programme in camp is not one that can be safely hurried. The Beduin dislikes intensely to be rushed over his meals, or to be deprived of those moments of leisure thereafter which are so essential to peaceful digestion and a contented spirit. The wise leader will see that these prejudices of his men are carefully observed.

Perhaps this is a good place to set down the outline of a typical day's trek under the conditions which prevailed until we reached Arkenu.

Although it is March, it is still cold in the morning and one gets up a little after dawn because it is too cold to stay in bed longer. Even the sleeping-bag and the Beduin blanket will not keep out the chill. A peep through the flaps of the tent shows that the stars are paling in the sky. Some one has the fire already started and the first impulse is to get to it without delay. Throwing my *jerd* about me and wrapping the *kufia* about my ears I dash out to the crackling blaze. There is nothing hot about the desert in these crisp morning hours. I stand by the fire and have a look round. There is little life in the camp yet, though all the men are up. They are huddled close to the warmth, muffled in *jerds* and every other garment that they can lay their hands on. When water is plentiful, steaming hot glasses of tea are handed round, and after they are drunk the activities of the camp divide. The camelmen go to feed the camels with dried dates, which the beasts munch reflectively, stones and all. A consultation is sometimes held over the camels, if some of them have suffered the previous day from too heavy loads. Perhaps a shifting of loads is decided on or better packing and loading recommended.

Other men are pulling down the three tents, which form the apexes of a triangle, with the camels parked at its centre. The luggage which had been set up as a barricade against the icy wind is sorted out and arranged ready for the loading.

Meanwhile I have been attending to the barometer and thermometer, registering their readings, filling in the spaces in my scientific diary, seeing that the cameras have fresh films. The voices of the men sound low through the camp, muffled by *kufias* and extra clothing. At last breakfast is ready.

It may be *asida*, the Beduin national dish, a kind of pudding baked of flour, oil and spices ; or it may be rice. It is an utterly simple meal in either case, but with what a keen appetite one attacks it. In the desert any disinclination for the first meal of the day that one may feel in city surroundings vanishes away. Breakfast is finished off with the inevitable three glasses of tea, taken slowly and reflectively. Whatever one does, one must not deprive one's men of their tea or hurry them over it. Give a Beduin a filling meal and let him sip three glasses of tea after it and you can get any work out of him that you want. Stint him or rush him and you will get worse than nothing.

After breakfast every one is warm and contented and ready to work hard. The loading goes on swiftly, diversified at times by the antics of the two or three young and frolicsome camels that seem to get into every caravan. These young fellows resist being loaded and even throw off their loads when the job is apparently all finished. Zerwali and Abdullahi are alert to see that the loading is done with the utmost care and precision. An extra half-hour spent now may save two or three hours' delay on the road later caused by slipping of the loads or improper distribution of the burdens.

When the caravan is all but ready, I have a few words with the guide about the direction of our day's march. He draws a line on the sand and says that there lies our way. I take a bearing of the line with my compass, a proceeding which doubtless seems to him an absurd if harmless idiosyncrasy of mine. But I like to be able to check with the compass the direction the caravan is taking as the day goes on. On the whole the precaution proves unnecessary, however, for Senussi Bu Hassan goes straight to his mark as a homing pigeon. Only in the middle of the day he sometimes wobbles a bit. In the daytime he travels by his shadow, and, as he explains, "When the sun is high and the shadow lies between my feet, then my head goes round." There is one other hour in the day when the guide's task is a perplexing one. In the twilight hour between the setting of the sun and the appearance of the stars, all directions on the desert's vast disc are the same. Then sometimes the compass is useful. Once, by means of the bearing I had taken in the morning, I caught the guide in the hour between sun and stars going almost 90 degrees off the right direction. But as a rule the accuracy with which a good guide, like Senussi Bu Hassan, steers his course is almost uncanny.

Our conference over and the last camel loaded, the

guide sets out ahead and one by one the camels follow. The men of the caravan have a last warm-up of hands and feet at the dying fire, thrust their feet into the Beduin shoes and hasten after the camels, singing gaily. The sun is getting warm by now, and unless there is a strong wind blowing from the north, one disposes quickly of wrappings on ears and neck and finally with the *jerd.* The extra garments are flung on the backs of the camels, jokes begin to crack, foot races are run, and everybody is happy to be alive. Gradually the men sort themselves into groups of two and three, spaced at intervals along the caravan, chatting about their own affairs or about things in general. Sometimes I walk at the head of the caravan and again some distance behind it to keep an eye on the direction it is taking, and especially to enjoy the sense of solitude and remoteness.

Towards midday, contemplation of the beauties of Nature is sometimes disturbed by other and less romantic thoughts. My mind occasionally wanders towards favourite restaurants in far-away civilization. As I stride along I imagine myself in Shepherd's Grill Room in Cairo and I order *Crevettes à l'Americaine* with that subtle variation of *Riz à l'orientale* which is a speciality of the house. Or I am at Prunier's in Paris ordering *Marennes Vertes d'Ostende,* followed by a steak and a soufflé. Perhaps it is the Cova at Milan and a succulent dish of *Risotto alla Milanese* ; maybe Strawberries Melba at the Ritz in London, or again a Circassian dish of rice with walnut sauce which is the masterpiece of the old and beloved retainer, once a slave, who really rules my father's house in Cairo, occupying the privileged position of a treasured " Nannie " of long service in an English family.

Suddenly Ahmed or Abdullahi comes along and without a word pushes a bag of squashed dates into my palm. Dreams vanish, and I eat with as much appetite as though there were no better fare in all the world.

There is no halt for lunch, as the camels eat only twice a day. If we have just left an oasis, there is fresh bread, half a loaf or even a whole one to each man, with dates. Later on that fresh bread becomes hard bread, and still later no bread at all. But there are always dates.

I have one camel fitted up with a folded tent over its back so that any one of us may lie and take his ease when tired of walking. Ahmed calls it " the Club." One day at the lunch hour Abdullahi demands where I am and whether I have had my portion of bread and dates or not, and Ahmed replies, with a twinkling eye in an otherwise grave face, " The Bey is lunching at the Club to-day."

It is entirely possible when you are used to it, to have a good nap on the camel's back and an occasional ride is not to be scorned. But generally one walks, for the camel's pace of two and a half miles an hour is an easy one to keep up with, and riding is often more tiring than going on foot.

Sometimes during a whole day's trek a narrow strip of water lies shimmering on the horizon ahead of the caravan. It never gets any nearer, but continues to beckon a cool and pleasant invitation until the sun has rolled round to the west and the mirage vanishes away. It is a purely optical illusion, for there is no water there. Another kind of mirage comes sometimes in the early morning. Then the country far ahead of one appears in the sky at the horizon, as the Beduins say, " upside down." This is not, as the other variety of mirage is, entirely an illusion. It is really the reversed reflection of the country 30 or 40 kilometres ahead of where the observer stands. As the sun rises higher above the horizon suddenly the mirage vanishes as magically as it came. There are also other tricks of reflection of light in the desert. Sometimes, for instance, a small pebble the size of a cricket ball seen from a mile away might assume the appearance of a big rock, standing like a landmark. The skeleton or part of the skeleton of a camel or a human being take on the most fantastic shapes, on the horizon, but the Beduins know it well.

It is absurd to say that the Beduin is lured by the mirage out of his way and even to his destruction. The seasoned desert traveller knows a mirage when he sees one. It is entirely possible indeed that the " upside down " variety may be a positive assistance, since it can suggest what kind of country lies ahead. The mirage is an interesting phenomenon, but it is not one of the perils of desert travel.

In the afternoon there are several hours of heat, the pace of the camels slackens and the whole caravan becomes quiet and somnolent. As evening comes on and it grows cool again, the camels pick up their speed and go into a final spurt before the time for making camp. The men sing to the camels then to stimulate their efforts and the beasts respond cheerfully to the encouragement.

The songs are simple and poetic, full of the atmosphere of the desert life. One of them represents a Beduin waiting at an oasis for the expected caravan.

He sings to the approaching camels:

> Gone is the night;
> Come are the Marazam? to the morning sky.
> You are here—
> And vanished are all our fears.

The Singer speaks of his camels:

> In companies the sand-dunes
> Marched to meet them,
> Pointing the homeward way.

The Singer addresses his camels:

> The sand-dunes hide many wells
> That brim with waters unfailing.
> You come to their margins like bracelets
> Wrought of gold and rare gems in far countries.

In another the Singer is still addressing his camels:

> The wells lie hid in the dunes
> Masked by the sands drifted over them.
> You approach them in ones and twos,
> Oh you who reveal hidden places.

The last song that I shall set down shows the traditional attitude of the Beduin to his camel. It is his most precious possession. To give it up without a struggle to the death is dishonour. A Beduin might wait to take revenge for the killing of a brother or a son, but if his camel were stolen he would not rest until he found it and brought it back, by force of arms if necessary. " He who will not risk his life for his camel," says the Beduin, " does not deserve to have it." So the camel-driver sings to his beast :

> For your sakes,
> Oh ye who cherish us
> As loving mothers their children,
> For your sakes
> The sons of nobles
> Have lain stark on the sands,
> Unsheltered by tomb or burial.

The men suit the song to the occasion. The first one that I have translated might be used when an oasis was not far off, the second when the caravan is approaching sand-dune country, the third and fourth when they are nearing a well, and the last when entering a hostile region.

At sunset I make it a point to be near the guide and unobtrusively to check him up with my compass in those uncertain hours before the stars come out. When the dark falls a lantern is lighted and given to the guide. Then we follow that elusive pin-point of yellow in the darkness. It winks a provocative invitation to follow, but we can never reach it. The camels like to have the lantern ahead of them and move briskly forward in pursuit. Twelve or thirteen hours of walking, if conditions have been good, bring us to the end of the day's trek, though sometimes we cannot go on so long.

" *Eddar ya ayan*—home for you who are weary," is shouted by the guide and repeated by every man in the caravan. Then the men collect the camels and divide them, the water camels here, those carrying tents over there, the camels with luggage for the barricade yonder. The camels are " *barrakked* "—kneel with grunts of satisfaction to have their loads removed. Now we must be vigilant, for men tired by a day's trek are likely to be careless and let boxes with precious instruments or cameras fall with disastrous violence.

The baggage is arranged in a barricade, if the night promises to be windy, and the tents are pitched in their triangle, unless the night is particularly calm and pleasant. I could never decide which moment was fuller of satisfaction, that in which the tent was set up after a hard day's trek or that in which it was pulled down preliminary to taking the road again.

Then the fire is built and the leaping flames of the *hatab* throw a warm glow over the sand. The first thing is tea. Now I realize to the full the virtues of the dark bitter-sweet liquid that the Beduins know by that name. They make tea by taking a handful of the leaves and a handful of sugar and boiling them briskly in a pint of water. The result would drive a housewife of the West almost insane, but it is a wonderful stimulant after a hard day's trek in the desert and a glorious reviver of one's energies and spirits.

The men of the caravan are not slow to prepare and eat the evening meal, to feed the camels and then to dispose themselves for sleep. But I must compare my six watches and wind them, record the photographs made during the day, change the cinema films in the darkness, no mean feat in itself, label and store the geological specimens I have collected, and write up my diaries. The glasses of Beduin tea which I have drunk help me to accomplish these duties and then probably stimulate me to a walk in the desert. If there is no bitter cold wind I go for perhaps half a mile, looking back from time to time at the silhouette of the caravan against the sky. The dark masses of the tents, the baggage and the kneeling camels, touched here and there with flickers of light from the dying fire, in the midst of that immense sea of sand, make a picture full of mystery and fascination. All about me is silence. There is no wind whispering in the leaves, no murmur of the waters of a brook, such as one hears in the wooded wilds ; no slap and plash and swish of waves against the ship's side such as are always present at sea. Nothing but silence. Silence, the sands, and the stars.

CHAPTER XI

The Road to Zieghen Well

FROM this point I shall set down the days as they are recorded in my diary.

Sunday, March 18th.—Start at 9 a.m., halt at 8.30 p.m. Make 46 kilometres. Highest temperature 21°, lowest 3°. Cloudy all day, clears in evening. Just a few drops of rain in the afternoon. Strong north-east wind, which develops at 2.30 into a sandstorm. Wind drops at sunset, and gets up again at 8 in the evening. The sun not visible and the guide's course not so straight as usual, as shown by the compass bearings which I take often during the day. At 5.30 the sun appears, and he corrects his course ; at 7.30 he is travelling by the North Star, which the Beduins call El Jadi. The ground is generally the same as yesterday's, though slightly undulating. At intervals all day we come across patches of big, dark-coloured pebbles.

In the morning there was excitement when we sighted on the horizon the series of hazy dots that meant the approaching vanguard of a caravan. My binoculars were brought into play and passed around among the men. Rifles were unslung from their places on the camels' backs and the Tebus ran to get their spears. The men ranged themselves on the side of the caravan nearest the oncomers and held themselves alert until we should find out whether they were friendly or hostile. It did not take long to recognize them for friends. Then men from each party met and squatted down between the two caravans to exchange the news, while the two lines of camels plodded past. Tongues flew as they heard and told who had been married, who was dead, who had made money, what new feuds had sprung up or what old ones had been ended. Then the envoys sprang up, bade each other God speed and hastened after their respective caravans. (This is the desert wireless at work.)

Monday, March 19th.—Start at 8.15 a.m., halt at 8.30 p.m. evening. Make 49 kilometres. Highest temperature 22°, lowest 5°. Weather fine and clear. Strong north-east wind, which drops at midday. Few white clouds in the afternoon. Sun is very warm, making our progress slow, but evening is cool and the pace is quickened. Ground very flat, hard sand covered with fine gravel. At 6 in the evening cross a slight depression, with a patch of grey stone on the right and a white stone on our left about 2 kilometres distant.

All of us, men and camels, were getting into our stride. The Beduins and Tebus indulged in foot-races and played practical jokes. The Tebus are simple primitive fellows, with delightfully naïve habits of mind. Being poor, they take the best of care of what possessions they have. They dress in a simple cotton shirt and pair of drawers, and devote much attention to making these garments last as long as possible. When a Tebu rides a camel, for example, he takes off his drawers to save wear and tear, and hangs them on his camel's back. When he sleeps also he removes his garments to protect them from friction against the sand, and wraps himself in his fur cloak.

While one of the Tebus was riding that day some of the Beduins took his drawers and hid them. When he alighted and looked for his garment, he immediately feared that it had dropped off and lay somewhere in the desert along our track. Without a moment's hesitation he set out on the back track, running briskly in search of his precious possession. He had become a tiny figure in the vast expanse of sand before we took pity on him and fired shots to call him to return. He turned reluctantly and soon rejoined us with downcast face. But the merriment of the jokers told him that something was up, and when his drawers were produced he was too pleased to get them back to resent the joke.

The previous night some of the camels paid a visit to my tent and threatened to have it down on top of me. They are clever beasts. They like to scratch their necks on the tent ropes, and when all the camp is asleep they hobble in quest of this innocent form of diversion. First the camel sticks his head through the flap in my tent to see if I am awake. If he does not hear me resent his intrusion, he then knows I am asleep and out he backs and sets to scratching vigorously. Soon he is joined by others and I awake under the impression that my tent is being assailed by a violent storm.

Each day I was more impressed with Bu Helega as a travelling companion. He was a man of few words, with a big heart and generous spirit. His years and his white hair and beard gained him the respect of all of us, for in the desert the man of experience, who is possessed of the wisdom that comes with age, is the invaluable one. Zerwali and I, therefore, referred continually to Bu Helega's judgment. He was tactful in offering his suggestions for my consideration, but I was wise enough not to disregard them.

He was constantly on the look-out for the well-being of the camels, and his splendid voice was heard at intervals through the day addressing the camels or the men.

"The white camel is weary. To-morrow, Ibrahim (his slave), we will shift its load to the old brown one," he says to his slave.

"Talk to them, men, talk to them," he commands, knowing how much better the camels travel under encouragement, and again, "Sing to them, Ibrahim."

"Follow the guide, you beautiful beasts," he exhorts the camels.

"Pray, Hamad, that saddle has shifted; it will irritate the camel's back."

When the twilight comes he gives the order, "Light the lantern; it pleases the camels."

The qualities of the camel are seldom, if ever, appreciated on a slight acquaintance. The camel is as clever as a horse, if not more clever, and in some ways is more human. "Patient as a camel" is an Arab saying and a very true one. If you ill-treat a camel he will never forget it, but he will not attack you on the spot. He will wait, and if you repeat the offence again and again, he makes up his mind to get his revenge. Not, however, when there are many people about. Here he behaves in a most human way. He watches his chance until you and he are alone and then he goes for you; either by snatching at you with his mouth and throwing you to the ground, or by kicking you and then trampling upon you. There is a case known where a camel trampled on a man and then sat on him, refusing to move even after punishment from the men who ran up to the rescue, wanting to make sure that he had finished his man, as, indeed, he had.

People imagine that in the desert a camel has to be roped in and led. As a matter of fact, it is very hard in the desert to keep a camel away from the rest of the caravan, for instinctively he knows that to be left behind is death ; so he keeps as near the bulk of the caravan as he can. It is a sad sight to see a camel straggling behind a caravan. It is like the soldier in retreat, unable to keep up with his comrades, knowing that nobody can carry him and that to fall behind means disaster.

The camel also displays his intelligence when he is taken from the oasis and pushed into the waterless trek. Instinctively he tries at night, even three or four days after the start, to go back to the oasis. There have been a few desert tragedies when all the camels have deserted the men at night, either on the outward or the home-coming journey, when the caravan was still a few days from its destination. Or in the event of some accident befalling a caravan, camels which have travelled a certain road for ten or fifteen years will complete the journey alone.

As we were approaching Jalo and three days' journey from the camp of the Beduins from whom I had hired three camels, one of the latter fell desperately ill. They divided his load between the other two and left him in the desert, I, all the time, urging the Beduins to kill him and save him the tortures of death. I even offered to pay them the price of the camel if they would allow me to put an end to him. But as the camel was a pedigree beast, they refused. They said : " He is only feeling tired, he will go at his leisure back to the camp." I learnt afterwards that the camel reached home safely and was feeling much better.

Instinctively, again, the camel knows that he has a guide, and if you halt in the middle of the desert to debate some point in regard to the route, the camels crowd round the guide; the moment he moves, they follow him, ignoring the presence of every other member of the caravan, but never overtaking the guide. Or if occasionally a camel ignores even the guide and goes right ahead of a caravan, then it is safe for the caravan to follow that camel, for he certainly knows the place that the caravan is coming to. The Beduins say that a camel who has once grazed in an oasis would find his own way back to that oasis even if he were a few days' journey from it. There is a famous Beduin story of the sand grouse and the camel who had a competition. The sand grouse said: "I could lay my eggs in the desert, travel for days, and come back and hatch them." The camel retorted: "If my mother drinks from a well when I am still in her womb, I could travel days and come back and drink from the same well."

I myself have seen a camel head the caravan when we were four days from a well, the waters of which he had tasted four years before. There is a well-known case of one camel that saved a caravan which was going from Dakhla oasis to the oasis of Ouenat. The guide, who had never been to the place before, but was heading towards it going by the description of another Beduin, had lost his bearings, and the caravan wandered for twelve days aimlessly. The water was exhausted and they had lost hope. Suddenly one of the camels headed the caravan and they followed him. That camel had been to Ouenat a few years before, and when he was two days' journey from Ouenat he " smelt the place," as the Beduins say, and landed the caravan right at one of the wells.

In winter the well-trained camel can go for a fortnight without water, in summer up to twelve days. The Beduins try to feed their camels always on grazing grass if they can, but when they take them to the *daffa*, or long waterless trek, they are fed on dried dates and, when the Beduin can afford it, on barley. Most of the camels found in Cyrenaica are *hamla*, or pack camels. The best trotting camels are Tebus or Touaregs, beautiful white beasts with slim limbs and graceful lines. The average good day's work of the pack camel is a distance of 25 miles. The thoroughbred Touareg does up to 40, and has been known to do 70 miles at one stretch.

The camel can become a very affectionate beast and very devoted to his master. Well-trained trotting camels, or *hegins*, refuse to get up with anybody on their back but their own master.

As a rule the water is carried on the older and wiser camels who go sedately with no attempt to frolic. They realize that they are carrying the most valuable asset of the whole caravan, and therefore, the moment the day's trek is over, and we are at the hour of unloading, these older and wiser camels stand apart from the rest for fear the sheepskins they are carrying be bumped. I have also seen camels walking round the camp and approach the sheepskins lying on the ground, arranged and covered for the night ; the camels would take great care to walk round them.

There was one camel that was trained for a long time to carry my tent and all my books and instruments. He was only chosen for that task because of his being a strong and an old camel. Every morning when the loading started he used to come of his own accord and *barrak* near my tent and, in his usual supercilious way, wait for the load to be put on his back.

The camel is a jealous husband, or a faithful wife as the case may be. The female camels will never leave their lord and master and always follow him, while woe betide any adventurous male camel who dares to attempt to "butt in."

Each morning and evening Bu Helega and I rode together and talked about camels and the desert and Beduin history. I was careful to ask no direct questions, for the Beduins are suspicious people ready to mistrust your motives. But casual remarks easily bring out interesting comments and information.

"There was a time," said the venerable old man, "when Kufra was unknown to our people. A Beduin of the Ghawazi tribe, from El Obayad, a small oasis near Buttafal Well, noticed a crow which kept flying away to the south and coming back again, as regularly as the sun rises. He watched it for some time and then set out to follow its course southward. He finally reached Taiserbo and after a day's stop on the outskirts of the oasis, managed to get enough water to take him back. On his return he told his tribe of date trees and water in the heart of the desert. They formed an expedition which set out for Taiserbo and conquered it, after which they went on to Buzeima, Ribiana and eventually to Kufra itself. So the Beduins came to Kufra."

I had been casting covetous eyes on Bu Helega's horse since first I saw it in Jalo. Abdullahi had inquired for me whether it could be bought, but the price was too high. So I affected indifference and bided my time. No one of Bu Helega's family rode the horse but himself. The old man's dignity would not permit. But he kindly allowed me to use the animal whenever I wanted to ride. In fact, on this journey it seemed more mine than his.

Three of the camels were tired and "*barrakked*" (knelt down) without orders. They do not behave in this way unless there is good reason for it, so we shifted their loads to let them have a rest. We lost time in the process, but made it up when the cool of the evening came.

I made it a point to talk with each man in the caravan every day. It kept things running smoothly and incidentally I picked up some interesting information. I learned on this day that the Beduins not only know the tracks of their own camels, but can often tell whether camels which have passed belong to men of the same tribe or not. Tebu camels they know at once because of the peculiar shape of their hoofs and the long strides they take. The Tebu camels are hardier than the Beduin animals and can be used both in the northern desert of Cyrenaica and to the south in the Sudan. The Beduins change camels at Kufra, when going north or south.

I walked with Senussi Bu Hassan the guide and he told me of a trick used by the Beduins when they are herding camels or sheep. They milk the beasts in the morning and bury the milk in a *girba* to keep it cool. But desert marauders are clever and can easily find where a *girba* has been buried. So the wily Beduin buries two *girbas*, one beneath the other. The bottom one is full of fresh milk and the top one of stale. The thief discovers the upper *girba* and looks no farther, while the owner of the *girbas* finds his fresh milk safe when he returns at night.

We met flocks of small birds winging their way north. Some of them were tired and eagerly accepted the water we offered them. One perched on my hand to drink.

Sometimes near a well, one of those that is better described as a waterhole, one sees a few wings, feathers, bones of birds that tell their sad tale. They were probably immigrants who came across the well and stayed for a few days to recuperate. The well had just been dug by a passing caravan, water was easily available and the birds grew accustomed to the spot. Little by little the sand drifted up and filled the well and one day there was no more water, just a damp patch of sand. Or perhaps the birds arrived there too exhausted to fly another 100 or 200 miles in search of water, so they remained and died.

In the morning at 10.30 we passed sand-dunes, called El Khweimat, 8 or 10 kilometres to our left, like small white tents on the desert as their name indicates. At 4.30 we sighted on our left at 30 kilometres the landmark called El Ferayeg, four sandhills in a row. The name means "the little band" of men. At 6.15 we sighted the top of another landmark known as Mazoul, "the solitary one," hazy in the distance to the south-east.

We were all cheered by the sight of these landmarks, which marked our progress. We were confident that we had a skilful guide, but, as the Beduins say, "the good guide is known only at the well." It is only when one has reached the end of the journey that there is certainty that the right track has been taken. Senussi Bu Hassan demonstrated his remarkably keen eyesight. Very early in the morning before breaking camp he announced that he saw El Khweimat landmark in spite of the morning mist. It was several hours before other eyes in the caravan could make it out.

In the afternoon we passed camel skeletons lying white on the sands. Strangely enough this is a cheering sign in the desert, for two reasons. First because in the trackless monotony any sign that others have passed that way is encouraging, and, second, because the camel bones are more frequent near the wells. Camels are more likely to die near the end of a trek, when, if water is scarce, they have been pushed too hard by their masters. The Beduins do not like to use the word "skeleton" when they find such a reminder that death has come this way. So they euphemistically call it "*ghazal*," which means gazelle.

Thursday, March 22nd. Up at 5.30 a.m. I watched the sun rise at 6.27 a.m. and recorded its time. We started at 8 a.m. and made 48 kilometres over very flat country, hard sand and gravel. All the morning the Mazoul sand-dunes were on our left, 25 kilometres distant, but by the afternoon we had passed them.

In the morning I heard Zerwali and Abdullahi discussing this land of astounding flatness through which we were passing.

"Yes, our country is a blessed one," said Zerwali.

"Yes, indeed, it has a wonderful future," answered

the man from Egypt. " It is here, I believe, that the day of reckoning will be held. It is the only place God could find that would be big enough and so empty."

The Tebus were running far and wide, ahead and each side of the caravan, in search of camel-dung for fuel. They lived their life a little apart from the others in the caravan and so they liked to have their own camp-fire at night a short distance from the main camp. Camel-dung was the only available fuel. The Tebus, who are sturdy runners, would go as much as 5 miles out of their way to find the precious material. But the Beduins objected to the Tebus' habit of running ahead and seizing all the dung. It is an inflexible rule of the desert that anything found on the way belongs to him who first touches it, and the Tebus appealed to that rule for justification. The Beduins, however, had a telling retort.

" You have no guide ahead, nor do you let your camels go first, where they will not go without the stick," they said. " You want us to lead the way for your camels, while you run ahead and seize the dung. That dung belongs to us who would come upon it first if you were back with your camels where you belong."

The controversy grew spirited and was finally brought to me for judgment. I decreed that the Beduins were right, and the Tebus should have no fire of their own. However, they should be given a hot meal from the general commissariat every night. The Tebus are quite different in many of their habits and customs from the Beduins. They often do not use fire in the preparation of their food, though, as

I have shown, they do not reject it for comfort and cheer. They dry the inside of the bark from the top of the date tree over a fire and powder it, to use as material for a kind of pudding. They mix it with dates and locusts, also powdered. They invite no one to share their meals as the Beduins invariably do, nor are they resentful if others do not ask them to share their food. The Beduins criticize vigorously this failure in hospitality, as they consider it. The Tebus leave nothing behind them on the track, having a superstitious fear that whoever picks up what they have dropped will get hold of them, too. They are fine physical specimens and good workers, but extremely simple in their habits of life and mind. They are mixing more and more with the Beduins, however, and learning the Beduin ways.

On this day one of the camels became ill. Bu Helega got down and walked behind it and then bled it from the tail. We hoped it would be better after a night's rest.

As we were sure of our water supply we decided to have a glass of tea. Bu Helega, Zerwali, Abdullahi and I went on ahead of the caravan, taking the guide with us to set our course right. When we were far enough ahead, we quickly made a fire and brewed tea. As the caravan came up, we handed a glass of tea to each man as he passed. The caravan did not stop. When the last camel was past us, we packed up our paraphernalia and hastened to catch up with the plodding caravan, Bu Helega on his camel, Zerwali and Abdullahi riding double on a trotting camel, and I on the horse. I must own Baraka was useful to me for several purposes. With him the camels could be easily brought back from the grazing ground, which they are reluctant to leave to enter the *serira* again. I could ride him to visit places of interest when we halted at oases, allowing the camels to rest or graze. I could go ahead of the caravan with him or remain behind to make observations or secure specimens unwatched by the men. On his back I could make a properly dignified appearance at the head of my caravan when entering or leaving an oasis.

Friday, March 23rd.—We made 36 kilometres. There was a strong north-east wind the previous night, starting an hour after midnight. This wind continued all day, increasing from 1 to 3, and dropped in the evening. It was fair and clear, but cloudy in the late afternoon. At 5 in the afternoon we sighted the sand-dunes called El Mazeel, 25 kilometres toward the south-east.

The men had become interested in making a full day's trek, and exerted every effort to be under way at 8, intending to walk for twelve hours. But the sick camel interfered with our plans. When the time came to start, it had to be lifted to its feet. Bu Helega shook his head and said, " This camel will be flesh to eat before the day is over." Two hours later the camel knelt and refused to rise. In a few minutes it had to be slaughtered. Three men and two camels were left to bring the flesh after us. Before we had gone far Bu Helega came trotting up on his horse and said, " It is a fat camel. Let us stop for a while."

Knowing the Beduin's love of meat, I halted the caravan while a fire was made and a feast prepared. Every one ate the meat but myself and my two Egyptian servants. Bu Helega asked why I did not join the feast, and I told him that I did not care to eat the flesh of a sick camel.

"It is better than the little fish," he said, referring to some tins of sardines which we had with us. "We have seen the camel slaughtered, but who knows what has happened to the little fish since they were in the sea."

The camel's flesh which was not eaten at once the Beduins dried, and cut into thin shreds for flavouring their rice and *asida* later on. When we started again in the afternoon Senussi Bu Hassan said to me, "We will walk until we knock off the young moon and then we will be able to lunch at the well to-morrow." But when evening came clouds hid *El Jadi* before the young moon had set and we had to stop and make camp at 10.30 for fear of losing our way.

In this part of the desert there was little to discover externally, but a great deal to discover in one's self, that could only be brought to light in the silence and calm. It makes all the difference in the world whether one goes through the journey with the intention of getting back as quickly as possible to civilization again, or whether one lives and enjoys every moment of it.

Just as the sun was going down, I saw Zerwali sitting by himself, drawing lines on the sand with a meditative finger. He was doing the *Yazerga*, or the "science of the sands," with which the Beduin tells his own fortune. At intervals his eyes lifted from the pattern before him and brooded dreamily on the vivid colours of the sunset. The Beduin has an appreciation of beauty and a reverence for nature. How could he help it?

Day after day it is exactly the same. The photographs I took in these seven days might be pictures of the same camp from different angles, so persistently the same was the immense desolate expanse of sand unmarked except for a camel's skeleton or a few pebbles the size of a walnut. There was nothing to distract one's mind or interrupt one's contemplation.

What a peculiar charm this desolate desert has! What a cleansing effect on one's mind and body! How this constant touch with infinity day by day, and night by night, affects the mind and the spirit, and alters one's conception of life.

How small and petty one's efforts in the round of ordinary civilization seem! How insignificant one's efforts in this desert actually are!

Saturday, March 24th.—We were up at 5.30 a.m., tired, for we went to bed at 2. It was fine and clear all day; a north-east breeze in the morning, dropped at midday, leaving it very warm. A strong north-east wind got up again at 10 p.m.

At 9.30 a.m. the country began to change slightly; the sand was softer and the ground a little undulating. At 10 we came across patches of black broken stone, which continued all day. At noon we sighted on our right the first *hatab*—dried brushwood —of Zieghen Valley. At 1.45 we halted for a hot meal and a rest near the first *hatab* we reached.

Our fuel supply was exhausted the previous day, and we had had nothing hot to eat or drink since the morning of the *day before.* At 5.15 we sighted sand-dunes to the south-east, about 40 kilometres distant. The dunes ran southward in a line toward Zieghen Valley. At 8.30 the hillocks of *hatab* increased in number and extent.

When we started in the morning we hoped to get to Zieghen that day. Later there was disagreement as to why we had not reached it. Bu Helega remarked that the guide must have gone too far to the west or we should have arrived at the well before this. Zerwali, who had selected Bu Hassan for our guide, came to his defence. It was because we lost time slaughtering the camel and feasting the day before that we did not arrive, he said. Hamid had another explanation. "The camels are not being driven at all," he said. "One sleeps long and gets up at his leisure and the camels are still in sight." (It was the custom of the men to drop out of line for a nap of half an hour or so, the slow pace of the camels and their track in the sand making it possible for them to catch the caravan easily on wakening.)

When we halted to make a fire and have the first hot meal in thirty hours, I remembered that this was just where we lost our way on the previous trip to Kufra in 1921. After our meal, Dawood, Zerwali's uncle, left us with his single camel to go to Taiserbo, which lay a day's journey west of Zieghen. He proposed to get his wife and daughter and take them to Cyrenaica, where there were better prospects for business. Zerwali had agreed to help him in his affairs in the new region. It must have taken a lot of pluck for the old man to undertake the long journey to the north with the two women and but a single camel. I asked him how he would manage it. He told me that the first day they would all walk. The next day, as the weight of water on the camel grew less his daughter would ride, and the third day his wife.

"But suppose something happens to your camel?" I asked.

"Protection comes from God," was his quiet answer. I gave him rice, macaroni, tea and sugar, and when we had said the *Fat-ha,* he departed very happy.

The Beduins were delighted with a great feast of rice and camel-flesh and went to bed in vast contentment. It was a beautiful night, and I left my tent and spent a few tranquil moments under the golden moon and the stars paled by her brighter light. Their serene cheerfulness and encouraging company sent me back to my bed, as always, with new hope and confidence.

This is the entry in my diary for the following day:

Sunday, March 25th.—Start at 7.45 a.m., halt at 1.45 p.m. Make 24 kilometres. Highest temperature 32°, lowest 14°. Strong north-east wind all last night and until 4.30 to-day. Cloudy all the morning, no sun; a few drops of rain at mid-day. It clears in the afternoon. We walk all the way among little hillocks of dry *hatab*, gradually increasing from a few inches to 8 feet in height as we near the well. The hillocks are interspersed with patches of sand strewn with bits of black broken stone. The sand gets gradually softer until it is moist a few inches under the surface.

At 9.15 we sighted to the south-west about 3 kilometres away the sand-dunes of El Washka, a small well of the Zieghen group. At 9.30 we passed on our left Matan Bu Houh, the old well of Zieghen. We camped near the few date trees that stand by the best well of the group, El Harrash.

In the desert a well does not mean a nicely excavated and stoned-up arrangement such as one finds in other parts of the world, with a bucket and windlass, or a pump. In this part of the desert a well is a spot where the water is close to the surface and can be easily obtained by digging. Between the visits of caravans the sands drift over the place and choke the waterhole, which the Beduins scrape open with their hands, getting water at 3 or 4 feet down. If it has been a long journey the first thing to think of is the camels. After they have been watered and a good meal digested, washing is the most important item in the programme. If the water is scarce, clothes have to wait until the next well, because the question of water for the trek has to be considered.

As soon as the men have rested, sheepskins are filled and left for the night. Early next morning two or three men go to see which of the sheepskins has leaked, and, if possible, detect the cause of the leakage. They also make a point of separating the bad sheepskins from the good ones, so that on the journey water should be taken on the first day or two from those which leak or are unreliable.

The first night at a well, however tired the caravan may be, is always made the opportunity for great rejoicing, singing and dancing. Before arriving at the well one's idea of a rest has been at least four or five days' stay and plenty of water to make up for past privation. Thoughts dwell on the pleasing idea of really having water to splash about with. Curiously enough after a single day's rest, a fever of restlessness gets hold of one again and the luxury of abundance is left most eagerly for the privations of the road. No matter if it be a big well surrounded by a fertile oasis, full of the comforts of life, one returns with a sigh of contentment to the twelve hours' trek and the lunch of dried dates.

The well, when scraped out, is probably about the size of a tea-table for two. The moist sand holds the walls together. Usually one leaves it alone a little for the sand to settle, but the water is always sandy and it is too much bother to strain it. Not on one single occasion did I drink a glass of water that was not cloudy and never did I see the bottom of my zinc cup while drinking. The filter which kind friends said I must take with me I never used at all until we got to the Sudan, and there the water was really bad—in an inhabited area you do not know what may have happened to it. And then, when we tried to get this famous filter working, we found there were no washers for it, so that was the end of the story of the filter.

Dirt in the desert, it may be necessary to remark, is quite different from dirt anywhere else. It is not unwholesome, for the sand is a clean thing and the clothes of the Beduins let in the air. Vermin are there, but it is inevitable and the Beduin pays no heed to it. I might have just had my bath and then I would go and sit down for a glass of tea with my men and—well, you are bound to collect these things!

CHAPTER XII

The Changing Desert and a Corrected Map

MONDAY, *March 26th.*—At El Harrash Well of the Zieghen group. Highest temperature 27°, lowest 6°. Fine and clear with north-east wind, which develops into a bad sandstorm at 11. The storm continues until 6.30 in the evening, and the wind does not go down until two hours later.

Our halt at Zieghen should have been only for a night, but the severe sandstorm kept us windbound for another day. Zieghen is merely a group of four wells, the two that we passed on Sunday, El Harrash, where we were camped, and another, Bu Zerraig, 20 kilometres to the east.

During the day Bu Helega talked to Abdullahi about my coming to the desert.

" You have audacity, you Egyptians," he said. " For your Bey to come twice to our country, which no stranger has visited before in my time, that is boldness. Why does he come here and leave all God's bounty back there in Egypt, if not for some secret purpose ? He comes to our unknown country to measure and map it, and, by God, not once but twice."

Even my good friend Bu Helega was suspicious of my intentions in penetrating into his country.

I finally discovered the real basis of the antagonism

of those who live in the desert to the coming of persons from the outside world. It is not religious fanaticism; it is merely the instinct of self-preservation. If a single stranger penetrated to Kufra, the cherished centre of the life of their tribe, it would be, as the Beduins say, "the camel's nose inside the flap of the tent." After him would come others, and the final outcome would be foreign domination. That would mean the loss of their independence and the paying of taxes. They can hardly be blamed for dreading either of these results.

The changes produced by time in the desert, which we are accustomed to think of as eternally the same, are interesting. When Rohlfs passed to the westward of Zieghen on his way to Kufra in 1879 he reported a broad stretch of green vegetation here. To-day there is no extent of greenness, merely a great deal of *hatab*, dead brushwood. Rohlfs' statement, however, is confirmed by Bu Helega, who says that when he was a child his father used to take him to Kufra when he went to get dates, because the Beduins believe that the waters of Shekherra, the headquarters of the Zwayas near Jalo, is bad for children in the summer. Bu Helega used to be carried on his father's back most of the way. It was in those days that the trip was made in three days and five nights, without halts. They gave the camels but one meal between Jalo and Zieghen; when they reached the latter place the beasts were fed on the green stuff that was then growing there. What has seemed like an error on Rohlfs' part in describing so much vegetation at Zieghen is thus demonstrated to be merely the result of a difference in conditions after forty-five years. It is probably a variation in the water conditions in the soil which has turned the living shrubs into firewood.

Our trek from Buttafal to Zieghen illustrated the uncertainties of desert travel. In spite of all the precautions that we could possibly think of, our fuel ran out, one camel died, and two others were so exhausted that they were to fail us soon. The food for the camels was used up also, and from Zieghen to Kufra they were fed on date-tree leaves, gathered at the former place, which was very poor food for them indeed.

I picked up from a Beduin a proverb, with a cynical slant to it. "Your friend is like your female camel; one day she gives you milk and the next she fails you."

On the two evenings at Zieghen I took observations of Polaris with the theodolite. When the observations were worked out I found that Zieghen was about 100 kilometres farther to the east-north-east than Rohlfs had placed it. He did not visit the place and therefore could make no observations on the spot, but relied on what he was told by the Beduins. I found also that Zieghen is 310 metres above sea level.

Tuesday, March 27th.—Start at 8.15 a.m., halt at 8 p.m. Make 47 kilometres. Highest temperature 26°, lowest 8°. Fine and clear, cold strong north-east wind all day and all night. A few white clouds. From El Harrash Well the guide points out the direction of Kufra as being 5 degrees south of south-east. For two hours we walk among *hatab,* which extends about 10 kilometres south-east of the well. Then we enter a region of soft sand, a little undulating. The undulations gradually increase until we get into the sand-dune country late in the afternoon.

At 2.30 we sighted a range of sand-dunes to the east, with a few black stone *garas* or small hills in between them. They were about 20 or 30 kilometres away, and branched off to the south-east as far as we could see. Later there were *gherds*—sand-dunes—to the south-west as well, and at 5.30 the *gherds* closed in across our track and we definitely entered them. So far, however, they were not high or difficult to cross.

The complete separation between the Beduins and the Tebus on the march impressed me again. The blacks say that they do not like the Zwayas and fear them. The Tebu camels were well kept and better behaved than those of the Beduins. Each Tebu camel had a lead rope and did not run loose as the others did.

In the afternoon we passed the landmark of Jebail El Fadeel. As with most desert landmarks, its name commemorates some one who lost his life there.

El Fadeel was one of the best guides in the desert. He was going toward Kufra from Jalo with a caravan. Sandstorms of great severity swept down upon them. While there is no direct evidence of what happened the testimony of what was finally found told the story eloquently. Fadeel's eyes must have been badly affected by the driving sand. He bandaged them, and thus deprived of sight, had those who were with him describe the landmarks as they reached them. Nevertheless they missed the wells of Zieghen and tried to struggle on direct to Kufra. The desert took them in its relentless grip, and of the entire caravan but one camel survived. The beast struggled on to its home at Kufra, led by its infallible instinct. There it was recognized by the markings on its neck as belonging to El Fadeel. A rescue party followed the camel's track back into the desert, but its help came too late. The bodies of the men lay stiff upon the sand, near the landmark now known by El Fadeel's name, the bandage on the old guide's eyes revealing the tragic truth.

Wednesday, March 28th.—There were heavy clouds all day, with little sunshine. It was cloudy too in the evening. A cold north-east wind developed at 8 a.m. into a sandstorm, lasting for three hours and a half. The cold wind continued on into the evening. A few drops of rain fell at 10.30 p.m.

We walked among sand-dunes for two hours, when we entered undulating country, covered with broken black stone. It was bad going for the camels. An hour later the black stone belt ended and we came into the sand-dunes again.

At 11.30 in the forenoon the chain of the Hawayesh Hills were on our left and sand-dunes and black stone *garas* on our right. At 12.15 passed on our left 4 kilometres away Goor El Makhzan landmark, hills of black stone ranging from 50 to 150 metres in height. At 1.45 we passed the landmark of El Gara Webentaha, which means " The Gara and its Daughter," two sugarloaf hills of appropriate proportions to suit the designation.

I talked with some of the Beduins about our losing our way in 1921. They showed no surprise. To these desert dwellers it is all a part of the day's work, losing one's way, one's camels, one's water, or one's fuel.

Thursday, March 29th.—The lowest temperature this day was not recorded, as the minimum thermometer was broken in the storm.

The Hawayesh Hills were on our left until midafternoon. At 11.30 we entered soft and very undulating sand-dunes, difficult going for men and camels. At 1.30 we passed Garet El Sherif to the right, the biggest landmark we had yet seen. It was a ridge-shaped *gara,* 150 metres long and about 100 metres high, with three smaller ones beside it, two to the south and one to the north. At 3 we got into heavy dunes again, and two hours later passed into flat country, with harder sand and patches of black stone. At 3.30 in the morning the worst sandstorm we had encountered began. It swept the tents from the moorings and mine collapsed on top of me, smashing a few of my instruments and also the small chronometer.

With the whole tent on top of me, weighted down with the constantly growing load of sand, I was threatened with suffocation, but fortunately I got hold of a tent-peg with which I held the canvas away from my face. Some of the men tried to come to my assistance, but I shouted to them to put the sacks of flour and pieces of luggage on their tents and mine to keep them down. I lay in my uncomfortable position under the tent for two hours or so. The sand came hurtling through the gap in the tent like shot from a gun. The men and the camels suffered badly. Had the pole of my tent fallen a fraction of an inch to one side, it would have smashed my big chronometer and then what a difference it would have made to the scientific results of the expedition.

To the outside world the work of an explorer is either failure or success with a distinct line between them. To the explorer himself that line is very hazy. He may have won his way through, amassed all the information that he sought, be within a score of miles of his journey's end; then, suddenly, his camels give out. He must abandon the best part of his luggage. Water and food take precedence; the boxes containing his scientific instruments, his records, have to be left behind. Maybe his plight is still worse, and he must sacrifice everything, even his own life. To the outside world he would be a failure; generous critics might even call him a glorious failure, but in any case he has failed. Yet how much is that failure akin to success! Sometimes on those long treks the man who fails has done more, has endured more hardships, than the man who succeeds. An explorer's sympathy is rather with the man who has struggled and failed than with the man who succeeds, for only the explorer knows how the man who failed fought to preserve the fruits of his work.

The Beduins understand this. There is a trait in their character that surprised, even astounded me sometimes, until I grew to understand it. There was often no hilarity, no rejoicing when the day's march came to its appointed end. "To-day we have arrived, but to-morrow . . ." they seem to say. Because you have succeeded to-day it is nothing to brag about. It was not by your skill; it was destiny. To-morrow you may start an easier journey and fail horribly. On my first long trip in the Libyan Desert in 1921, between the oases of Buseima (one of the Kufra group) and Kufra, a three days' journey, we came across the remnants of a perished caravan. There was a hand still sticking out of the sands, the skin yellow like parchment. As we passed, one of the men went reverently and hid it with sand. A three days' trip and yet those men had lost their way and died of thirst.

There are many gruesome tales of the remnants of a caravan perishing within sight of the well. So far from being deterred from taking the same route, the Beduin only says that it was God's decree that they should die on the road. "Better the entrails of a bird than the darkness of the tomb," one Beduin told me, meaning that he preferred to be eaten by vultures.

It was a very tiring day, what with the disturbance to our rest during the night and the heavy going through the soft dunes. But the men were cheerful because we were getting near to Kufra. The news that Bu Helega, who lived at Hawari, the first halting place on the outskirts of Kufra, was going to slaughter a sheep and provide a feast was an added incentive.

The camels were weak and thin, but three of them whose home is in Kufra led the way all day without being driven, in spite of the difficult walking over the dunes.

At 6.45 we sighted Garet El Hawaria, the great landmark that indicates the approach to Kufra.

Friday, March 30th. We started at 7.45 a.m., halted at 5.45 p.m., made 35 kilometres and arrived at Hawari. A few drops of rain fell in the late evening. The ground was flat, soft sand, undulating a trifle, and marked with patches of black and red stone. At 9.30 we entered upon the zone of red sand of Kufra. We came across pieces of petrified wood all day. At 1.15 we passed Garet El Hawaria, and at 3.30 sighted the date trees of Hawari. An hour and a half later we entered the oasis, and soon camped at Awadel.

We had arrived at the first outpost of Kufra. This name was given in Rohlfs' time to the four somewhat widely separated oases of Taiserbo, Buseima, Ribiana and Kebabo—Rohlfs' designation for the present-day Kufra—but now it is restricted to the last named.

Hawari is the northernmost part of the present Kufra, a comparatively small oasis with the three villages of Hawari, Hawawira and Awadel. Seventeen kilometres south lies El Taj, the seat of local government and the principal settlement. It is situated on a rocky cliff overlooking the depression of the oasis proper, which lies to the south and contains the villages of Jof, Boema, Buma, El Zurruk, El Talalib and El Tollab.

I had intended to go straight on to El Taj, the chief town of Kufra, the next day, but Bu Helega claimed the right of hospitality and insisted that I should stop a day at the oasis which is his home. After a good night's rest—undisturbed by sandstorms or collapsing of tents—and a shave, I was quite ready to do full justice to the breakfast sent by the Beduins of a caravan which had just arrived from Wadai. At the same time I gathered some interesting information which made me consider making a change in my plans.

I sent a messenger on to El Taj with letters to Sayed El Abid, the cousin of Sayed Idris and the chief Senussi in Kufra, and to Jeddawi, Sayed Idris's personal *wakil*.

In the afternoon Zerwali escorted me to Hawari, where I was received at the *Zawia* by the *ikhwan* and the notables of the town. After the usual words of welcome and exchange of compliments, I went to dinner at the house of Zerwali's uncle. The Beduin chiefs protested that I should not have come direct to Hawari, but should have camped outside to give them an opportunity for a ceremonial reception. They had apparently heard how I was received at Jalo and would have liked to duplicate it for me here. I heard rumours of intrigues among some of the Zwaya chiefs, who were suspicious of my purpose in coming a second time to Kufra, and as a protest had refused to attend the dinner. They were influential chiefs and the news made me determined to press on to El Taj before they could send word there in prejudice of my coming.

After the meal I rode home through the beautiful moonlight, and on my arrival found a difficult task before me. Egaila, Bu Helega's eldest son, had been bitten by a scorpion. With more confidence in my medicine chest than I had myself, Bu Helega asked that I should cure him. I took the anti-scorpion serum and went to the house, where I found the boy very ill indeed, burning with fever.

At the last moment before leaving Cairo these serums had been included in my equipment and a doctor friend while he was shaking my hand and I was saying good-bye to people all around me, explained to me (perhaps most lucidly) just how to employ the serums. It was the first time I had ever attempted that kind of injection, and I tried to conjure up the scene and recall fragments of those parting instructions, but it only struck me how different was that dimly lit room with the anxious friends and relatives watching my every movement from the hearty send-off when the serum had been added to my stock-in-trade.

However, in spite of my doubts whether the case was not too far advanced for treatment, I administered the serum, and went to my camp wondering what the outcome would be.

Before long I heard a crowd approaching my tent with loud outcries which sounded hostile to my ears.

Probably, I thought, the boy is already dead and his death would be laid at my door instead of at that of the scorpion.

I summoned my men to protect the box of instruments which I suspected would be the first object of attack, and prepared myself for a hostile approach. It was a disturbing moment.

But great was my relief when I detected in the cries of those who were coming a note rather of rejoicing than of hostility. Presently Bu Helega entered my tent and thanked me with impressive warmth for the relief which I had given his son.

"It was like magic," he declared with fervour. "Allah is great. That medicine of yours has made the boy well again."

In appropriate terms I answered, "Recovery comes from God." Already the fever was abating and the boy evidently on his way to recovery. I thanked God internally for the good fortune which had attended my ministrations. If the boy had died, my position would have been a dangerous one. When my visitors had left, I went out into the moonlight for a walk among the graceful palms.

TUAREG (CAMEL MAN) WITH HIDE SHIELD, SPEARS AND WAR KIT.

A TEBU WITH HIS CAMEL.

CAMELS CROSSING SAND DUNES.

A SENUSSI PRINCE AT KUFRA.
A nephew of Sayed Idris.

THE SON OF THE GOVERNOR OF KUFRA.
Note the gold-embroidered robe under the desert head-dress.

SAYED MOHAMMED EL ABID,
Governor of Kufra and Cousin of the Head of the Senussi sect.

THE "KING" OF OUENAT
with his Mohammedan rosary.

SIDI HUSSEIN WAKIL,
a representative of Sayed Idris, head of the Senussi sect, and a friend of the explorer, at Jaghbub.

THE COUNCIL OF KUFRA, CONSISTING OF THE OLD SENUSSI BRETHREN.

A VIEW OF THE DESERT FROM THE HILLS OF ARKENU, THE SMALLER OF THE TWO OASES WHICH THE EXPLORER DISCOVERED

In the foreground is the explorer's tent and camp. The hills are of granite and are about 1,500 feet high.

THE VALLEY OF OUENAT

THE CARAVAN ARRIVING AT OUENAT.

CHAPTER XIII

Kufra—Old Friends and a Change of Plan

SUNDAY, *April 1st.*—We started at 9.45 a.m. and halted at 2 p.m., making 17 kilometres and arrived at El Taj. At 11.15 we entered a broken, rocky country very rolling, covered with patches of black and red sandstone until we reached Taj.

Egaila came to help in loading the camels. He had quite recovered from his scorpion bite, and was to go with us to Taj. Breakfast was sent by Bu Helega for me and my men. When I protested that he should not have taken the trouble, he retorted that I should have given him an opportunity to provide the customary three days' hospitality. A little later a slave girl came from him with a huge bowl of rice, chicken and eggs.

She was evidently dressed especially for the occasion and was quite charming in her dainty attire of blue cloth with a red sash about her slim waist.

I told her that we were starting at once and should not need the food.

"You may need it on the way," she replied shyly. "I cooked it myself."

"If that is the case," I assured her, "I will accept it gladly." She was obviously pleased and immediately went back for another bowl quite as large and inviting. I bowed to the inevitable and sent my thanks to her master.

We were given a pleasant send-off by the people of Awadel and I set out at the head of my caravan on Bu Helega's horse. We needed no guide just now, for I knew the way myself.

"Aye, the Bey knows the way too well," said Senussi Bu Hassan. "He will soon become a guide in this country of ours."

The approach to Kufra from the north has an element of surprise in it that makes it doubly interesting. We marched through a gently rolling country with an irregular ridge of no great height forming the horizon ahead of us. Suddenly the top of the ridge resolved itself into the outlines of a group of buildings, their walls hard to distinguish at any distance from the rocks and sands they match so well in colour and in form. This was El Taj, the headquarters of the Senussi family in Kufra. As we entered the town, we saw that the ground dropped abruptly away beyond it, down to the valley of Kufra. This pleasant valley is a shallow roughly shaped oval bowl, 40 kilometres in extent on its long diameter and 20 kilometres on the short one. It is dotted with palm trees and across it in an irregular line from north-east to south-west are strung the six settlements of Boema, Buma, Jof, Zurruk, Talalib and Tollab. Close to Jof lie the blue shimmering waters of a fair-sized lake. At this mid-point in the sand waste of the desert this expanse of water is both a boon and an aggravation. The mere sight of so much water brings refreshment to the eyes weary of looking at nothing but sand; but to the parched throat it is worse than a mirage to the vision, for its waters are salt.

On our entry into Taj I was met cordially by old

friends. Sayed El Abid, the cousin of Sayed Idris and the chief Senussi in Kufra, was ill with rheumatism, but Sidi Saleh El Baskari, the Kaimakam, Sidi Mahmoud El Jeddawi, Sayed Idris's *wakil,* and several *ikhwan* brought words of welcome from him and conducted me to the house of Sayed Idris where I was to stay. It was here that we lived on the first trip to Kufra two years before, and immediately I felt at home.

"You will have to initiate your men into the ways of Kufra," said El Baskari whimsically. "Even Zerwali has not been here for thirteen years."

At once the hospitality began, with coffee brought by the commandant of the troops. I had just time for a short rest before a slave came to take me to the house of Sayed El Abid for a meal. Led by the same messenger that came for us two years ago, I walked through the same streets, and entered the same wonderful house of the Senussi leader with a curious feeling as though time had stood still or gone back. El Abid's house is a labyrinth of corridors, lined with doors behind which live the members of his family and his retainers. We passed into the familiar room whose spaces seemed more richly adorned than ever with gorgeous rugs, many-coloured cushions and stiffly embroidered brocades. On the walls hung the well-remembered collection of clocks, barometers and thermometers in which my host takes naïve delight. The clocks, of which there are at least a dozen of assorted shapes and sizes, were all going strong.

Sidi Saleh came to bear me company and to apologize for the enforced absence of my host, Sayed El Abid. There was set before me a feast fit for the gods, or for mortals fresh from the monotonous living of the desert —lamb, rice, vegetables, *mulukhiah,* an Egyptian vegetable rather like spinach, delicious bread, sweet vinegar, milk, sweets, followed by coffee, milk with almond pulp beaten up in it, and finally the ceremonial three glasses of tea, flavoured with amber, rose-water and mint.

When the meal was over and I had returned to my house, I had barely time to see about the disposition of my baggage and discuss the question of camels for the next stage of the journey, when the slave came to conduct me again to El Abid's house for dinner. El Baskari was again my host, a dignified, kindly figure in a beautiful *gibba* of yellow and gold, having changed the classical soft Beduin *tarbush,* which he had been wearing, for a white silk *kufia* and a green and gold *egal.*

When this second meal had reached the point of scented tea and incense, suddenly the clocks began to strike, each with its own particular tone, the Arabic hour of three—which then meant nine by the standard of the outside world. I closed my eyes for a moment and felt myself back in Oxford with the hour striking in endless variety of tones from all the church towers of the University town.

I went out into the moonlight with the fragrance of the rose-water and the incense lingering about me. I stood on the edge of the ridge overlooking the waters of the lake and reflected on my former visit to Kufra when this was my goal. Now it was the beginning of the most interesting part of my journey. I heard the voices of *ikhwan* and students reading the *Hezb* in the evening quiet. Abdullahi slipped out of the shadows and stood beside me.

"This is the night of half *Shaban*" (meaning the middle of the month before Ramadan), he says in a low tone as of a man who thinks aloud. "God will grant the wishes of one who prays to-night."

For several minutes we two stood there silently. My face was toward the south-east where lay an untrodden track and oases that are "lost." But Abdullahi turned to the north-east—where lies Egypt and his family and children. I did not need to ask him for what he prayed.

Monday, April 2nd. At Hawari I had been told by the Beduin caravan from Wadai that a French patrol had come north as far as the well at Sarra over the main trade route from Wadai to Kufra. This was the route I had intended at first to follow, but it seemed that only the small portion of it which lay between Sarra and Kufra remained unexplored. Again I had heard vague stories of the "lost" oases on the direct route south which I had planned some time to explore, although I knew that this direct route to Darfur in the Sudan was practically never used either by Beduins or by Sudanese because of its supposed difficulties and dangers. The story of the French patrol turned my mind again to these oases and I determined to try and find them rather than to follow my original plan.

I set out decided to do all that was possible to explore these lost oases, but failing that I was to cross the Libyan Desert by the beaten road through Wajunga and Wadai and then turn eastwards towards Darfur.

Zerwali and Suliman Bu Matari, a rich Zwaya merchant, came to discuss the trip southward. Bu

Matari had discouraging counsel to offer as to the route I had now decided to take.

"Eight years ago," he said, "the last caravan to go that way—of which my brother Mohammed was the leader—was 'eaten up' and slaughtered on the frontier of Darfur. They went, not as you wish to go, but by the easier route from Ouenat to Merega (a small oasis about 290 kilometres south-east of Ouenat). This journey you propose to make is through territory where no Beduin has passed before. The *daffa* (a long waterless trek) between Ouenat and Erdi is a long and hazardous one. God be merciful to the caravan in such heat. Your camels will drop like birds before the hot south winds. Even if you get through safely, who knows how the inhabitants of the hills over there will receive you? Do not let your anxiety to travel fast overrule your wisdom and keep you from choosing the safe trade route to Wajanga and Abeshe."

I thanked him for his advice—but I knew that I should not take it.

After luncheon royally provided by El Abid, I went to visit his son Sharrufa. He is an intelligent young man, thirsting for knowledge. He has gone as far into the outside world as Benghasi, and that by no means metropolitan community is still for him "the" city of the world. He apologized for the illness of his father and I offered to send medicine which might possibly help him.

Tuesday, April 3rd. It was very warm, with heavy clouds and a bad south-west wind. After luncheon as usual I went to visit Shams El Din, a cousin of Sharrufa and his young brother. The older boy is very intelligent and has eyes that seem to be asking questions of the world. They offered me three cups of milk with almond pulp and home-made jam. I knew that to refuse such an offer is to offend; so I left the house in a state of torpor. Dinner later at Sayed El Abid's did not improve matters internally.

Again I discussed the plan of going by way of Arkenu and Ouenat. I was more determined than ever. We would see what Bu Helega had to say when he arrived from Hawari.

Wednesday, April 4th. I was awakened by Jeddawi, who as usual brought me a pot of fragrant tea.

This is comparative civilization, I thought, as I saw Ahmed preparing my shaving kit. There are of course times when one welcomes the conveniences and comforts of civilization, but having trekked so far one feels more at home when on the move than when resting in an oasis.

The early part of the day was spent in cutting down most of the wooden boxes and re-arranging the luggage in preparation for the long trip south. It requires particular care, since from now onwards there will be no chance of changing the camels until our arrival at El Fasher in the Sudan, about 950 miles.

The question of providing new shoes for the men of my caravan had to be attended to, as the Beduin shoes that were made for them at Jalo had been worn out. Before lunch I had a visit from a few Zwaya chiefs who came officially to pay their respects, and also unofficially to satisfy their curiosity and suspicion as to the size of my caravan and the equipment I was carrying, and if possible to find out what plans I had made for my journey to the Sudan.

Lunch, as usual, at Sayed El Abid's. I had the cheerful news that the medicine I gave to him had the good effect. The afternoon I spent in attending to the question of arms and ammunition. Later I took a long walk in order to make compass observations of the vicinity of Taj.

Thursday, April 5th. Zerwali had a long talk with Bu Helega, who arrived in the night from Hawari. The latter refused point blank to go to El Fasher by the Ouenat route.

Bu Helega came to visit me and tried to persuade me to go by way of Wadai. When he saw that his advice would probably not be taken he became desperate. I had clearly pointed out to him that nothing could change my decision to cut across by the Ouenat route to El Fasher.

"By God, it's a dangerous route," he said, "and many a caravan has been eaten up by the inhabitants of the hills on the way. They do not fear God and they are under the authority of no man. They are like birds; they live on the tops of mountains and you will have trouble with them."

"We are men and we are believers," I responded. "Our fate is in the hand of God. If our death is decreed, it may come on the beaten track to the nearest well."

"Many a Zwaya beard has been buried in those unknown parts," he declared. "The people are treacherous and they fear neither God nor man."

"May God's mercy fall on those Zwayas who have lost their lives," I replied. "Our lives are no more precious than theirs. Shall our courage be less?"

" The water on this route is scarce and bad," he argued again. " God has said, do not throw yourselves with your own hands unto destruction."

" God will quench the thirst of the true believer," I answered, " and will protect those who have faith in Him."

He felt himself in danger of being beaten in argument and shifted his ground.

" None of my men are willing to accompany you on this route," he asserted, " and I cannot send my camels either. It is sending them to death. If you find anybody who is willing to hire his camels I am ready to pay for them, but neither my men nor my camels are going to take you on this journey."

" Do what you like," I retorted with spirit. " I am going by this route. It will be between you and Sayed Idris when he knows that Bu Helega has not kept his word."

There the argument rested. I had already learned that the few owners of camels at Kufra had been urged by Bu Helega and his men not to help me in my new plan. He hoped by so doing to force me to accept his plan of the safe route through Wadai.

An enormous lunch was provided by Jeddawi. The three days of official hospitality of El Abid having ended yesterday, Jeddawi, as Idris's *wakil* at Kufra, can now entertain us.

Bu Helega was about to leave, but I invited him to partake of our meal and he accepted. He hoped still to persuade me to change my mind. I hoped even more strongly to convince the old man that the route was not as dangerous as he made it out to be. After the third glass of tea we parted, neither of us having succeeded in convincing the other. But I felt that my last words had an effect on him.

In the afternoon the slave came to tell me that his master, Sayed El Abid, would like to see me. I had already intimated that he need not be in a hurry to give me an audience, as I knew he was suffering badly from his gout and it was very difficult for him to come down to the reception room. But he was not willing to have me think that he had violated the rules of hospitality by delaying the audience, so he very kindly allowed me to see him in spite of his suffering.

It was the first time that I had seen Sayed El Abid on this journey, and as I was ushered into his presence I thought that he might have come out of a gorgeous illustration of the *Thousand and One Nights*. He was dressed in a yellow silk *kuftan* embroidered with red braid, a rich white silk *bornus* carelessly hung on his shoulders. On his head he wore a white turban with snow-white gauze flowing from the sides. This is the classical headgear of the chiefs of the Senussi family. He carried in his hand a heavy ebony stick with a massive silver head. He was a picture of simple and benign dignity, and no one would have suspected him of being the redoubtable warrior that he really is. He was sitting on a big upholstered arm-chair and as I entered he tried to get up. I hastened to him, grasped his hand, and begged him not to make an effort to rise. He was suffering badly from his gout and the conversation started easily on the subject of his ailment. He has been suffering for many years. At times at night, he said, when the pain is at its worst, " I pray to God that He may shorten the number of my days in this world, for I cannot even perform my prayers as I should."

We then discussed the question of my trip to the Sudan, and he too, I found, had been prevailed upon to urge me to take the safer route through Wadai. I pointed out to him that Sayed Idris was now in Egypt and that I had to hasten to my country to try to repay a little of the hospitality that had been lavished upon me by the Senussis. It was fortunate that the route to the Sudan through Ouenat is known to be shorter than that through Wadai.

"You are a dear friend of ours," he said, "and the Sayed, I am sure, would rather have you arrive in Egypt late and safe than hear that any harm had befallen you."

"Our fates are in the Hands of God," I replied; "our efforts are decreed by Him and I carry with me the blessing of the Senussi Masters."

I spoke with an air of determination. Sayed El Abid was pensive for a few moments. Slowly he raised his head, and lifted his two hands toward Heaven.

"May God make your efforts succeed and send you back safe to your people," he said, yielding to my desire. "You have visited the tomb of our grandfather at Jaghbub and the Kubba of Sidi El Mahdi here and you have their blessings. 'He who struggles and has faith is rewarded by God.'" He quoted from the Koran. We then read the "Fat-ha"—he gave me his blessing and again prayed that God might guide our steps and give me and my men fortitude. I felt very happy as I wound my way through the multitude of corridors and courtyards. I was relieved to know that I had an ally in Sayed El Abid, and that he would not prove an obstacle in my new plan of going to the Sudan by way of Ouenat.

All the men of my caravan were there when I entered the house. One look at their faces told me with what suppressed excitement they had been waiting since my departure to Sayed El Abid to hear his verdict on the journey south. Slowly I made my way to my room and asked them to come in. I too had to suppress my excitement; but mine was the excitement of success and not of expectation. There was a long pause before I could control my voice and make it as indifferent as it should be.

"The Sayed has blessed our journey to Ouenat and has given me the 'Fat-ha' for it."

I dared not even look in the men's faces.

"We have the blessings of the Senussi Masters with us, Sayed El Abid has assured me, and God will give us fortitude and success; and guidance comes from Him."

CHAPTER XIV

Kufra—Its Place on the Map

FRIDAY, *April 6th.* The day began with the arrival of an immense bowl of roses, gloriously fragrant, sent by Sayed El Abid. This is the way the desert belies its name every now and then. I defy the Riviera to produce anything finer than these, or more fragrant.

It was Friday, the Moslem Sabbath, and I attended prayers at the Mosque. The young Senussi Princes were expected, and some of the Beduins came in their best clothes, but side by side with the richest of silk *kuftans* were the shabbiest *jerds.* Every one took off his slippers as he came in. I watched them for a while. There came a prosperous Zwaya or Majbari merchant with the crease still fresh in rich robes just removed from the chest, and *kohl* in his eyes, put in with a *madwid* (*kohl* stick) of ivory or brass. The prosperous man, maybe, has everything upon him new, and he smells strongly of scent, perhaps pure rose-water distilled in Kufra, or else musk or other strong perfume from the Sudan. He enters in a dignified way and takes his place. There comes another and his *jerd* is tattered and his face bronzed and withered, not flabby, but he is no less dignified. Clothes play but a small part in this assembly owing to the natural dignity and courage of these people, and those qualities are brought out in relief even more by the tattered *jerd* than by the fine silks and scents, which sometimes take away something of the personality of the individual.

A slave comes. He is the favourite slave and confidant of one of the Senussi chiefs. His silks are as rich and even more vivid, and there is little to suggest servility. He feels his importance and walks with equally dignified grace through the ranks of the worshippers to take his place, maybe next to a dignitary, maybe next to a beggar. At the Mosque the poor not only stand on level ground with the rich and the prosperous, but in a subtle way they have their revenge, for in the house of God the master is God and the beggar may feel as great or greater than the rich man since he is not submerged in the luxury of the world and forgetting God. The old and shabby *jerd* is, to the Beduin going into the Mosque, as fit a garment for worship as silken brocades are proper raiment for a man going to see the Senussi chiefs.

The worshippers are now ready. The *muezzin* has finished the call to prayer. There is a hush. The young Senussi Princes are entering the Mosque. They take the places that have been reserved for them. All eyes turn towards them and, on account of their youth, they look a little shy and embarrassed. No one rises as they enter, for this is the House of God, wherein God alone is the Master. Then the *Imam* mounts the pulpit and delivers his sermon. On the few occasions that I have been able to attend Friday prayers in an oasis mosque, the theme of the sermon has often been the same ; advising the congregation to shun the world and its luxury and to prepare for a life of happiness in the next world by doing good. " Beware of the ornaments and the luxuries of this world, for they are very enticing. Once you fall a victim to them you lose your soul and stray farther from God. Draw nearer to God by doing good deeds and obeying His commands. This life will pass away. Only the next world is everlasting. Prepare yourselves for it that you may be happy in eternity."

The interior of this Mosque is beautiful in the simple dignity of its lines. The walls are bare, whitewashed, scrupulously clean. The floor is covered with rugs or with fibre matting. The worshippers squat cross-legged upon the floor in a very reverent attitude. There are perhaps 200 of them, ranged in rows, all facing towards Mecca. There are some who count their prayers upon rosaries of amber beads ; others, too poor to have rosaries, record the number of their prayers by opening and closing their fingers. There are some whose very movement betrays opulence and prosperity ; others, Beduins of the desert, have a far-away look. The most striking impression is the serenity and contentment written on their faces. Even upon the pinched and haggard face there is an expression of equanimity which shows that the man has accepted his fate. It is written there that he is living on the verge of starvation, yet he does not rebel.

After lunch at El Abid's, Soliman Bu Matari came again to talk about the trip south. He reported that Bu Helega, and Mohammed, who was to be our guide, had met and talked things over, but Bu Helega was still unwilling to go.

Abdullahi had spent the day at Jof, gathering what information he could about the Ouenat route and trying to find out if the Tebus would let me hire camels from them for the journey thither.

After dinner at El Abid's I spent some time in Sayed Idris's library, which he had instructed Jeddawi to throw open to me.

Imagine a room of medium size filled with chests containing books. The ceiling is decorated in vivid colours, the work of an artist, a lover of the Senussis, who came from Tunis simply to do them a service, just as in mediæval Europe painters and sculptors devoted their lives to adorning churches. Every bit of wood in the room has come from Egypt or Benghasi. There is a window open to the air with only wooden shutters as a protection against the sun.

It is not easy to move about, for books and chests of books are ranged along the walls and in the middle of the room as well.

There are many very ancient chests used as cupboards and at the same time fitted with attachments at the sides which enable them to be straightway loaded upon a camel in case of need. The library is somewhat out of order, books piled carelessly one on top of another, for Sayed Idris has long been absent. There is a great number of manuscripts enclosed in beautifully tooled morocco covers. There are modern books printed in Cairo and in India. There are manuscripts from Morocco, Algeria, Tunisia. With the exception of a few books in the Persian language, all are in Arabic. There are two or three manuscripts of the Koran illuminated in gold. It was a great privilege for me to be allowed to go into this library, for as a rule no one is admitted.

I found many manuscripts laboriously written on

ancient parchment, works on philosophy, the Arabic language, theology, Sufism, a few on poetry and mysticism, another on talismans and magic. Many were the interesting and pleasant hours that I spent among this collection. The surroundings and the atmosphere were just right ; so remote, so many miles from the world, one felt in the mood to absorb the thought to be found in these manuscripts. Sit in a comfortable chair in the midst of civilization and try to read such books—one ring of the telephone would be enough to make them appear archaic.

Saturday, April 7th. A fine pair of shoes came as a present from Sharrufa. The chiefs of the Zwayas came to pay me another visit. We talked over our coffee about Zwaya history. I learned that it was not the Zwayas who first conquered Kufra from the Tebus, but the Ghawazi and Jahama tribes. The names of two of the Kufra villages, Tollab and Zurruk, are family names of the Jahama tribe.

I gave each of my visitors a photograph of the group which I had taken several days before, and they were delighted with them.

I realized to the full that day the perils of Kufra. Rohlfs almost lost his life here by violence ; I almost lost mine by kindness. I lunched prodigally at El Abid's, as usual, and the meal was followed by coffee, three glasses of tea, with amber, rose-water and mint, and three glasses of milk enriched with almond pulp. Then Sharrufa insisted that I should come to his house, and offered me three glasses of perfumed tea, followed again by three glasses of almond-flavoured milk. I reflected that to refuse was to offend, and gulped down the beverages, which, by now, had become somewhat nauseating. The end was not yet. Shams El Din hauled me off to his house and set before me biscuits and nuts and a huge glass of sweet syrup. It was almost more than flesh and blood could endure, but—to refuse was to offend. There followed three glasses of coffee, but I stalked forth with all the dignity of a man going to the gallows or the Spartan boy with the fox gnawing at his vitals.

As I lay down in my room to recuperate, many thoughts surged through my brain. Would that the Beduin, whoever he was, who selected " three " as the mystic number to characterize desert hospitality, had died unborn! But it was lucky that he did not hit on seven instead of three. I came to the desert perfectly prepared for destruction by the hand of Nature or hostile men, but the idea of perishing through indigestion did not commend itself to my sense of the fitness of things.

And yet at the proper time, I went to El Abid's again for dinner. Some of the Beduin chiefs were my fellow-guests and once more the route to the southward was discussed. Bu Helega persisted in his refusal to go by way of Ouenat.

" The conditions laid down by Sayed Idris," he said, " call for a journey to Wadai and not to Darfur." He would send neither his camels nor his men that way. I argued like a lawyer that since he had contracted to provide thirty-five *marhalas*—or day's journey from Kufra southward—it should make no difference to him whether I use those *marhalas* to go to Wadai or to El Fasher or back to Egypt. He was unconvinced by this ingenious reasoning, but when he realized that I was determined, that El Abid was not opposed to my plan, and that I was willing to take fewer camels than originally stipulated, he gave a reluctant consent. But he would not go himself or send his men.

Sunday, April 8th. The affair of Bu Helega's horse came to a head. I bought him for £33. He was sturdy and a splendid traveller, needing to drink only every second day.

After luncheon I took El Abid's photograph and had a long talk with him about his malady, which he bore with true Beduin fortitude, about conditions in Cyrenaica and Egypt, and about my plans for the trip to the Sudan.

I had had bad luck with my scientific work at Kufra. I did not find it easy to escape surveillance and to move about unattended or to use my instruments without arousing suspicion. What was worse, it had been cloudy every day since I arrived there and I had been unable to take observations of the sun or Polaris with the theodolite.

After dinner I was thoroughly tired. I had used up all the indigestion tablets which I brought with me. I felt that it would be a relief to get back to the simplicity of the open desert again.

Monday, April 9th, was still cloudy, but a cool breeze was blowing. I spent a quiet day, reading in Idris's library, developing a few films, and buying *girbas* and barley for the journey. Sayed El Abid gave me copies, written with his own hand, of letters by El Mahdi to various *ikhwan.* He made me presents of a Moorish knife in a silver scabbard and a flint lock pistol also beautifully inlaid.

Tuesday, April 10th. The clouds cleared away in

the afternoon, and I took photographs of the valley. I arranged with the shoemaker for shoes for myself and my men, and for bandoliers, which the men insisted on having, in view of the alarming rumours they had been hearing.

I met Mohammed Sukkar, who was to be our guide over the Ouenat route, for the first time, and liked him.

Wednesday, April 11th. El Abid had heard of my purchase of Bu Helega's horse, and sent me a Tuareg sword and Italian carbine to carry when I ride him. At last I was able to make observations with my theodolite. I was anxious to see how my results would agree with those of Rohlfs.

Thursday, April 12th. I sent Sayed El Abid my shot-gun as a gift.

In the afternoon I rode with Sayed Mohammed Bu Tamanya and Zerwali to Jof. We were met by the chiefs of the village. I visited the *Suk,* where the weekly market was being held, the *Zawia,* which is the oldest Senussi school in Kufra, and the Mosque. Jof is the trade centre of Kufra. It was interesting to find side by side in the *suk* rifle cartridges whose marking showed them to be thirty years old, Italian tomato sauce in tins from Benghasi, blue and white calico made in Manchester and imported from Egypt, and leather, ivory and ostrich feathers from Wadai. These products of the South, however, are not plentiful now in Kufra, except when a merchant who has brought them from Wadai is prevented for some reason from going on to the north to sell them in Egypt or Cyrenaica. Kufra had seen its best days as a trade centre before the occupation of the Sudan. Then it was easier to find an outlet for the products of Wadai and Darfur through Kufra than by way of the country to the East. Even now, however, there is a contraband trade through Kufra in female ivory and ivory of less than 14 lbs. weight, the exportation of which is prohibited by the Sudan Government.

In addition to the trade that passes through Kufra, most of the big Zwaya chiefs who have enough slaves go in for agriculture. They raise barley and maize. The Senussis are more progressive and grow melons, grapes, bananas, marrows and other vegetables of the more delicate kinds, all of which are a great treat after the monotonous fare of the desert. They raise mint and roses, from which they make the rose-water and mint essence, so essential in their ceremonies of hospitality. From a few olive trees some olive oil is produced in primitive presses. The animals of Kufra are camels, sheep, donkeys and a few horses. Meat, however, is very expensive, as there is little grazing for sheep in the valley. The animals are fed on pounded date stones, which do very well as a staple diet. But some green stuff is necessary at intervals. The Senussis, who are in everything more progressive than their neighbours, raise chickens and pigeons.

The price of slaves, I learnt at Kufra, has risen a great deal during the last few years because there are no more slaves coming up from Wadai on account of the vigilance of the French authorities in that province. Occasionally the Beduins get round this by contracting a marriage with a slave girl in Wadai, and then, when they come back, divorcing and selling her. On one of my travels in 1916 I was offered a slave girl for six gold louis (120 francs) ; now the price varies from £30 to £40. A male slave costs less. The Beduins sometimes marry their slave girls, and if one of these bears a male child she automatically becomes free. The Beduins have no prejudice against colour; that is, if a slave bears the head of a tribe his eldest male child, that child *ipso facto* becomes in his turn the head of the tribe, however black he may be. Whereas the children of slaves are slaves, the child of a slave girl and a free man, however poor, is always free, and even though his father dies and he is left an orphan, he can never be a slave. The lot of a favourite male slave especially is preferable. They have more power and are taken more into the confidence of their masters than free men. They are very well treated and become members of the family. They are well dressed, for an ill-dressed slave reflects badly on his master, just as a shabby footman would detract from the glory of a millionaire's Rolls-Royce. The favourite slave of Sayed Idris, Ali Kaja, is not only the most trusted man of Sayed Idris, but he has more power and authority among the Beduins themselves than many a free man. Such a slave is treated as a confidant. If the slave of Sayed El Abid came to me with a message, I took it to be absolutely true, knowing that it is his duty to report exactly what he is told. In the same way, if I wished something to reach the ears of Sayed El Abid, and only his ears, I knew that I could tell it without a moment's hesitation to his slave and be perfectly confident that it would not go anywhere else.

A man slave is permitted to buy a slave girl. Once when I asked Ali Kaja about the price of slaves, he complained: "They are very expensive nowadays. The other day I bought one and she cost me £40 in golden sovereigns." He said it with such an air that he might never have been a slave himself.

The shabbiest slave that you see in an oasis is generally the freed slave, who curiously enough is looked down upon by the other owned slaves, and himself feels ashamed that he is a freed slave and belongs to no one!

There are many date trees all through the Kufra Valley, and many of them belong to the Senussis. When the Zwayas invited Sidi Ibn El Senussi to come to Kufra, each one of them gave the Senussis one-third of his property, land and date trees. The proportion of two to one between the date trees owned by the Zwayas and those of the Senussis has, however, in the years since then, been considerably altered in favour of the Zwayas. These regular inhabitants of the valley naturally planted new trees faster and thus increased their own holdings. One can still see in the valley the walls separating the Senussi lands from those of the Zwayas.

On our way back from Jof we met a wedding party. The officer commanding the troops at Kufra was being married, and the father of the bride invited me to "empty gunpowder" in honour of the occasion. I was glad to pay a compliment to the officer, who was an old friend of mine, and, when they fired their guns in salute, in good Beduin style I rode my horse at a gallop up to the party, pulled him to a sudden halt in front of the bride, and fired my gun into the ground before her. It was astonishing how Baraka, the moment he heard the sound of the guns, took to the gallop and brought me at a rush within the prescribed distance for firing. It was all a part of his training.

Friday, April 13th. A slave of Sayed Idris came to be treated for an illness which had lasted for two months. It seemed to be a digestive upset, with continual vomiting. I gave him ether on a piece of sugar, milk and rice, and by evening he was better.

Bu Helega arrived from Hawari with seventeen camels. I told him to complete the twenty-five we had agreed upon.

I received a visit from the bridegroom and his father-in-law, who came to thank me for the compliment I paid the wedding procession.

Saturday, April 14th. Bu Helega brought the rest of the camels. He was in a dilemma about sending a man with us. He did not wish to send his son, or even a slave, on such a hazardous journey which none of us might get through alive. On the other hand, there was the off-chance that Fate might be good to us and let us escape. In that case, remote though it seemed to him, if he had no representative with us, how should he get his camels back, or rather their value, for it would be the natural thing to sell them at the end of the trip?

The afternoon was spent in packing and the evening in making observations. The weather was now more gracious. This was only the third night since reaching this spot that I had been able to see Polaris. I determined that I would not leave Kufra until I had made at least twice as many observations on different nights.

Sunday, April 15th. The morning was spent in loading. Bu Helega was still in a quandary about sending a man with us. But since I had the camels it did not make any particular difference to me what he decided.

The slave whom I had been treating was astonishingly improved in health. He came to thank me. No one was more surprised than I at what I had been able to do for him.

At two the caravan set out for Ezeila, the last well of Kufra Valley on the south. There we were going to do *tag-heez* properly, taking several days for perfecting our final preparations. I had bought two sheep for "Bu-Zafar," as none of us had made this journey before.

All my men had been newly clothed, and made a cheerful sight in spotless white with red shoes. Their carefully cleaned rifles glittered as they hung on their backs. Most of the new camels looked fresh and strong.

Monday, April 16th. Abdullahi took the horse to Taj for shoeing, as I found that the stony ground was too hard for him. I sent a brass tray to the Commandant as a wedding present, and the last three bottles of Bovril to Idris's sick slave. Our departure was postponed because the guide was still occupied before the *kadi* with a legal matter over a camel.

Tuesday, April 17th. I had breakfast at Soliman Bu Matari's in Jof with Zerwali, Abdullahi, the Commandant, Saleh, and Mohammed Bu Tamania. The rest poked fun at the Commandant because, being a new bridegroom, he would not partake of a dish cooked with onions. "They do not forgive when they are young," said Bu Tamania, winking at the Commandant.

I bought a *hejin*, or trotting camel, for my own use, paying £9 for it. We were at last ready for the start the next day.

As I made my last observation of Polaris, I had a

strong hope that I should have succeeded in putting Kufra into its proper place on the map. I had been keen to check Rohlfs' determination of the position of Kufra, which he made from the observations of his companion Stecker at Boema. Taj had not been built in Rohlfs' day. When I made my first observations at Taj, I discovered that they were not in agreement with the results of Stecker's observations at Boema, which is 2 kilometres from Taj in a direction 54° east of true south. I thereupon determined that I would not leave Kufra until I had secured a sufficient number of observations to preclude the possibility of any appreciable error. Polaris was observed with the theodolite by me on six different nights, under conditions which Dr. Ball, in his scholarly paper on my work published at the end of this volume, declares to leave no room for an error greater than a single minute of latitude or longitude.

The net result of my observations, when they were finally reduced after my return to Egypt, was that Kufra is some 40 kilometres south-south-east of the position assigned to it by Rohlfs from Stecker's observations. I found the altitude of Kufra to be almost precisely the same as that ascertained by Rohlfs, 400 metres for Boema on the floor of the valley, and 475 metres for Taj on the valley's ridge.

CHAPTER XV

The "Lost" Oases—Arkenu

WEDNESDAY, *April 18th.* Bu Helega had at last found two men, Bukara and Hamid, who would go with his camels. They were poor men and the money they would make loomed larger in their eyes than the danger.

Sayed El Abid sent three representatives to see us off. They brought a letter of farewell from him that touched my heart.

Bu Helega came to say good-bye. At the final moment there were tears in his eyes, and I do not think they were caused by fears for his camels or for the men whom he was sending with us. In spite of our controversy over the route, we remained true friends, with affection and respect for each other.

My men were greeted by their friends as though this was to be their last meeting. It was the most touching farewell of the whole journey. "May God make safety your companion . . . what is decreed is decreed and that will happen. May God guide you to the true road and protect you from evil."

There was little about this parting of that sense of assurance which attends both those who go and those who stay behind when it is a case of starting for a holiday with some certitude of safe arrival. There were a few quivers in the last phrases of farewell, and knowing what had passed in the preceding days and the intimidation to which the men had been subjected, I could guess what was in their minds. Whereas I was excited by thoughts of the "lost" oases and taking the unexplored road and going into the unknown, they were thinking that this might be the last time they would shake hands with their friends. There was even a pitying look on the faces of some of those who came to bid us God-speed as to doomed men, yet being Beduins they also felt: "It is decreed that they should go thus."

We recited the Fat-ha, the first chapter of the Koran: *Praise be to God, the Master of the Universe, the Merciful, the Compassionate, the Lord of the day of Resurrection. It is You Whom we worship, and it is You Whom we ask for help. Guide us to the straight path, the path of those whom You have rewarded, not those upon whom displeasure has fallen nor those who have gone astray. Amen.*

There followed the Call to Prayers: *God is great and I testify that there is no God but God and that Mohammed is the Prophet of God. Haste to prayers, haste to that which is beneficent. Prayers are ready. God is great. There is no God but God.*

It was upon the edge of the valley of Kufra where the oasis ends and the desert stretches out ahead. They had walked with us until then, and as we passed from the valley into the flat desert we looked back upon the date palms. The sun was setting, dusk falling and Kufra itself in the waning light was glimpsed as through the aperture of a camera. Those who had come to say farewell straightway returned and looked back no more. I was eager to get away from

Kufra, and let my men turn their minds to the task ahead.

At last the real start had been made. Before me all was unknown, full of the mystery and the fascination that lie in those parts of the earth's surface yet untraversed by men from the outside world.

We started at 4.30 p.m. and halted at 8.15, making 15 kilometres. It was fine and clear, with no wind. Hard sand covered with very fine gravel, slightly undulating. After leaving the date trees of Ezeila and Kufra, we crossed a zone of *hatab*, similar to that at Zieghen, and entered the *serira* at 5.45. At 6.30 we passed hillocks which form the south side of the Valley of Kufra. At 8.15 we arrived at Hatiet El Houesh, marked by dry *hatab*, which must once have been green. We left two men behind us to bring two loads that were to be carried on Tebu camels.

Our caravan comprised twenty-seven camels and nineteen persons—myself, Zerwali, Abdullahi, Ahmed, Hamad, Ismail, Senussi Bu Hassan, Senussi Bu Jaber, Hamad Zwai, Sad the Aujili, Faraj the slave, Bukara and his young brother Hamid, the camel man, Hassan, Mohammed our guide, and three Tebus.

An entry from my diary again :

Thursday, April 19th.—Start at 1.45 p.m., halt at 7.15 p.m. Make 24 kilometres. Highest temperature 32°, lowest 11°. Fair and clear, with few white clouds. South-east breeze which drops at midday. After leaving Hatieb El Houesh we enter into a *serira* again, flat expanse of hard sand covered with fine gravel. East of the *hatia* is a chain of sand hillocks covered with dark brown stones ; to the west is another similar chain about 4 kilometres away.

At 2.15 we pass the end of the Hatieb El Houesh. The *hatia* is about 2 kilometres broad. At 3.45 there is a *gara* on our left about 2 kilometres away, and at 5 another *gara* 4 kilometres distant on our right. At 6.30 the sand is softer, with patches of red and black stones. The surface is undulating.

We were delayed in starting through waiting for the two camels which had been left behind, and used the time in collecting *hatab*. It was very warm and the camels grew tired quickly because of the heat. The country was similar to that between Buttafal and Zieghen. With my new *hejin* I found it easy to fall behind to take observations without exciting suspicion. We had to camp early because of the condition of the camels.

Friday, April 20th.—Start at 2 a.m., halt at 9.30 a.m. Start again at 3.30 p.m. and final halt at 8 p.m., make 48 kilometres. Highest temperature 32°, lowest 10°, at 12.30 a.m. Fine and clear, with cold south-east wind in the early morning. It drops at midday and gets up again at 4. In the evening it shifts to north-east.

At 4 a.m. passing through undulating country strewn with stone. At 6 enter *serira* again, flatter. Sunrise is as 5.50. Immediately thereafter on our right and left are low sandhills from 8 to 10 kilometres distant. See a swallow in the morning and a hawk in the afternoon. At 4.20 cross low sand-dunes, and sight a black *gara*, a long low mound, 10 degrees south of south-east.

This was the worst part of the journey for travelling, so far as temperature conditions were concerned. In the middle of the day it was too hot to march, and at night it was too cold. So we broke the trek into two parts, starting soon after midnight, and resting in the heat of the day. We had trouble with the baggage because of the difficulty of good packing and loading in the dark. The camels, however, went better on this day.

This was the fourth day of the lunar month. The Beduins observe the weather conditions on that day, believing that the weather for the rest of the month will be the same. It was to prove true in this case.

Saturday, April 21st. We started at 2.30 a.m. At 6 in the morning we came across stony and hilly country which lasted for 12 kilometres. We passed on our left the *gara* called Garet Kudi. At 9 we entered again into *serira,* with distant sand-dunes on the right and left.

One camel fell ill shortly after our start and refused to go even when its load was taken off. Two Beduins were left behind to bleed it, but all efforts at cure were in vain, and it had to be slaughtered. I forbade the Beduins to eat its flesh. Later, after the midday halt, two Tebus dumped the loads from their camels and went back to dry the flesh and leave it until their return from Ouenat. They were to catch us later. This all delayed us about an hour.

The men had little sleep the previous night and were very tired after sunrise. But it was chiefly the intense heat from noon to 4 o'clock that exhausted both men and camels. It was a very tired caravan that started again at 4.30 p.m. and moved slowly along.

I saw two hawks and fresh sleeping camps of birds on the sands.

Sunday, April 22nd. We travelled over flat hard sand, with occasional sand hillocks, 3 to 10 metres high, covered with black stones. At 5.30 a.m. we sighted a chain of hills on our left running from north to south-west across our path. At 8 a.m. we entered into broken, hilly country, which continued all day. It was called Wadi El Maraheeg. We came across broken ostrich eggs.

We had better loading to-day, but the men were

tired. Many of them fell out to snatch a half-hour's sleep, catching up the caravan when they woke.

Bukara brought me two little eagles which he had taken from their nest on the top of a *gara*. I ordered him to put them back and saw that it was done.

The *hejin* was ill and had to go all the afternoon without load or even saddle.

At the midday halt the men fell asleep immediately and snored heavily. This kind of travel is gruelling, tedious work. But we were getting on.

Monday, April 23rd. We started at 2.30 a.m., halted at 9.15 a.m., second start at 3.45 p.m., halt at 9 p.m., making 46 kilometres. This was the most exhausting trek that I had yet known. For eight days we had had only four hours of sleep a day. We had hardly started before the men with one accord fell back to snatch a half-hour's sleep, leaving the camels to follow the will-o'-the-wisp of the guide's lantern. I could not avail myself of this privilege, because of my anxiety for my instruments. The loading, done in the dark, was insecure and a slipped fastening may mean a broken instrument or camera.

At intervals one or another camel would halt and kneel and refuse to get up. Then a Tebu would come and press his thumb on a certain big vein in the camel's forehead and manipulate it. It seemed to give the beast relief.

We were having a hard time of it crossing the high steep sand-dunes when suddenly mountains rose before us like mediæval castles half hidden in the mist. A few minutes later the sun was on them, turning the cold grey into warm rose and pink.

I let the caravan go on and for half an hour I sat

on the sand-dune and let the sight of these legendary mountains do its will with my mind and heart. I had found what I came to seek. These were the mountains of Arkenu.

It was the outstanding moment of the whole journey. Any hardships I might have endured, any hardships that might still await me, were as nothing compared with the joy that filled me at the mere sight of those hills. It was not like going to seek a hidden treasure that had to be dug out of the ground. There they were standing right up high before me so that I might feast my eyes upon them. Up and down, up and down we had plodded across the sand-dunes in the chilly greyness of the hours before dawn, until suddenly at the last dune it was as though somebody had rung up a curtain upon these magical hills of which I have not seen the like in the whole Libyan Desert. From the time I left Sollum until I reached this spot there had been nothing like the mountains of Arkenu. The sight of them so gripped me that for a while I dreamed that I was not in the desert any more.

Tuesday, April 24th, was the 111th day from Sollum and the 140th from Cairo. We covered broken country, sand covered with stones, undulating. At 5 a.m. heavy sand-dunes. After the dunes the country became stony again, and later there was hard sand covered with gravel. North of Arkenu Mountain and only 100 metres from it was a big sandstone hill about 2 kilometres long and 100 metres or so high.

There was a glorious sunrise, with shades of red and gold splashed on the few grey clouds in the east. The cool wind soon dropped and it became close and warm.

Arkenu Mountain is a mass of granite, its grey

surface weathered to a ruddy brown, rising uniformly along its length some 500 metres from the desert surface. It is made up of a series of conical masses which run together at their feet, without intervals between them. We approached it at its most western point. As we came toward it, we could not tell how far it extended to the east. At the farthest point which we could see in that direction it rose into a peak. We marched around the north-western corner of the mountain mass and came to the entrance of a valley which runs to the eastward. There is one solitary tree of the species, called by the Goran "*Arkenu*," standing in the desert here. From it the oasis takes its name. We made our camp near it. This was a bad spot for camel ticks, who lived in the shade of the tree and came literally running by the score when our camels approached. We were obliged to camp some distance from the tree, as the insects did not seem to care to forsake its shade, even to attack the camels.

I once picked up a tick that was like a piece of petrified stone. I hit it with a stick and it just clicked like a piece of stone. I turned away and pretended to be busy with something else. It took about three or four minutes before it gave any sign of life. The tick knows instinctively that safety lies in pretending to be petrified. Then, without warning, it scooted like lightning. When there are no camels these ticks live on nothing. They absorb the camel's blood, get inflated, and then they can live—the Beduins say years, but certainly a few months.

Immediately on our arrival the camels were sent into the valley to be watered and to bring back the supply of water of which we were much in need.

Two hours after we pitched camp the two Tebus left behind arrived with a supply of meat from the slaughtered camel, which was eaten with enthusiasm for dinner. A hot, gusty wind blew all the afternoon. While I was resting in my tent I was suddenly aroused by something tickling my ear and tried to brush it away, without discovering what it was. In a moment a gust of wind blew in one of the side walls of the tent, which had been raised for ventilation, and I felt something darting across my body. I grasped at it instinctively and, fortunately for my peace of mind, missed it. It was a snake some 4 feet long, which was subsequently caught by my men and dispatched.

The men held a shooting competition in the afternoon. It started as a perfunctory affair, but the interest quickened when I put up a *mejidi*—a Turkish dollar—as a prize. Senussi Bu Jaber, though short-sighted, won the contest. Hamid expressed the feelings of the other contestants when he said: "It was the *mejidi* that worked on my emotions and made me nervous. I had hit the mark before."

I made observations and took photographs, and, incidentally, treated the guide's teeth.

Goran, the black tribes of the neighbourhood, suddenly appeared from the valley and were kept to dine with my men. No one had dreamed of their presence until they appeared. The mountain looked desolate and deserted and one would not suspect that inside it lies a fertile valley which is inhabited. As a matter of fact, Arkenu is not inhabited all the year round. In the valley is good vegetation, to which in the past Beduins, Tebus, and Goran brought their camels during the grazing season. They closed the entrances to the valley with rocks and left the camels there unattended for three months.

"When they came to take them back," said Mohammed the guide, "they had as much fat on them as this." He puts his closed fists one on top of the other.

Wednesday, April 25th. The Goran family in the valley brought a sheep, milk and *samn,* which is butter in a curious liquid state because of the heat, as *diafa* or hospitality. They also drove their sheep to the camp to be milked for the men of the caravan.

After luncheon I rode into Arkenu Valley with Zerwali and Bukara. It is a *karkur,* or narrow winding valley, extending some 15 kilometres back into the mountains. There are grass, shrubs and an occasional tree. We visited the Goran hut, where I took photographs of a girl and two boys of the family. The boys wore white robes, the sign of the sons of a *sheikh.* When I got back to camp, I sent presents of cloth, handkerchiefs and rice for the three children.

It was a beautiful moonlight night. I decided to spend three days more at Arkenu because the grazing was good and the camels still seemed tired from their hard trek. My *hejin* was doing well. I picked up stones for geological specimens and aroused the suspicions of some of my men. They thought there was gold in what stones I picked up or else I would not take the trouble to carry them back home.

Thursday, April 26th. At Arkenu. Highest temperature 36° ; lowest 9° Centigrade. Fine and clear, with very strong and hot south-east wind. Twice the wind blew the tents down. We sent the camels to be watered and to graze. It was a sweltering day, over

100° Fahrenheit in the tent, and only a little less in the shade outside. Making observations was difficult on account of the wind. I did not like to shelter myself behind the tent while making them for fear of arousing the inevitable curiosity and suspicion. The wind dropped in the evening and we were repaid for a hot and scorching day by a beautifully cool evening with a fine moon. There was dancing and singing by Bukara and the other men until midnight.

Friday, April 27th. Arkenu was the first of the two "lost" oases which it is my good fortune to place definitely on the map. There had long been a tradition that two oases existed close to the south-western corner of Egypt. But the position that they had been conjecturally given on one or two maps was from 30 to 180 kilometres out of place. No one had described them from an actual visit. My observations showed that Arkenu is situated in north latitude 20° 12′ 32″, and east longitude 24° 44′ 15″, and has an altitude of 598 metres at the foot of the mountain. It is thus well within the boundaries of Egypt.

The principal interest of this oasis—as of Ouenat—lies in the possibilities it offers for exploring the south-west corner of Egypt, which has until now been unreached either by military patrols or by travellers. No one has known with any certainty of water supplies in that part of the desert which could be relied upon. The water at Arkenu is apparently unfailing and is drinkable, though not as wholesome for human beings as one could wish. Arkenu may conceivably prove to have strategic value at some future time, standing as it does almost precisely at the meeting-point of the western and southern boundaries of Egypt.

Both Arkenu and Ouenat differ from all the other oases of the Western Desert of Egypt in that they are not depressions in the desert with underground water supplies, but mountain areas where rain-water collects in natural basins in the rocks.

The mountain chain of Arkenu, as I saw it, is about 15 kilometres in extent from north to south and some 20 kilometres from east to west. But there was no opportunity to explore it to the eastward, so that I cannot say whether it may not extend farther in that direction than I have stated. I could only observe it as far as I could see from the desert at the western foot of the mountain. It may well be that off to the east Arkenu Mountain runs into a chain of hills of which the Ouenat Mountains are also spurs to the south. There is an opportunity for more exploration of the eastern portions of both these rock masses than I was able to make in the time and with the resources at my command.

The nearest known point to Arkenu and Ouenat to the east or rather the north-east is Dakhla Oasis, some 600 kilometres distant. There is a tradition that there is an old track to Egypt between these two points, but a journey from Dakhla to Arkenu and Ouenat with caravan, which would take at least fourteen days, would be a formidable undertaking.

THE HILLS OF OUENAT.

THE EXPLORER'S CAMP AT THE FOOT OF THE GRANITE HILLS OF OUENAT.

THE ROCK VALLEY WELLS FOUND AT OUENAT.

THE VALLEY OF ERDI.
The end of the long, waterless treks, although far from the end of the journey.

THE VALLEY OF ARKENU.

THE FIRST TREE SEEN APPROACHING ERDI.

THE WELL OF ERDI.

A BIDIYAT FAMILY.

A ZAGHAWA GIRL
with her baby on her back.

CHAPTER XVI

The "Lost" Oases—Ouenat

SATURDAY, April 28th. We started at 9.30 p.m. for the first all-night trek, halt at 7 a.m. of the 29th. We made 40 kilometres. Fair and clear with a very strong hot wind from south-east all day. The wind blew from same quarter, but warm rather than hot, all night. The ground was *serira,* with large stones making bad going for the camels. At 6 a.m. we reached the western corner of Ouenat Mountain and camped an hour later.

The day was spent quietly, chiefly in rest for the coming night trek. In the early evening we sent men to bring the camels from their grazing. Bukara hired a camel from a Tebu, to relieve his own, which he wanted to be able to sell at the end of the journey for a high price. I hired three Tebus and their camels to go with us, but not for the same reason. Our transport was inadequate, for the trek from Kufra had shown me that our loads were too heavy. The camels became quickly exhausted.

The camels were brought in at 8 in the evening and we started an hour and a half later. They were lightly loaded this time because we were taking no water from Arkenu. The water there, while its taste is not particularly unpleasant, is hard on one's digestive apparatus. We had three bad cases of dysentery among the men. The invalids rode camels from the start, and the rest of the men took turns during the night.

The caravan started out in the best of humour. At intervals some cheerful spirit stopped and began to chant. In a moment half a dozen of them were lined up beside him, all chanting, stamping and clapping their hands rhythmically as the camels filed past. The words of the song were always the same :

En kàn azeèz alaih lanzàr
Hàtta laù ba-èd biddàr.

The accents are strongly pronounced and differ in the two lines, as I have marked them. I would translate the verse thus, without making any attempt to fit it to the jazz rhythm that would be needed to complete the effect for the Western ear : " O Beloved, our eyes gaze after you, even though your camp is far away."

Again and again the chant was repeated until the performance ended in a sudden shout. I had been the whole audience for the little show, beating the rhythm with my whip, and when the shout went up I called out " Farraghu barud ! " " Empty gun-powder ! " was the signal for a *feu de joie* from the rifles, after which we all took our places in the caravan and went on exhilarated.

A night march has its advantages. The time, unless one is dead tired, passes more quickly than during the day, and the stars are cheering company for any lover of Nature. On the horizon ahead of us loomed the dark masses of the Ouenat Mountains. It is so much easier to march with one's destination distinct before one than to be walking on that flat disc of a desert where every point of the compass looks like every other and the horizon keeps always at the same maddening distance. We steadily approached the mountains until the sun was rising over them, tinting and gilding their peaks and throwing out on the desert a heavy shadow whose edge marched steadily toward the mountain foot as we approached it from another direction. Shortly after sunrise we were opposite the north-west corner of the mountains, and an hour later we made camp close under their rocky walls. At this point there was an indentation in the mountain-side, with a well in a cave at its inner end. We pitched our tents at the mouth of this little arm of the desert sea, and ten minutes later we were all sunk into sleep. This was our first full night of travel, and we had some arrears of sleep to make up.

However, we did not sleep as long as we had expected to, but roused ourselves before noon and turned our attention to food. The French saying, *qui dors dine*, may be true under some conditions, but we of the desert find it more satisfactory when we are able to do both. We all found pleasant distraction in roasting parts of the lamb which was provided by Mohammed as *diafa* for Ouenat.

I spent the rest of the day in visiting the well, which is situated in the cave in the mountain-side, in taking observations and in looking over our surroundings. At this point the mountain rises in a sheer cliff, with a mass of boulders, great and small, heaped against it at its foot. The stones that make up this *tabre*, as the geologists call it, have been carved by ages of wind and driven sand into smooth, rounded shapes that giants of the heroic days might have used in their slings to kill monsters or for some enormous games of bowls. The *ain*, or well, lies a few metres away from the camp, in a cavity walled and roofed with the great rocks. It is a pool of refreshing water kept cool by their protection from the sun. The desert knows two kinds of wells—the *ain*, which properly speaking is a spring, and the *bir* or *matan*, which is a place where water may be obtained by digging in the sand. We call these wells of Ouenat *ains*, for lack of a better word, although they are not springs but reservoirs in the rock where rain-water collects.

There are said to be seven of these *ains* in the Ouenat Mountains, of which I was to see four before I moved south again. I also heard rumours of one or two *birs* in the oasis, but I did not see them.

In the evening the camp was full of life and gaiety. The men danced and sang as though there were no tedious days of hot sand and scorching wind behind or ahead of them.

Monday, April 30th. Up early and went with Zerwali, Abdullahi, Mohammed and Malkenni, the Tebu, to the big *ain* up the mountain. It was a stiff climb of an hour and a half. The *ain* has a plentiful supply of splendid water and is picturesquely surrounded with tall, slim reeds. I took some of the reeds back with me to make pipe stems. They give a pleasantly cool smoke.

In the early evening I set out on the *hejin*, with Malkenni, Senussi Bu Hassan, and Sad to explore the oasis. It was a fine moonlight night with a warm south-east breeze. For four hours we marched over *serira*, skirting the north-west corner of the mountain, and at midnight we entered a valley with a chain of low hills on our left and the sinister mountain with its fantastic rock formations on our right. The valley is floored with soft sand strewn with big stones, which made hard going for the camels. At the hour when men's spirits and courage are proverbially at the lowest ebb we halted a few minutes for a draught of strong tea from my thermos flask, and then pushed on. But our spirits were by no means low. There was something magical about the night and the moonlight and the mountains, to make this an experience stirring to the imagination and uplifting to the soul. I speak for myself; but the men seemed to be getting something out of it, too.

At 5 the valley opened out on to a wide plain of flat *serira*, with hills 10 or 15 kilometres away to the north-east. We turned sharply to the south, around a spur of the mountain. At dawn we stopped for morning prayers.

The camels were *barrakked* and we took our stand on the sands facing toward Mecca. When Moslems take part in their ceremonial prayers, they stand before God—not, as some misinformed persons say, before Mohammed, who was not God but man, a prophet and not the Deity, and the first essential is cleansing, of body, heart and soul. In the desert the cleansing of the body can be only symbolical, since water cannot be spared. We take sand in our hands, rub it over each hand and forearm, then gently over our faces. With hands uplifted, palms upward, we say the prayers appointed, then kneeling touch our foreheads to the cool sands of the morning.

In the desert, prayers are no mere blind obedience

to religious dogma, but an instinctive expression of one's inmost self. The prayers at night bring serenity and peace. At dawn, when new life has suddenly taken possession of the body, one eagerly turns to the Creator to offer humble homage for all the beauty of the world and of life, and to seek guidance for the coming day. One prays then, not because one ought, but because one must.

Seven o'clock found us entering a wide valley, running a little east of south, with mountains rising high on both sides. The floor of the valley is as flat as a table, patterned with tufts of grass and marked here and there with mimosa trees and small shrubs, whose leaves when crushed give off a fragrance similar to that of mint. At intervals the ground is carpeted with creeping plants of the colocynth, expanses of green leaves dotted with brilliant yellow globes like grape-fruit. It is from this fruit that the Tebus and Goran make *abra*. They boil the pips thoroughly to get rid of their bitter taste and then crush them with dates or locusts in a wooden mortar. *Abra* is their staple dish.

For three hours we proceeded up the valley, and at 10 we camped hot and tired, but not ill-content. We ate a good meal of rice, drank our three glasses of tea, and went to sleep in the shade of a ridge. It was uncomfortable slumber, what with swarming flies and the moving shadow of the ridge, which made each of us shift position from time to time.

As I opened my eyes a figure stood near me that seemed to be part of a pleasant dream. She was a beautiful girl of the Goran, the slim graceful lines of whose body were not spoiled by the primitive garments she wore. She carried a bowl of milk which she offered with shy dignity. I could only accept it and drink gratefully. Then she asked me for medicine for her sister, who had borne no children. When she refused to believe that I had no medicine that would be helpful to her sister, I fell back on my malted milk tablets, a harmless remedy for ailments which were beyond me. I also gave her a *mejidi* and a silk handkerchief for herself.

A Tebu appeared with a parcel of meat of the *waddan* or wild sheep. I gave him macaroni and rice and he went away happy.

After we had eaten I went to see some relics of the presence of men in earlier times. At Arkenu I had got talking with one of the Gorans, and having satisfied myself about the present inhabitants of Ouenat, I asked him whether he knew anything about any former inhabitants of the oasis.

He gave me a startling answer. "Many different people have lived round these wells, as far back as anyone can remember. Even *djinns* have dwelt in that place in olden days."

"Djinns!" I exclaimed. "How do you know that?"

"Have they not left their drawings on the rocks?" he answered.

With suppressed excitement I asked him where. He replied that in the valley of Ouenat there were many drawings upon the rocks, but I could not induce him to describe them further than saying that there were "writings and drawings of all the animals living and nobody knows what sort of pens they used, for they wrote very deeply on the stones and Time has not been able to efface the writings." Doing my best not to show anything like excitement, I inquired whether he could tell me just where the drawings were.

" At the end of the valley, where the tail of the valley wags," he answered.

The whole time I remembered this, and after a little time spent in making sure about the water, which is the most important thing, and having a look round from the top of the hills at the surrounding country, there came the exciting task of going round the oasis. But the most exciting part of it was to find these rock inscriptions, especially as the history that I had been able to collect about the oasis was very scanty. I gathered that Ouenat was the *pied-à-terre* of Tebus and Goran, who were going eastwards to attack and despoil the Kababishe. Arkenu and Ouenat, indeed, were very well placed for that purpose, since they provided water for the attacking party and at the same time were too far away for the Kababishe to dare attempt reprisals or try to recover their own belongings.

With these drawings in mind, then, I took Malkenni, who had joined the caravan at Arkenu, and towards sunset he led me straight to them. They were in the valley at the part where it drew in, curving slightly with a suggestion of the wagging tail. We found them on the rock at the ground level. I was told there were other similar inscriptions at half a day's journey, but as it was growing late and I did not want to excite suspicion, I did not go to them.

There was nothing beyond the drawings of animals, no inscriptions. It seemed to me as though they were drawn by somebody who was trying to compose a scene. Although primitive in character, they betrayed an artistic hand. The man who drew these outline figures of animals had a decorative sense. On their wall of rock these pictures were rudely, but not unskilfully carved. There were lions, giraffes and ostriches, all kinds of gazelle, and perhaps cows, though many of these figures were effaced by time. The carving is from a quarter to half an inch in depth and the edges of the lines are weathered until in some parts they can be scraped off easily with the finger.

I asked who made the pictures, and the only answer I got came from Malkenni, the Tebu, who declared his belief that they were the work of the *djinn.*

"What men," he demanded, "can do these things now?"

I did not find any traditions about the origin of these interesting rock markings, but I was struck by two things. There are no giraffes in this part of the country now; nor do they live in any similar desert country anywhere. Also there are no camels among the carvings on the rocks, and one cannot penetrate to this oasis now except with camels. Did the men who made these pictures know the giraffe and not the camel? I reflected that the camel came to Africa from Asia some 500 years B.C.

At 5.30 we started for the home camp. We wound our way up a steep mountain path, hardly wide enough in places for a single man and exceedingly dangerous going for the camels. We reached the highest point of the path and then picked our way down to the desert level south of the mountains. At the highest point we reached there were a few peaks around some 200 or 300 metres higher than we were. The camels went up and down the steep path wonderfully well in spite of the darkness, and at 10.30 we were at the foot of the mountains.

It seemed best to give the camels a rest and we halted at 11 for two hours. We had tea, and a Tebu family whose camp was near came to visit us. We snatched a brief sleep and awoke refreshed. There was a cool wind blowing and the ride home over the level desert was a pleasant relief after the hot work of climbing about among the rocks.

We reached camp at 10 a.m. of the 2nd and were met with firing of rifles and an agreeable welcome.

Wednesday, May 2nd. On reaching camp we found Sheikh Herri, the Goran chief who is called " King " of Ouenat, and its 150 inhabitants. He came the day before to visit me and waited for my return. He was a very nice old man with a calm, dignified face. He brought two sheep, milk and *abra* for *diafa*. He was keeping Ramadan, and I insisted on his staying the night with us. Otherwise I could not offer him hospitality, since he might not eat or drink until sunset.

I had a long talk with him and with Mohammed. The old chief was still fond of his own country north of Wadai and sighed when it was spoken of. He belonged to the Rezzi family, which is a ruling family of Goran in Northern Wadai. He came to Kufra as a voluntary exile, when the French entered Wadai, and later he settled in Ouenat.

I found myself tired after our twenty-eight hours of trekking with only nine hours of rest, but a bath, a meal and a short sleep made life worth living again in the evening.

Bukara had organized a chorus among the men, and

the evening was spent with Beduin, Tebu and Sudanese songs.

Thursday, May 3rd. Herri came to my tent with a bowl of milk when I got up. When I thanked him, he shook his head sadly.

"This is all I have to offer," he said. "It is not worthy of you. But you will forgive us for not being able to give you the hospitality that you should have."

I assured him that it is the spirit that counts in these matters and not the intrinsic value of the offering. The day was spent in preparations for the start south, which I hoped would be made on the morrow.

Friday, May 4th. I made an arrangement with Herri to go with us to Erdi, as an additional guide. Mohammed had not been through this country for a number of years, and I felt that Herri should know it better.

In the afternoon I went for a long walk and took photographs of the mountains. By this time all the Tebu and Goran settlements, which are scattered about the oasis wherever there is grazing for their beasts, had heard of our presence, and the people came to visit us. There were many guests for dinner, and it was a very gay camp. It was one of the pleasantest evenings of the trip.

Before we leave Ouenat I must say something about Bukara, who is one of the most interesting people in the caravan and a romantic figure. He is tall, slim and wiry, a typical Beduin, always cheerful and with a song at his lips at those critical moments in the day, early in the morning or late at night, when the men are tired with the night march and need encouragement.

I did not know that he smoked until one day as

I was saddling my horse I caught him collecting the cigarette ends from the spot where my tent had stood. After this I shared my cigarettes with him. It was great fun to hand him a packet of the precious articles and see him break into a song and dance of joy.

Bukara is one of the most travelled Beduins that I have come across. He is only thirty-three and yet he has travelled to Wadai, Borku, Bornu, and Darfur. He has seen days of good fortune in the past, but to-day he owns but one camel. He has thrown in his lot with my caravan, arranging with Bu Helega that he is to have a share of the money received from the latter's camels when they are sold at the end of the journey.

He speaks most of the dialects of the Black tribes and knows a great deal about them. He is also a wonderful mimic. One evening he put on the green cloth that formed a partition in my tent as a *burnoos*, and with Sad and Hamid bleating like sheep behind him came to the camp pretending to be a Beduin *Sheikh*, bringing the two sheep as *diafa*. We were kept in roars of laughter and suddenly Bukara flung away the green cloth and, snatching a spear from one of the Tebus, broke into a Tebu war-dance. A Tebu assisted him by beating a rhythm on one of the small empty *fantasses*. This droll exhibition was followed by a concert of Beduin songs from Cyrenaica, Fezzan and Tripoli.

I have seen Bukara refuse to mount a camel to ride when all the Beduins have yielded to the temptation.

" Why don't you ride, Bukara ? " I asked. " There are several unloaded camels."

" What would my *washoon* (wife) say if she heard

that her Bukara had ridden between Arkenu and Ouenat?" he replied, with scorn in his voice for the thought.

He told me that on one occasion he had been entrusted with some fifty camels to take to Ouenat for grazing. He was alone and ran short of food.

"For twelve days I ate no meal, except the pips of colocynth, which upset my digestion," he replied simply. "Then I reached Kufra. The men at Kufra who had sent me for the camels had forgotten to send me food. They had expected me at Kufra earlier."

"But why didn't you slaughter a camel?" I inquired.

"Should I permit the men of Kufra to say that Bukara could not endure hunger and had killed a camel?" he retorted proudly.

Bukara is very fond of his wife. When we reached Arkenu he said to me, "I am feeling better now, but I cried like a child when I said good-bye to my *washoon* at Kufra. It is always like that when I begin my journeys. If the company is good I forget more quickly."

CHAPTER XVII

Night Marches to Erdi

SUNDAY, *May 6th.* We got away at 6.45 p.m. and made a good twelve hours' trek of 54 kilometres. It was a thoroughly tiring performance, however, as the first night's march was likely to be. The men had had no chance to sleep during the day, but, on the contrary, had been busier than usual. In spite of our weariness the loads had to be carefully watched and readjusted every now and then. At dawn most of the men dropped back for short naps.

One of the camels broke away and ran back toward Ouenat. Malkenni had to leave the caravan at midnight and go after it.

There was moonlight the latter half of the night and a refreshing cool breeze at 3 in the morning. The camels grazed, as they went, on the grass which grew here because of the water coming down from the hills.

When we came to make camp one of our best *girbas* was found torn and half empty. It was a misfortune, for we could not spare water on the trek that was before us. We had to go ten days before reaching a well. Malkenni and the runaway camel did not appear during the day.

My diary runs :

Monday, May 7th.—Cloudy all day. Strong north-east wind which drops in afternoon. Highest temperature 38°. When travelling at night cannot take minimum temperature, which occurs about 2 or 3, as we are on the move at that time. Start at 6.30 p.m., halt at 11.30 p.m. Make 20 kilometres. Very soft sand, undulating, with dry *sabat* for grazing.

In the afternoon a Tebu arrived with a camel loaded with the luggage that had been on the runaway. He told us that Malkenni's camel had thrown off its load and run back to the grazing-ground at Ouenat, with Malkenni after him. At 11.30 we halted on very soft sand with patches of rock about and grazing ground near Baret Shezzu, to wait for the runaways. They appeared shortly after our arrival ; but I decided not to go farther that night. The rest would do us all good.

Tuesday, May 8th. We started at 4.45 p.m. in an oppressive atmosphere under heavy clouds. Two hours later it rained a little and the Beduins, whose life depends on rain, instinctively shouted with joy and sang fervently to the camels.

The ground was undulating, hard and covered with stones and large gravel. We crossed some small *gherds* soon after starting and then the country flattened out again, with softer sand. At 3.30 a.m. we entered a belt of high sand-dunes and crossed it in an hour and a half. After the dunes the ground became the old familiar *serira* again. Here I found bits of ostrich eggshells.

Early in the day Arami, Malkenni's brother, had taken a sack and gone to collect *hatab*. His name tells his story, for among the Tebus and Goran a man who has killed another is known frankly as Arami. He had said that he would meet us later on. We had no anxiety about him, especially as we were told that he knew the way well.

But when we had been two hours on the road and it was growing dark we became anxious, and halted to wait for him. We fired many shots to attract his attention and direct him to where we were. The men shouted his name as loud as they could, but all in vain.

I turned to Malkenni and asked him what he intended to do.

"My brother is mad," he said. "No one asked him to collect *hatab*. He left the camp without even having his breakfast. It may be that he has been called by God to his death. When the moon rises I shall leave my camel's load and return to look for him. If he is alive I shall bring him back with me; if he is dead I shall bury him and join you later."

It was said quite simply and as though it were all a matter of course. The load was shifted from Malkenni's camel to another, and he set out on the back track. Arami had already had many narrow escapes from death and every one hoped that it might be so this time. But Mohammed was doubtful.

"God is merciful," he said, "but I think Arami has walked to his fate."

I was afraid he might be right. There was something strange about Arami from the first. I learned that on a trek once from Erdi to Ouenat his water supply had run out and he had had a "bad thirst," as the desert people call it. He had reached Ouenat half dead. Such an experience leaves its mark on a man and it is likely to be long before he is himself again. I had noticed the queer, strained, vague look in his eyes and wondered about it. If he did not come back, the desert, in one of its moods of cruelty, would have claimed its own.

In the desert upon the long, waterless treks, the men, from exhaustion, thirst, fatigue, sleeplessness, often lose their heads, and, as the Beduins say, " walk to their fate," which means that unless their comrades are on the look-out and keep them with the caravan they walk away into the desert, disregarding even the animal instinct of the camel to keep with the herd. In such a case, if the wanderer suddenly returns to his senses, he has to sit down where he finds himself and not move. It is understood that his comrades when they are aware of his absence will retrace the tracks of the caravan and then his own tracks upon the sand and so rescue him. I met a Beduin at Kufra who had been lost for eighteen hours, cut off from the caravan. When he was rescued he was unconscious, suffering badly from thirst. " God was merciful," he told me, " for I was just able to do my prayer and face God before what I thought was my inevitable death. But we live and die only by the decree of God," he added with a smile.

Wednesday, May 9th.—Start 4.15 p.m., halt at 10.15 p.m. Make 24 kilometres. Highest temperature 37°. White clouds and very strong warm wind from the north-east which continues all day and at night develops into a sandstorm. A few drops of rain fall at 7 p.m. The sandstorm lasts from 8 to 10. The ground is ordinary *serira,* with soft sand in places. There are no landmarks and no dry grass. We sight distant sand-dunes on our right in the early morning.

We marched fourteen and a half hours last night, but we were not very tired. Breakfast and four hours' sleep found us all refreshed a ·ain. Mohammed wanted us to make an early start, as there was a difficult *gherd* ahead which could not be crossed in the dark. So 4.15 found us under way, with *serira* under our feet and a cool north-east wind behind us.

Shortly after 8 I felt the wind in my face. I was startled, for the wind does not usually shift so suddenly. Besides, the quality of the wind had not changed. This wind in our faces should be coming from the south and yet it is not warm. There is something strange about it. I look above for the stars, but the sky is completely covered with dark clouds. I take out my compass and am startled to find that we are heading full north-east instead of south-west. Then it is clear to me that Mohammed has "lost his head," as the Beduins say, and is leading us in the diametrically opposite direction from the right one.

It was a serious moment and one that required tact and careful handling. It is dangerous to undermine a desert guide's confidence. I got off my camel and, mounting my horse, galloped to where Mohammed was leading the caravan.

I realized as I went that the men of the caravan, most of whom were accustomed to this sort of country and this kind of weather, had also a feeling that we were going wrong. But it is the etiquette of the desert that no one may interfere with the guide in any way. The guide of a caravan is exactly like the captain of a ship. He is absolute master of the caravan so far as direction is concerned, and must also be consulted as to the starting and halting times.

I had fortunately asked Mohammed before leaving Ouenat as to the direction we were to take and had set my compass to it. As I approach the guid I find him agitated and lacking his habitual cheerful smile and air of self-reliance. I show him the compass and suggest that we are going in the wrong direction. He says nothing, but scans the sky anxiously for his favourite *Jadi*, but in vain, for Polaris is behind the clouds.

At this moment, the sandstorm which had been rising blew out his lantern. The caravan had caught up with us, and every one realized that we had lost our way. Men and camels were huddled together, with the gale and hurtling sand beating upon them. The wind made it impossible to hear one's own voice, to say nothing of any other man's.

Mohammed's confidence had completely deserted him, and I could see its effect on the men's faces. They were all travelled men of the desert and they knew what it meant to lose one's way in a *serira*, where there are no landmarks.

"We must camp until the sky clears," is the chorus.

But I know how fatal such a policy would be. They would spend four or five hours brooding over their fate and growing more and more despondent and hopeless. There is no need for a halt, as my compass is a reliable one, and I have checked it many times with the directions pointed out by Mohammed.

"This wind comes from the north," I asserted quietly but with assurance during a lull in the storm, "as it has for the past few days. If it came from the south it would be hot. There is the *Jadi*, and this is our route."

I pointed to where Polaris must be, unless the compass is all wrong, and then swung around and indicated the way that we should go.

"Allah bless you," replied Mohammed, pulling himself together. "What you say is true."

Senussi Bu Hassan, who was our guide to Kufra, came close to me, and in a loud voice confirmed the statement.

"Wallahi, you speak truth," he said firmly. "I had thought of it, but could not speak as I had no proof, since the *Jadi* hides himself behind the clouds."

That was enough for us. We lighted the lantern with difficulty and with Mohammed and Bu Hassan beside me I led the way.

"How are we going to march?" demands a voice from the darkness.

"Let the wind fan the back of your black neck and you won't go much wrong," answers Bukara with a laugh.

A few hours later Mohammed grips my hand, and pointing to the sand-dunes ahead, ejaculates with deep feeling, "The *gherds*! Praise be to God! God is generous!" He is perfectly cheerful again.

The storm soon subsided completely and we were among the sand-dunes. The sky was perfectly clear now and even the most pessimistic of the men could have no more anxiety. But our little experience in this sandstorm demonstrated what a touch-and-go business desert trekking could be at times. It was only my compass that saved us from a very serious situation.

Mohammed was doubtful of the wisdom of trying to cross the *gherds* in the darkness, so we made our camp where we were.

Thursday, May 10th.—Start at 4.15 a.m., halt at 8.45 a.m.; start again at 4.30 p.m., halt at 7 a.m. (of the 11th). Make 75 kilometres. Fine and clear. Strong cold wind in the early morning, moderating later. Highest temperature 38°. Sand-dunes, 2 kilometres in width, of very soft sand, dangerous in places. Then ordinary *serira*. At 5.30 p.m. country is interspersed with patches of black and white stone like that before reaching Kufra. At 3 a.m. of the 11th enter zone of dry grass on flat soft sands. At 4.30 a.m. pass belt of sand-dunes.

In the early morning we got under way to cross the *gherds*, and speedily realized how serious a mistake it would have been to tackle them in the darkness. They were very steep and the sand was treacherously soft. The camels sank to their knees and had to be helped by the men. It took us three-quarters of an hour to cross them. We halted at 9 a.m. very hungry, for we had not eaten since lunch the day before. We needed food more than sleep, since the few hours of rest during the night were quite refreshing.

It was still hot when we started again at 4.30 p.m., but a pleasant north-east breeze tempered the oppressiveness. Herri asked me for a few yards of white cloth to make a turban, because the heat of the sun was affecting his head. I was glad to give it to him. Among the Tebus and Goran only *sheikhs* wear white.

I felt like walking that night and rode my camel less than usual. Since leaving Ouenat I had been walking six or seven hours a night, but that night I did nine. We made good progress until 3 a.m., when I suddenly felt or heard something rustle against my ankle boot. I reached down and found grass. The desert had changed its aspect. The camels were hungry, for we set out from Ouenat with only two days' food for them, trusting to the opportunities for grazing that we expected to find. So we let them eat as they went along instead of driving them at their best pace.

That night's march was tiring for everybody. We had arrears of sleep to make up and keeping the camels going in grazing country was hard work. Mohammed and Herri both rode most of the way, with Hassan carrying the lantern. Just before dawn, however, Mohammed got down and relieved him. When we rounded up the camels for our morning prayers the men looked more weary than I had ever seen them.

Friday, May 11th.—Start at 4.45 p.m., halt at 3.15 a.m. (of the 12th). Make 42 kilometres. Clear and fine. No wind. Warm all day and night. Highest temperature 39°. Soft sand covered with dry tufts of grass like a field of ripe corn. At 12.45 a.m. pass an ordinary *gherd*. At 1 enter flat *serira* without grass. At 3.15 halt at sandstone hills, having missed our way.

The day was spent in sleeping and eating, and at 4.45 p.m. we started with the intention of marching all night. But by 10 everybody was tired and sleepy. Even Mohammed was riding his camel. In the next few hours he fell asleep at intervals, and because of his fatigue did not look back to correct his direction by Polaris. When a guide neglects the *Jadi* he is far gone indeed. Senussi Bu Hassan and I felt certain that he was not taking the right course, but did not want to interfere with him again after the previous night.

At 3.15 a.m. we came to a ridge of hills and Mohammed stopped dead. Until now I had been walking behind the caravan and checking from time to time the bearing on which we were going. We had been walking since 10 o'clock more to the southward than before.

When the caravan halted I rode forward to Mohammed and asked why we were stopping.

" This opening in the hills," he says, pointing in front of him. " I do not recognize it and I do not know what kind of ground follows it." Whatever his faults, he is perfectly frank.

I did not want to arouse any feeling of anxiety in the men, so I said casually, " Let us camp until daybreak. We are all tired to-night." I have hardly spoken the words when the camels are *barrakked* and their loads are on the ground. I have never seen men fall so quickly to sleep. Each one wraps himself swiftly in his *jerd* and takes shelter from the cold north-east wind behind a piece of luggage.

Mohammed goes up the ridge to look about him and I follow.

" I think you have been following the *Jadi* too much," I suggest, meaning that he had been going too directly south. I do not intimate that he has been asleep on his camel. I do not want to shake his self-confidence and have him become demoralized.

" Allah bless you," he murmurs, scanning the horizon anxiously. " I must have done so, for we should not have reached hills so early. I counted on getting to them at dawn. But in the morning God will bring solace."

I am somewhat troubled as I leave him, and lie awake a few minutes, hoping that we have not gone far from our proper path. But I am too tired to worry long and go quickly to sleep.

Saturday, May 12th. At 4.30 a.m. Mohammed's voice is heard. " To Prayers, O ye Moslems! " We quickly get up and are under way in an hour.

Mohammed puts himself at the head of the caravan and I join him. He is still troubled, but as we round a corner of the hills he sighs with relief.

"Allah be praised. There lies our way."

He points to the north-west corner of the chain of hills and we make for it. We reach it at 9.45 a.m. and pitch camp. The camels are sent a kilometre or two into the hills to graze. Men and camels are in bad shape and water is getting scarce.

In the afternoon Mohammed and Herri go ahead into the hills to make a track in the sand with a tent-pole for us to follow. At 5 p.m. we follow them into the sand-dunes and thence into the hills. The *gherds* are fortunately not many, though they are steep enough. But it is the hilly country beyond them that takes it out of us. Our feet keep bumping into stones in the dark and Beduin shoes are little protection against such painful encounters. The collisions are particularly numerous and correspondingly trying in the early morning hours when we are terribly sleepy and walk with eyes half shut.

On previous nights I have tried the experiment of suddenly firing two or three shots from my rifle to rouse the men to life, and with good results. Each time they have responded with a loud cheer and mended their pace forthwith. But to-night the scheme fails. About 3 in the morning, the most deadly hour of all, I "empty gunpowder," but not a voice responds.

There is one small compensation, however, in the midst of this dead expanse of fatigue and depression. The crescent moon rises in the early morning, a curved silver thread with a brilliant star above it, an exquisite piece of celestial jewellery. I fix my eyes on their beauty and forget for a moment the bruises that my poor feet are getting.

When a little later we reach a patch of dry grass, we are all ready to let the camels graze for a while and to give our tired bodies a brief respite. At dawn we halt again for morning prayers. We have barely risen from our knees when most of the men wrap themselves in their *jerds* and fall on the beautiful red sand like white stones. The caravan goes limping on and the sleepers join us presently, I hope a little refreshed.

My limbs ache this morning and cannot be made comfortable. I try every possible position on my camel and every possible pace and stride in walking, but none of them are of any avail. My eyelids, too, seem weighted with lead.

At 6 we have the good fortune to come across a few patches of green grass and make camp, having marched for thirteen tormented hours. Eyes are bloodshot and bodies are protesting in every muscle and sinew. In a half-hour it is a dead camp.

Sunday, May 13th. We were up at 10 a.m. for breakfast. The men went to sleep again, but I could not. We started again at 5.15 p.m., and this evening things were worse than ever. The country had become more undulating and broken, and both camels and men found the going disastrously painful. Camels were continually being left behind as we wound about among the dunes and little hills of rock. They found bits of grass and fell to grazing. It was very difficult to see them against the red sand spotted with patches of dark stone.

The singing stopped early that night, the surest sign that the men were dead tired. Zerwali told me that Mohammed had come to him to say that we had better camp early and not try to march too long to-night. The going was so difficult and we changed directions so often to go around the elevated points and stone outcroppings that there was danger of our losing our way. But Zerwali, knowing how averse I am to any delay, had told the guide that I wanted to make a night's march of it.

At last the walking was so hard and camels were so continually left behind that I felt there was no use in going farther. If I had needed any more proof that the men were spent it would have been supplied by the fact that Hassan the Wajangi, ordinarily a sturdy walker, had taken to a camel early in the evening, and had not come off it.

We camped at 11.30 p.m. I wrapped myself in my *jerd* and told the men not to bother about making a shelter for me. I am sure I did not move from the first position I dropped into until 5. I got up with a stiff back and aching legs.

The morning air was serene and refreshing, and the sight of the men busy and eager to go ahead made me forget my physical discomforts. In spite of the new spirit of cheerfulness which the morning brought, however, things were not too encouraging for us. The country was nearly as bad for trekking as it could be. The men seemed to be losing confidence in Mohammed and Herri. The camels were in bad condition and our water was very low.

Monday, May 14th.—Start at 6 a.m., halt at 9 a.m.; start again at 5.30 p.m., halt at 10 p.m. Make 30 kilometres. Fair and clear. Cool north-east breeze at 7 a.m., which drops at midday. Calm evening and night. Highest temperature 32°. Soft sand covered with grass, both green and dry. Shortly after start in afternoon country changes into undulating ground with valleys full of green grass and dry *nisha*. This is one of the signs that we are approaching Erdi. At 8.30 p.m. hilly again for about 4 kilometres, and then we pass a big valley with grazing and trees.

As we started again in the morning I intended to go forward for four or five hours, but it speedily got too hot and we camped at 9. The four hours' rest had its good effect and no one went to sleep until we had had breakfast.

In the afternoon Mohammed and Herri went ahead again to mark the way, as there was even more difficult going before us.

The caravan got under way at 5.30 p.m. Our water had become scarce and bad and the camels looked weak and exhausted. We were anxious to reach Erdi as soon as possible. Shortly after the start Bukara and Arami—not the one who went away into the desert and disappeared, but another who had also killed his man—found the track of a big *warran* or lizard, and we followed it to its hole. A little sport was a pleasant relief. We dug into the hole, but the lizard was not at home. We traced its track to a pile of rocks and after twenty minutes of excavation caught the creature.

The Beduins and blacks use the fat of the *warran* as medicine for rheumatism, and say that if one carries its head about with him he is safe against black magic. Its skin hung in a house is reputed to keep snakes at a distance. The *warran* does not bite, but it has a tail like a whip with which it can do damage. Arami skinned the creature for me.

We followed the track made by our guides, but lost

it many times in the dark and wasted time finding it again. At last it began to wobble about and I realized that Mohammed was by no means certain of his direction. I ordered the men to camp and fire shots into the air. Shortly we were joined by Mohammed and Herri, who were relieved that I had decided to halt. The guide told me that he could not be sure of his road in this country in the darkness, but that he knew we were not far from the well.

For the first time since leaving Ouenat we had five solid hours of undisturbed sleep. Before going to bed I talked to Arami about Erdi and its wells.

"Mohammed is a good guide by daylight," he said, "but he is old and at night he does not see much. Besides, he has not been to this country for several years. We should have camped at the first well this evening, but we have missed it. But God knows best." I told him to say nothing of this to the men, lest they should grow more panicky and blame Mohammed.

I prepared my sleeping-bag and sat down to think. This was the most discouraging moment of the journey. The men had lost confidence and had suffered much from the heat, the camels were dead beat, largely from the same cause, the guide was not sure of the way, and the water was scarce and bad. Any one of these circumstances would have been enough to make one anxious, but all together made a devastating assault upon one's nerve.

As I reviewed the difficulties and dangers of the trip thus far, there flashed through my mind the thought that neither the mad Arami nor his brother Malkenni, who went to find him, had been seen again. I found myself wondering whether Fate intended to rob me of what I had been able to achieve. If Fate is malicious, this was an opportune moment to strike. If I had missed Arkenu and Ouenat it would not have been so hard. But now that I had made my modest achievement, I felt I should like to get back home with it. But—God knows best. I wondered if it would be a sleepless night. But the magic of the desert again came into play, and I was surprised to find my eyelids growing heavier. The sleep that came was sweet.

Tuesday, May 15th. We were up at 4. Still uncertain where we were, Herri, Mohammed and I went forward to make a reconnaissance, when suddenly the red hills of Erdi leapt into view. I satisfied myself by a good look through my binocular that we were not mistaken, and an hour later we started toward them. Before we started there was a discussion as to whether we should camp on the hills above the valley in which the well lies or go down into it. The descent would be hard on the camels, but nevertheless we decided to make it and camp on the floor of the *wadi*. In case of an attack by marauders we should at least have possession of the water supply.

We had been steadily climbing through rough defiles between cliffs of red rock and suddenly we came out on the top of a high cliff with the pleasant *wadi* of Erdi lying stretched out below us. It is a narrow valley, about 10 kilometres long by not more than 100 metres wide, surrounded by sheer cliffs of red rock. Trees and green grass, after the monotonous *serira* and the bare, unfriendly rocks that we have been traversing since Ouenat, suggest all the traditional connotations of the phrase "an oasis in the desert."

As we approached the well, Mohammed and Herri went forward again to reconnoitre the ground. The blacks are always cautious when they come to a well. They do not approach it directly, but send a man or two ahead to make sure that, if anyone is already there, he is not a stranger or at least not an enemy. So that the two guides will not only mark out the path we are to follow, but will discover if we need be on our guard when approaching a well.

We picked our way laboriously down the rough path into the valley and pitched camp at its northern end. The well lies at the extreme south, and there is no way of getting to it safely from above—without great risk to the camels—except where we came down.

A huge meal of rice and freshly baked bread, combined with our pleasant surroundings, made us all as cheerful as a wedding party. My anxious thoughts of the previous night seemed now like an absurd nightmare ; and yet there was plenty of truth in them. There is often in the desert only a hair's breadth between safety and comfort and disaster.

After three glasses of stimulating tea, over which we all lingered luxuriously, the men went off to the well to water the camels and to bring back water for the camp. When they returned, a shave, a bath and clean clothes restored all my self-respect and confidence, and life seemed very good again.

At 5 in the afternoon I climbed the wall of the valley with the theodolite and took observations. Zerwali went with Senussi Bu Hassan and Arami on a hunt for *waddan*, the mountain sheep, but they came back unsuccessful. I asked Arami if it were the fault of the sportsmen. " Wallahi (By God !), no, they shoot straight, but God was merciful to the *waddan*."

Night fell on a camp of rested camels and cheerful, singing men. I felt I should have none but pleasant dreams to-night.

CHAPTER XVIII

Entering the Sudan

I GOT up early in order to open the film box and refill the cameras while it was still cool. At 7, with Mohammed and Hamad, I set out to visit the well. The valley of Erdi is what is known as a *karkur*, a long narrow depression in the hills which winds like a snake. It runs to the southward for 7 or 8 kilometres, ending in a cul-de-sac where the well lies in a shadowy hollow under the rocks. The pool is semicircular in shape, half a dozen metres long and half as broad. The well is like those at Ouenat, although I suspect that, in addition to the rain-water, it may possibly be fed by a spring. The approach to it is a rocky and somewhat dangerous climb. The night before one of the camels bringing water slipped and hurt itself rather badly.

We climbed up to the *ain*, had a rest and tea, and rode home under a hot sun. The valley is beautiful, with its sheer walls of red rock, and the green grass and trees scattered about below them. Mohammed told me that it is the most difficult valley in this region to enter and therefore the easiest to defend.

In the late afternoon I climbed the valley wall to watch the fine sunset and the play of the light on the red sand and the rose-coloured rocks. The men shaved their heads, trimmed their beards and washed and mended their clothes, which were becoming very tattered.

The grazing here just saved our camels and it was wise to take this day for rest and recuperation. Mohammed and Herri told me that from now on it would not be practicable to travel at night. The country was too hilly to be safe to traverse in the darkness. All the Beduins gave Mohammed credit for the way he led the camels over the steep rocks to the valley yesterday.

In the evening the dog had a fit of barking and we suspected that some one was near. We quickly put out the fires, gathered the camels together, made ready the rifles and put sentries out around the camp —but it was a false alarm.

These precautions, like those we take when approaching a well, seem absurd when it is all over and nothing has happened. But in unknown country like this the caravan that did not take them would be very foolish. An attack by hostile tribesmen or outlaws is far from being an improbability.

Thursday, May 17th. We were up at 4 and under way at 5.30. The climb out of the valley was as difficult as the descent, and one camel fell, but fortunately without serious results. As we reached the edge of the *wadi* and looked back I realized the difference between the valleys in these hills and those at Arkenu and Ouenat. There the floor of a valley is on the same level as the plain outside, and one goes into it by a pass as through a gateway. In the region we were now in, the valleys are depressed below the general level of the country and one drops down into them by winding, rocky paths.

In an hour we were out of the *wadi* and turned to the south-east. We were in a mountainous country of black and red rocks and it was clear that we could not travel over such *terrain* in the dark. At 9.30 we descended into a large valley by a steep path, on which two camels stumbled and threw off their loads. One, carrying water, very nearly broke its neck, but the presence of mind of Abdullahi, who drew a knife and cut the girths, saved the situation. The wooden stopper of one of the *fantasses* came out and the water was three-quarters spilled. Fortunately the next well was only three days ahead, and we had an ample supply for even a longer trek. Such an occurrence as this would have been a disaster if we had been in a *daffa*, as a long waterless trek between wells is called.

On this morning a serious situation arose suddenly which might have had fatal results had it not been for two pieces of luck. Ahmed, the cook who came with me from Egypt, was riding a camel without a bridle. He had asked Hamid, the camelman of Bu Helega, to provide a bridle, but the other, being wise in the ways of camels, knew better than to do so. It is important that the camels shall be able to graze at will. They are more in need of food than of guidance.

Ahmed's camel, spying a fine tuft of grass, went directly to it. On the way he passed under a tree set thickly with thorns. The rider could not escape the sharp projections and his face was badly torn. Annoyed by the pain, Ahmed proceeded to curse the camel and the owner of the camels. Hamid instantly retaliated by cursing him and telling him not to curse the noble owner of the animals. I happened to be near and in my heart I praised the camel-man for his loyalty to Bu Helega, his master.

Ahmed came quickly off the camel, his face streaked with blood, and went hotly at Hamid. Senussi Bu Hassan, the other Hamid and Sad, the Aujila, rushed to take the side of their brother Beduin. Abdullahi ranged himself beside Ahmed, two Egyptians shoulder to shoulder.

I had had experience of such quarrels before and I quickly looked to see where the rifles were. It was with deep relief that I saw them safely fastened on the camels' backs. The men had only sticks to fight with, but, even so, prompt action was necessary before the trouble became more acute.

I galloped my horse among the men and pushed him between the two groups of combatants, brusquely ordering Ahmed and Abdullahi to stand back. It was a most difficult moment, with one side my own men and the other the men of my caravan.

Senussi Bu Hassan and Hamid looked back, and for the flicker of a second I saw their eyes rest on the slung rifles. One word of encouragement from me to the other party would have meant disaster, for the Beduins outnumbered us. On the other hand, it was not the time even if my own men were in the wrong, to humiliate them before the Beduins.

"What do you mean by behaving like children?" I demanded impartially of the men on both sides. "Men like you ought to be ashamed."

Hamid started to speak.

"He insulted me."

Ahmed interrupted him.

"He attacked me as I came off my camel."

"I don't care who insulted whom or who attacked whom," I declared sharply. "You are all my men and it is a shame to have you behave like a batch of children."

Just then Zerwali came up. I turned to Abdullahi and then to Senussi Bu Hassan.

"And you, older men, instead of bringing peace, actually take part in this disgraceful quarrel," I said severely. "Perhaps I have made a mistake. I should have chosen men for my caravan and not boys."

By this time both parties had begun to cool down and to lose their tense look of men about to spring to the attack. Zerwali, who probably expected me to take the side of my compatriots, Abdullahi and Ahmed, was disarmed, and did the unexpected thing.

"Put Hamid on the ground," he ordered the slave Faraj. "I will beat him with my whip."

In a flash the stalwart Faraj laid Hamid unceremoniously on the ground and pinned him there with his knee. Before I could interfere Zerwali's whip descended twice. But by that time I had dismounted and caught Zerwali's arm.

"This is no matter for punishment," I asserted. "We don't know who is to blame. I shall inquire into the matter and punish with my own hands the man who is proved guilty."

Turning to the men, I commanded, "Follow the camels."

To Mohammed and Herri, who had kept tactfully out of the affair, I gave the order, "Lead the way," pointing with my stick.

All moved off, and I walked alone, trying to preserve for their benefit my expression of stern disapproval. Zerwali gradually edged nearer to me and spoke deprecatingly.

"The Bey is not angry over what has happened?" he questioned. "God knows when I got up this morning there was something weighing heavy on my heart. I felt sure that something unpleasant was going to happen. My feeling was reflected in your salutation to me."

I realized that I also had had an uncanny feeling. There was no reason for it, for everything was going smoothly and well. But still something had oppressed me.

In a short while both parties felt like children who had been naughty. I observed furtive glances stealing toward me from both sides to see if my anger was abated. But I kept my stern countenance until luncheon.

Those who have travelled in the desert, and know the Beduins, will realize what a serious possibility this incident contained. A single harsh word interpreted as an insult means shooting if guns are close at hand. If both men had had their rifles and if I had been some hundred yards away, as was generally the case, there would almost certainly have been bloodshed. The Beduins would probably have killed Ahmed and Abdullahi out of hand. Then, what could I have done, as an Egyptian, but avenge the killing of my countrymen at whatever cost to myself?

How lucky it was that the rifles were lashed to the camels and that I was close at hand!

"We are getting near the end of our journey,"

said Zerwali. "The men are always quarrelsome then."

By the time this dangerous incident was over, the sun was very hot, and we camped in the valley in the shade of some fine trees. The camels had good grazing while we ate and rested. Before we started in the afternoon Mohammed, Senussi Bu Hassan, Bukara and Hamid the camelman came to ask me to forgive Hamid for having let his anger get the better of him with Ahmed. I pardoned him readily and he went to Ahmed and kissed his head. Ahmed returned the compliment and then the quarrel was ended in the best Beduin tradition.

We made our way down the big valley for three hours and camped near its mouth at 7.15. Shortly before halting we saw ahead of us the distant hills of Agah where the next well lay. The ground before us was flat *serira* and it was a relief to see it. On this morning when we were going down into the valley it looked as if all our baggage would be in bits if there were more of these precipices. In places the descent was so rough that for safety we had to unload the camels. The men had to carry the baggage down the steep rocks—often a drop of 3 feet from boulder to boulder.

The new moon had risen as we camped. The next day was Bairam, the feast marking the end of Ramadan, and Zerwali came to say that the men would like to feast according to our Moslem custom. I willingly agreed, since the Agah hills were in sight before us and the water supply was ample. Besides, the excellent grazing in this valley would do the camels good.

We all rose early the next day (Friday, May 18th)

and put on clean clothes for the feast day. We exchanged good wishes and followed them with the prayers appointed for Bairam. There was a look on every face as of men who are thinking of those left behind at home.

I produced a few *mejidies* and Egyptian notes and distributed them. The coins went to Mohammed, Herri, Hassan and Arami, who were to leave us before we reached territory where Egyptian notes are current. The rest got the notes, which they would be able to use at El Fasher. To Zerwali I gave twenty rounds of revolver ammunition and a bottle of scent. Another bottle of scent was divided among the men, Bukara received one of my pipes and tobacco to go with it and he declared that he did not know what to do to return all the kindness I had shown him.

" I have only my camel and the clothes on my back," he said. " He has given me the value of my camel in tobacco."

It was a cheerful camp at breakfast ; the men were pleased with their gifts and I enjoyed their satisfaction. After breakfast we all lay down for a siesta, but got up again promptly, our bodies itching furiously from the assaults of white ants.

At 5.45 p.m. we made our start and half an hour later emerged from the valley on to the *serira*. In front of us lay a chain of hills running east and west, in the middle of which was Jebel Islingah, and to the right of it Jebel Agah, to which we were going. Herri said that there was a well also in Jebel Islingah, but that it was difficult to get at. The valley where we had camped was marked by trees on the east side of the entrance to it.

It was a hot day and we moved slowly for six hours, when we reached a belt of sand-dunes which stopped our progress for the night.

Saturday, May 19th. We started at 5.15 a.m. and made our final halt at 8 p.m. There was a hot north-east wind from the hills which dropped in the evening. We travelled over soft sand, very undulating, covered with dry grass. As we approached the hills the country became flatter with patches of small black stone.

The sun got hot quickly in the morning, and a hot wind was blowing, so we camped at 9.30 in the shade of a *tumtum* tree. Its protection was welcome and its bunches of red berries made an attractive pattern over our heads.

We started again at 3.30 in spite of the heat, with the hope of reaching the hills of Agah before dark. The camels had to be beaten in order to get them away from the shade of the tree and into the hot sun. By 7.30 we were at the foot of the hills, with the slim moon just coming up. Mohammed suddenly raised the alarm. He had found the fresh tracks of two men leading toward Merdi. A stranger in the desert is an occasion for vigilance until he proves to be not unfriendly. Rifles were quickly unslung, the oil rags were stripped from their breeches, and cartridges shoved in. The men collected the camels which were scattered out grazing and Mohammed, Herri and Senussi Bu Hassan went forward to the valley to reconnoitre. After a careful search they came back to report that there were no tracks leading into the valley, but that there were fresh tracks leading out of it. We made camp at the entrance, keeping clear of trees and vegetation in case anyone approached in the night. We ate dinner rapidly and extinguished our camp-fire. The camels and *girbas* were put in the centre of the camp, and the luggage arranged around its edge. Four sentries were posted for the night, and we went to bed. But sleep was difficult because of the oppressive heat and the suspense.

Early on the Sunday morning we got up and approached the valley cautiously. We came across fresh tracks of sheep and men and were convinced that some one had a camp in the valley. Mohammed and Herri went ahead, as the inhabitants of this district were Goran and no one else spoke their language. They soon returned with three Gorans. I met them and we solemnly went through the ceremony of giving and receiving the *aman*. We advanced toward each other and lay whatever weapons we might be carrying, sword or rifle, on the ground. I addressed them in the time-honoured phrases: " I swear by God that we are peaceful men, that we wish you no harm, and that we have no intention of robbing you." One of them did the same in his turn and we indulged in brief questions and answers on each side. Who are you? Whence do you come? Whither are you going? On what business? Then we shook hands formally, each took up his weapons, and both sides retired.

We tried to buy sheep from them, but they refused to sell. In a short time they went away and returned with three sheep which they offered as *diafa*, refusing to accept any money for them. I gave them *etkias* of blue cloth as a return courtesy, with which they were delighted. The camels were sent off to the well to drink and to bring back water for the camp, while the men busied themselves with preparations for the great feast of meat. In the afternoon I took photographs and in the evening made observations. The electric torch which I used in reading the theodolite first frightened the Goran boys and then delighted them.

The valley of Agah is very picturesque, a long narrow defile between high cliffs, with more vegetation and trees than we had seen thus far. Half-way down its length it divides, one branch leading south-westward to the well and the other southward toward the open desert. The well is similar to that at Erdi, but its water is badly fouled by sheep and camels. The valley is full of birds, whose pleasant songs make one think one is at the aviary in the Zoo.

We were up while it was dark and the stars were still shining in the clear sky. The Goran came to say good-bye. Arami and Hassan had declined to go farther south and left us to return to Ouenat, with Arami's camel. We wound our way down the eastern fork of the valley, its steep sides protecting us from the sun. On the way we sighted three gazelle and some of the men gave chase, but the nimble animals climbed the hills and escaped. Hamid the Zwayi fired at one and missed, to the scornful delight of the others. Hamid, however, refused to admit complete failure.

"By God," he stoutly maintained, "I hit it. I saw the blood spurt."

It did not matter so much, however, as we still had meat left from the *diafa* of the Goran.

It quickly got too hot for comfort and the camels,

fresh from drinking, refused to go on. We camped in the shade of a tree, but soon discovered that better protection from the sun was to be had in crevices in the rocks. The camels were allowed to graze and the men settled down to prepare the midday meal. Two sheep were slaughtered and their flesh, impaled on sticks, was slowly revolved before the fire to roast in the Beduin fashion. It was delicious. While the meat was being prepared, Sad cut his hand. I saw the blood and asked where it came from.

"From Hamid's gazelle!" said Bukara, and once more shouts of laughter went up over the unsuccessful hunter.

After lunch I wound my watches, recorded the readings of the aneroid and the maximum and minimum thermometers and wrote up my diaries, when Hamid the camelman came running to say that a herd of ostriches was near by. We all grasped our rifles and stood ready. Soon the ostriches appeared, thirty or forty in number. The Beduins were impatient and opened fire while the distance was too great. The ostriches dashed off into another valley with the men in hot pursuit. Many shots were fired, but Zerwali soon came back to say that nothing had been killed.

In a little while Hamid appeared carrying a small ostrich and followed by Senussi Bu Hassan. Both men claimed to have shot the creature, and since there were two bullet wounds in it, either of which might have been fatal, they appealed to me for judgment. I asked the opinion of the men who saw the shooting and all agreed that Hamid's shot felled the bird. I decided in his favour.

Later Hamid the camelman, small and sharp of features and afraid of no animals, not even of snakes, came upon an ostrich in a closed part of the valley, and after attacking it unsuccessfully with stones, rushed at it and caught it round the neck. He wrestled with it manfully, but it landed a kick on his side from one of its powerful legs and ran away. I was watching the contest through my binoculars and nearly split my sides with laughter. The ostrich mounted a ridge, looked back scornfully at Hamid who stood cursing it, arranged its feathers and trotted off with the gait of a gay dowager, leaving him with his hand pressed to his maltreated side.

"Has the ostrich hurt you?" I asked solicitously when he returned.

"Oh no," he replied, quickly taking his hand from his side.

"Why didn't you bring it back, then?" I asked again.

"I had to let it go," he explained with great plausibility. "She was only a female."

One of my great regrets on this trek was that I was unable to follow game as I would have liked to. The night marches between Ouenat and Erdi left me too exhausted in the morning to do anything but record the readings of my scientific instruments and try to snatch two or three hours of sleep before it was too hot. Then our food supply began to get less and less. I could not stay at Agah where there was plenty of gazelle, ostriches and wild sheep. Besides, the scarcity of water made me lose no time there, where the well had been so fouled by animals.

An old Egyptian army Martini and an Italian

cavalry carbine which I was given at Kufra, handy as they would have been for self-defence, were of little use for long-range work on game, especially gazelle. Hunting, therefore, was a diversion which I had to deny myself.

It was very hot and we could not start until 5 p.m. We followed the lovely valley for an hour and then began to climb the hills. As we got to the top we had a fine view of its beauties, all the various shades of green of the trees and shrubs making picturesque patterns with the rosy sand and the redder rocks of the hills guarding the valley. The soft notes of innumerable doves floated up on the cool evening breeze. A gorgeous red and gold sunset completed an ensemble not easy to forget. I stopped my horse and spent a pleasant half-hour lying on a patch of soft sand drinking in the delights of this little bit of paradise. It soon grew dark. The crescent moon showed herself and far away I heard the Beduins of my caravan singing. Reluctantly I rose and took the track again.

We were soon in different country, broken and very undulating, with distant jagged hills surrounding us. The camels were suffering from the foul water of Agah and so were the men. We camped early, both on this account and because it is dangerous country to travel by the weak moonlight.

We dropped into a soft sand valley about 200 metres from our route and camped.

We got up with the stars still in the sky on the Tuesday, May 23rd, and made our start with a gorgeous sunrise on our left hand. We moved slowly because of the thick shrubs and scattered stones and also because Mohammed and Herri had not been in this country for ten years and were picking their way cautiously.

" Mohammed is riding, I suppose," I said to Hamid the camelman, as I walked in my favourite place behind the caravan, " or we would not be moving so slowly."

" The grey-haired man is walking, O Bey," said the shrewd fellow quickly. " His track is on the ground."

Once more I was impressed with the keen observation of the Beduins, especially the camelmen. Hamid had already learned the characteristic footprints that each man of the caravan leaves. Of course he knew the track of each camel also.

On Wednesday we were up much earlier than usual in our anxiety to reach the well of Enebah. The water of Agah was the worst we had yet tasted and it was having its effect on both men and camels. A three-hours' trek brought us to the edge of the valley in which the well lay. We dropped down into it and discovered from tracks of sheep, donkeys and men that the place was inhabited. Mohammed went forward to meet the men who live there, gave and received the *aman*, and soon we were camped by the well. The water was excellent; animals and men both enjoyed the change.

There was quite a large Bidiyat camp here, with hundreds of sheep and a few horses for the *sheikhs*. Presently the whole population, led by the *sheikhs*, came to greet us. I shook hands with them and distributed scent, putting a little on the hand of each one.

In the afternoon they brought sheep as *diafa*, and

the women (who have a keen business sense) produced *samn*—butter—and leather to sell to us. We gave them *mejidies* and cloth in exchange. In the evening I took observations. The Bidiyats were frightened at the theodolite and the electric torch and their suspicions were aroused.

One of the *sheikhs* entered my tent and caught me opening the instrument case. I shut the case quickly and instantly realized my mistake. I could see in his dark cruel face, with yellow eyes like those of a fox set close together, that he believed I had gold in the box. As he left my tent I ostentatiously ordered Senussi Bu Hassan and Hamid to stand as sentries in the camp. I pointed to them and told the *sheikh* not to allow the women and children to approach the camp at night lest my men might make a mistake and shoot at them. It was just a hint that we were wide awake and that there was no hope of catching us off our guard. I could see that the hint went home.

CHAPTER XIX

To Furawia on Short Rations

THE valley of Enebah was covered with soft sand, dotted with shrubs both green and dry, and with trees.

I had a good night's rest and was awakened by the hubbub of the Bidiyat women bargaining with the men of my caravan for empty tins. They offered a kind of dry shrub that they called tobacco and milk in return. Five more sheep were brought as *diafa,* and more presents were distributed.

Encouraged by a cool south-east wind, we started at 3.15 p.m., but the wind soon dropped and we made slow progress in the heat. The evening was cooler, however, and we made up a little for lost time. The night was cold.

On *Friday, May 25th,* we were up at 4 and started an hour and a quarter later. The country was very undulating and broken and Herri was not sure of the way. We moved slowly because of the difficulty of the going and the uncertainty of the guide. Shortly after 9 we dropped into a valley and camped an hour later.

Senussi Bu Hassan, who was walking beside me, gave expression to his opinion of the guide and his Beduin pride.

"Those Goran wobble about like camels," he said.

"They do not walk like Beduins, who fly straight to their goal like birds."

When we took the road again in the afternoon the sun was still very hot. The camels moved slowly and the men's singing sounded like broken bagpipes. It was perhaps as well that we were compelled to move slowly, for Herri was more uncertain of the way than ever. Some of the time we followed the track left by a flock of sheep going presumably toward Bao, but at intervals it was lost in the tracts of broken stones.

A little after 5 we dropped into a big valley whose name we discovered later to be Koni-Mina, running east and west and filled with fine trees. Just before reaching it we met a Goran with a few sheep. He came up to me, dropped his sword and spears on the ground, and took off his sandals. We shook hands with many ejaculations of "*Keif-halak, tayibeen.*" "How are you? Very well." It was all the Arabic he knew. Mohammed and Herri then talked with him and learnt that there was a Goran camp in the valley before us. A cattle merchant had also just arrived from Fada in Wadai with sheep and cows on his way to El Fasher. Mohammed and Herri left us and approached the few straw-thatched huts that constituted the Goran camp. We went across the valley and camped on its farther rim.

Soon a man came running to ask us to return to the camp and start again the next day. I appreciated the hospitable suggestion, but felt that we could not afford to retrace our steps even for 2 or 3 kilometres. I thanked him for the invitation and told him that we were in a great hurry. We should camp near-by to wait for our two guides. An hour later Mohammed appeared, full of news from Fada and El Fasher, obtained from the merchant.

We were busy that evening overhauling our baggage and repairing damages. All the ropes were getting worn and the Beduin woollen bags too. We had been losing much time on the way with reloading and shifting things about. But it was a consolation to know that in a fortnight we should be in El Fasher.

We had the most beautiful sunrise on May 26th that I have seen. The brilliant white light on the red and black stones near-by and the distant hills made everything wonderfully clear and distinct. Soon it changed to a warm red glow and then the golden rays of the sun broke through the thin clouds and flooded everything. The long shadows cast by rocks and shrubs on the ground looked like black stencilling on the yellow sand. The shadows of the slowly moving caravan made a fantastic pattern.

It soon proved to be an oppressively close morning.

Herri joined us later in the forenoon with a slaughtered sheep slung on each side of his camel—the *diafa* from the Goran camp.

We followed sheep and camel tracks and marched from one valley into another, until we camped in one of the largest of them which had many shady trees.

It is always a problem whether to stop under the shade of a tree and suffer the attacks of white ants and all sorts of sinister-looking insects or pitch tent in the broiling sun. In future, I shall be inclined to take my chance in the open, as the insects are always with you, while the sun's heat is over by 5 or 6 in the afternoon. The valley in which we camped is called Kap-Terku.

We started again at 4, with a south-east breeze that made walking not so tedious. There were also a few clouds which tempered the heat of the sun. The camels walked better. In the late afternoon we passed a Goran family, a man, wife and naked child, and later we found a well. It was 7 metres deep and had good water, though the roots of a near-by tree had rotted in it, giving it an unpleasant odour.

We camped at 8, fortunately in a clear space free from shrubs and stones. At 1 in the morning a hyena visited the camp, and had it not been for the vigilance of Hamid the camelman, it might have got Baraka, who was tied at night and therefore unable to defend himself. Hamid fired at it impulsively and with my glasses I saw a dark object running far away in the brilliant moonlight.

Sunday, May 27th.—Start at 5.15 a.m., halt at 9.15 a.m.; start again at 3.45 p.m., halt at 7.45 p.m. Make 30 kilometres. Highest temperature 38°, lowest 7°. Fine, clear and calm in the morning. At midday strong hot south-east wind, which drops in afternoon. Few white clouds. Warm and calm in the evening. Very cloudy, with few drops of rain at 10 p.m. Valleys of soft sand as before, with low sandstone hills 20 to 80 metres high. Patches of the same stone crop out through the sand.

Herri proved himself a bad guide. He predicted that we would reach Bao this morning, but when night came we were not yet there. He knew the places when he saw them, but his sense of direction was faulty. Our water had given out, except for one last *girba*, and it was very hot.

We marched until 7.45, when we reached rocky ground, dangerous for the camels even in the clear moonlight. We were on the edge of a large valley which Herri declared to be that of Bao, but we could not believe him. Experience had taught me not to permit the last of the water supply to be used until we had not only seen the well, but approached it to make sure that there was drinkable water there. I insisted that the last *girba* should not be touched that night. We went to bed without dinner, since we could not cook without water.

There was, however, the consolation of a beautiful night. I lay in bed watching the play of the moonlight on the clouds. A few drops of rain announced the approach of the rainy season. We were astir early. Empty stomachs do not encourage long sleep. We drove the camels as we had not driven them before. How tired they looked and how weak! When camels and men are hungry and thirsty, all the other defects in the caravan come out. There was no singing that morning, merely silent, relentless urging forward of the camels and ourselves.

The descent into the valley was steep and dangerous. Three camels threw off their loads, which had to be carried by the men down to the level ground and loaded again. At last we saw a few sheep and a straw hut or two. We stopped and I let the men drink the water from the last *girba* for which they had asked many times that morning.

Herri and Mohammed went ahead and made their way to the huts. The caravan meanwhile moved directly down the valley toward the well. Soon some blacks of the Goran and Bidiyat tribes came to meet us. We fired our rifles as usual, as if in salutation, but in reality to impress the natives with our preparedness.

I noticed that by a curious coincidence those who met us, men and women, were all old. There was not a single young person amongst them, especially no young woman. However, it did not strike me as extraordinary, but a little later I was surprised to see batches of slim and beautiful girls, brown or black, half-naked in their tattered clothes, but holding themselves gracefully erect. As they came along in groups of three and four, I turned to Bukara and asked, "From where are these girls?" Bukara looked at them with great admiration and replied, "Allah be great! These girls are of the village. They thought we were going to rob the village and take away the young girls as slaves, so they sent them out to hide as soon as they sighted our caravan. Now that the men know that we are a peaceful caravan, they have sent word to the girls to come back."

As the girls passed my horse they shyly dropped on their knees in salutation, as is the custom there when addressing a person of higher rank. In this part of the world, when one is addressed by some more exalted person the etiquette is not to stand up but to sit down in token of reverence. One after another these girls dropped to their knees and in return I gave them the usual Arab blessing, "May God's Peace be on you and His Mercy and Blessings." As they rose again the girls bashfully turned to look at my company of admiring Beduins.

We camped at the end of the valley near the well. An hour later the *sheikh* of the camp came to greet us. We discussed the roads to El Fasher and the direction to be followed. Here Herri looked thoughtful and sad. This was close to his own country, for we were across the frontier of French Wadai now. He had thrown away his rights and run away from the French, leaving all his property and relatives, and gone to the solitary oasis of Ouenat to live in self-inflicted exile.

We were getting into a different kind of country. There were many more varieties of birds, including crows, owls, parrots, doves, and others whose names I do not know.

In the night a lioness had killed two donkeys, and some of the natives captured one of its young and sent its skin to Fada to be sold. There are several score of blacks of the Goran and Bidiyat tribes at Bao. The women are graceful creatures, clothed with the utmost simplicity. Their dress is either a length of cloth wound skilfully around the body, with a narrow strip of cloth for a belt, in which is carried a small knife, or a sheepskin wrapped round the lower part of the body. Their hair is arranged in small plaits. They wear ornaments of silver and ivory, heavy rings in the hair, and bead and amber necklaces. Young girls wear only an apron of cloth or leather. The men have splendid physique, go naked, except for a loin cloth, and carry two or three spears, a sword and throwing knife. Only *sheikhs* wear white robes and large turbans.

We gave the women and children macaroni, but they refused to eat it. Instead, they threaded the pieces on strings and made necklaces which they wore proudly. The business instinct of the Beduins at once displayed itself. They made necklaces from our little store of macaroni and exchanged them for butter and leather.

Herri and Mohammed were to leave us here. They

did not care to venture farther south. I had some difficulty in finding a guide to take us to Furawia, but at last succeeded. A sheep was brought to us as *diafa*, and we dined early on the Tuesday, intending to make a prompt start in the morning.

The guide did not present himself, and I began to feel that the Bidiyat were suspicious of my caravan. At 11 p.m. he appeared, however, and I immediately woke the men and set them to loading the camels before he had any chance of changing his mind.

Wednesday, May 30th.—Start at 1 a.m., halt at 8.30 a.m.; start again at 4.15 p.m., halt at 7.15 p.m. Make 40 kilometres. Highest temperature 36°. Fine and clear. Strong and dusty south-east wind. The wind changes to north-east in the afternoon and drops in the evening. Country same as before, except flatter, and with no large valleys and no big trees. At 8.15 a.m. cross a small *wadi* running east and west.

When we started at 1 o'clock there was a beautiful moon, which made it as clear as in daylight.

Herri and Mohammed started with us, as they wished to give the impression to the men of Bao that they were going with us to El Fasher. Otherwise they feared that they might be waylaid. In an hour we had climbed out of the valley. We halted to say good-bye to the two guides, who were going to travel only by night on their way back to Ouenat, to avoid detection.

As I stood a little apart from the caravan in the moment of farewell to them, I realized that the difficulties through which we had come had drawn us close together. Mohammed was tall, erect, with a piercing eye and an interesting illustration of the self-assurance that life in the desert gives and the fatalistic resignation with which one accepts whatever comes. Herri was a gentle-mannered, unassuming old man with a benign smile and charming manners. There was unquestioned dignity in his movements in spite of an injured left foot which he had to drag when he walked. He was a prince by nature.

This was not merely a parting of companions of the trek, but a symbol of the old, having run the race, pointing the onward road to the young. We all forgot that I was the head of a caravan and they my guides. Herri put his hands on my shoulders and spoke with feeling in his voice.

"May God bless you and give you strength," he said. "There is your road." He pointed to an opening in the distant hills. I murmured a few words in a voice that I could scarcely trust not to tremble and turned away to my caravan. The two dignified but somehow pathetic figures—both exiles from their own land—faded away in the moonlight.

We halted at dawn for our morning prayers and at 8.30 to camp for the day. There were tracks of lions about. We started again early in the afternoon, but the men were tired, having had little sleep the previous night, and we marched only three hours. The sheep which had been given us escaped, and in the moonlight Hamid and Sad went after it, bleating like sheep themselves to attract it, but with no success.

Thursday, May 31st.—Start at 3.45 a.m., halt at 8.45 a.m.; start again at 3.30 p.m., halt at 7.30 p.m. Make 36 kilometres. Highest temperature 37°, lowest 5°. Fine, clear and calm. South-east wind in the afternoon, which changed to north-east and dropped toward evening. Calm evening and night, with full moon and few white clouds.

An uneventful day.

Shortly after an early start on Friday, June 1st, the guide got sleepy and "lost his head." We were soon travelling due west instead of south-east. I did not interfere until we stopped for morning prayers at 5, but then I asked him quietly if he had intended to march to the westward. He was surprised, but admitted frankly his error. Fortunately, we had not been going wrong for long.

At 6.30 we passed a hill called *Tamaira*, on which stood a dry tree marking the boundary between Wadai and the Sudan. From the boundary post we dropped into Wadi Hawar, a large valley full of big trees, which is said to extend westwards to Wadai and eastwards towards the Sudan. In Wadai it is called Wadi Hawash.

The soil in the *wadi* is very fertile and the men from Wadai and Darfur come to it in the autumn for grazing. We camped here for the midday halt and found tracks of giraffe. In the afternoon we walked through high dry grass as though in a great field of ripe corn.

The men of the caravan were getting worn out, all the more as clothing was tattered, shoes at the last gasp, and to add to our inflictions we had much trouble with *haskanit*, a small, very hard, hooked thorn which grows on a low bush and attaches itself to whosoever brushes against it, when it is extremely difficult to extract.

I heard Bukara describing to Hamid a giraffe and an elephant. The giraffe, he said, has the head of a camel, the hoofs of a cow, and the hindquarters of a horse. His word picture of the elephant was grotesque and much exaggerated, to impress the man from the North.

We made a very early start on Saturday, June 2nd, to make sure of reaching Furawia that day. At 5 a.m. we passed on our right the landmark of Hagar Kamra-ra, 10 kilometres away, and an hour later passed another, Hagar Urdru, a hill about 80 metres high and 200 metres long. *Hagar* is the Sudanese word for *gara,* or small hill. Then we started dropping into the valley of Furawia. It was the largest valley and the most inhabited that we had come across. Its people are Zaghawa and a few Bidiyat.

We camped at 9 near a Bidiyat camp and soon heard the distressing news that no food was to be obtained at Furawia. This was contrary to my expectation. I made haste to find a messenger to take a letter to the Governor of Darfur at El Fasher, asking him to send me provisions and cloth to clothe my men, who were in rags. After much hesitation, caused apparently by fear of my men, the Zaghawa *sheikh* of a camp near-by came, driven by curiosity, to visit us. He was under the Sudanese Government and I pounced on him and offered him £3 to take a letter from me to Saville Pasha, Governor of Darfur. It was liberal pay, and in addition I threatened him with much unpleasantness should he hesitate or refuse. I told him he must start at dawn the next day. After murmuring something about having no animal to carry him, he went away and soon returned to say that he would take my letter to El Fasher. He intended to go on horseback. This was good news, for we had had no sugar for three weeks and had been obliged to sweeten our tea as best we could with pounded-up dates. Flour and rice had also given out and a scanty diet of macaroni prepared with bad water is very monotonous.

I moved the camp near to one of the wells in the valley and tried to buy a sheep to cheer up my men. But it was getting dark and none of the inhabitants came near our camp. We watered the camels and settled down for the night, not very well satisfied with life.

I was suddenly surprised to hear my men singing and apparently as cheerful as though they had had a good meal. I called Zerwali and Bukara over and asked them what was the singing about when there was no sugar and little food and things were generally disagreeable.

"We can breathe now," answered Zerwali. "We have entered the Sudan and feel ourselves at last in safety."

"Were you so fearful, then, of this journey we have made?" I asked.

"At Kufra all our relations said that we were 'walking to our fate,' when we took this road," explained Bukara. "'Your fates are written,' they said to us, 'but may God protect you.' We wondered if, perhaps, they might not be right."

"You heard at Kufra," said Zerwali, "how some people offered you encouragement to take this route, while many advised against it. Those who favoured it were malicious men who simply hoped that they would never see you again."

It was then also that Zerwali—who now that we were nearing the end of the trip felt himself more free to talk—told me that the houses of Sadaida and

Jehilat of the Zwaya tribe at Hawari and Kufra had strongly resented my second visit and held a meeting to discuss the best means of either destroying the caravan or preventing me from coming back.

Then I realized what pluck it had taken for these men to come with me by the strange and unknown way without a murmur of protest. I was proud of them.

At 2 a.m. Hamid who was acting as sentry, woke me to say that the messenger had arrived and was ready to take my letter to El Fasher. Two letters were all written and ready under my pillow, one to Saville Pasha and the other to the Officer in Command at Kuttum, the outpost, on the way to El Fasher, asking him to make sure that my letter to El Fasher reached its destination. I was glad the messenger had come so early. The sooner we got new supplies the happier we should all be. I promised him a few extra dollars if he would deliver the letter to El Fasher in four days. I bade him a very warm God-speed and watched him ride off in the moonlight on a quite strong if ragged-looking horse.

CHAPTER XX

Journey's End

SLEEP came slowly to me that first night at Furawia. I was excited as I had not been since saying good-bye to Lieutenant Bather at Sollum and beginning the journey. Now I was in touch again with the outside world and the journey was really over, even though it would still be a month or more before I should exchange my caravan for other methods of travel. The "lost" oases of Arkenu and Ouenat were no longer lost, and, if my observations proved to be as accurate as I hoped they were, a good map could now be made of this strip of the Libyan Desert from Jalo to Furawia.

We spent three full days at Furawia getting used to the damp climate we had come into and trying to get enough to eat to keep us from feeling miserable. Dark clouds hovered over our heads much of the time and every day it rained. My men gorged themselves with mutton, but the lack of sugar for the tea and other provisions rather took the edge off their enjoyment of these feasts.

On June 6th we started south in the afternoon and climbed slowly out of the valley. We passed many flocks of sheep and cattle going home, followed by slim girls and boys clad in nothing but a loin-cloth or strings of beads.

It was quite different from the desert we had come through. We were following a beaten track and passing frequently small villages of straw huts, women carrying *hatab*, and other signs of habitation.

Near one of the villages I told the caravan to go ahead and pointed out to them where we would camp. I followed with my horse. There were a few points of interest geographically and I had to take some observations. As I was nearing the camp I heard voices curiously upraised, a mixture between men wailing and singing. My first thought was that some of the men of the caravan had got into trouble with the natives. I spurred on my horse and as I was approaching the camp my mind was relieved, for I heard the "tom-tom" of the drum and women's voices singing. It was just after sunset and in the dusk I could not distinguish clearly the crowd that was moving towards me, but soon one of my men came rushing up to tell me they had had the most cordial reception from the men and women of the village, who insisted on coming out to receive "the Sheikh of the Caravan." He had hardly broken this news to me when a bevy of young girls, some singing, others dancing, surrounded my horse, who responded as befitted a Beduin horse, and started prancing. The women raised "lu-lias," and I was urged by my Beduins to "empty gunpowder." The crowd made way for my horse and I walked him a short distance off, turned back, came rushing back and pulled him up dead. By that time I had got out my rifle and as my horse stopped dead I fired my shot, in Beduin fashion, at the feet of the first row of beautiful damsels. They were half frightened and half delighted. Then six of them surrounded the horse, circling round me, and gave me the *shabaal*, that is to say, with a sudden twist of the head they whirled their tresses towards me as a woman of Southern Europe might throw a rose. In response, I put my finger on each girl's forehead and holding my rifle high in the air twirled it round her head, crying, "Abshiri bil kheir!" (Rejoice in the bounty of God.) We then formed ourselves into a procession and proceeded to the camp. The moment they saw me coming surrounded by all these girls the Beduins fired in the air in honour of the occasion. The Beduin is very chivalrous and such is his idea of honouring the ladies. Afterwards I distributed scent to all the girls, who went away very happy, and it was a most cheerful evening in the camp.

The next day we reached Um Burn, 38 kilometres from Furawia. We camped near the well, and the next morning I was awakened early by sounds of cattle and sheep coming to water. An hour later a busy market was being held alongside our camp. We had unwittingly pitched our tents close by the big tree that marked the centre of the market-place. Only women took part in the market, bringing butter, leather, mats, maize, cotton and salt, which they bartered with each other without the use of money. Meanwhile, the men lay about at their ease and did nothing. As I watched such a scene as this and others not unlike in the villages of the Sudan, I found myself wondering whether the black women were not after all better off as slaves in a Beduin household. Here they do all the work that is done, caring for cattle and sheep, doing the housework, and preparing meals and making the favourite beverage *merissa* for their men, carrying on the business of the market—everything. As slaves they would have only certain circumscribed duties and some opportunity for leisure. As I turned this over in my mind, however, I seemed to catch something in the sound of their talk and their laughter that slaves do not have. Perhaps there is something in the feeling of liberty after all, even when it is accompanied by drudgery.

We stopped at Um Burn for two days. Abdel Rahman Jeddu, *wakil* of Mohammedin, the head of the Zaghawa tribe, visited me and brought sheep and chicken as *diafa*. On the second day we were given an official welcome, the *wakil* coming with a retinue of retainers on horseback beating drums. Mohammedin's family, in the absence of the master of the household, sent a lunch of *asida*, vegetables, *merissa* and pastry.

The next stage of our journey was a five-days' trek to Kuttum, 129 kilometres to the southward. The weather was generally good, though hot, with an occasional shower. We travelled as usual in the early morning and late afternoon. There was a beaten track with fairly good going, through hilly country covered with dry grass and small trees. At intervals there were patches which had been burnt in preparation for being cultivated.

On the third day my messenger to El Fasher arrived, with two companions, but it was a disappointing meeting. It had taken him five days instead of four to reach his destination, and he had not brought the answer to my letter back with him. It was waiting for me, he said, in the possession of a soldier at Mutarrig Well, twelve hours' journey from where we were. The soldier also had provisions for us, but they did us little immediate good at that distance.

There was little for dinner when we camped that night. After dinner I sent our guide off post-haste with orders to ride all night and until he reached Mutarrig. There he was to tell the soldier to come to us as fast as he could.

We started before 4 the next morning and in an hour the men came rushing to me with the news that there was a soldier ahead on a camel. In a few minutes I had a letter from Mr. Charles Dupuis, acting Governor of Darfur, in the absence of Saville Pasha, who had resigned from the service, and a small supply of rice, flour, tea and sugar. I was especially pleased to be handed a supply of cigarettes.

I had not smoked since soon after leaving Erdi. At Ouenat I had suddenly realized that there were only a few cigarettes left. I then laid down a strict rule for myself : one cigarette a day after dinner. It was hard work waiting all day for that brief smoke, but it was worth it when the moment came. I would get into a sheltered corner, light the precious cigarette and shield it carefully from any breath of wind that might make it burn ever so slightly faster. When the few cigarettes were gone there was nothing left but memories and expectation. Now at last the expectation was gratified with a vengeance, for I smoked until my throat was sore.

Bukara, with a handful of the newly arrived cigarettes, put on his long tasselled red *tarboosh*, got on the guide's horse and did a little *fantasia* of joy. But it was when we camped at the Government rest-house at Marahig that general rejoicing broke loose with singing and dancing. The corporal, looking on while the men set the sugar-loaf on the ground and executed a wild dance about it, thought us all a little mad.

"Why all this rejoicing?" he demanded.

"Because for a month we have had no sugar and now our tea is sweetened again," said Abdullahi.

Until one has tried going without any sugar whatever one does not realize how keenly it will be missed.

The corporal shook his head and smiled. "I must return at once to Kuttum and bring you more provisions," he said. "We never realized that you were so short of food." Before he left he was kind enough to go to a camp near-by and bring us a sheep and butter, which were to be paid for by the Moawin of Kuttum since the seller refused to accept Egyptian paper money. The corporal then left with letters from me for Mr. Dupuis and the Moawin, the Deputy-Governor of Kuttum.

The provisions which he had brought us were good as far as they went, but we should very soon be in need of more. I decided to push on at once. We made our midday halt at the Government rest-house at Marahig Well and our stop for the night only a few kilometres farther on. The camels were in very bad condition. The backs and sides of some of them were sore and bleeding, and two camels refused to move until their loads were taken off. It rained for an hour that evening, but it could not dampen our spirits. The men sang and danced round a big fire. The humidity and the smell of the wet grass reminded me of my walks in English country.

We made an early start the next morning in order to reach Metarraj Well for the midday halt. We lunched at the rest-house near the well and received a visit from the *sheikh* of Metarraj, who brought a few chickens as *diafa*. He wanted us to stop the night so that he could entertain us properly the next day, but I felt the necessity of going on as fast as possible.

The camels were getting steadily worse. We had to leave one of them with the *sheikh* of the village on the understanding that if it recovered he was to get a quarter of the price it brought when sold, while if it died he was not to be held responsible.

An hour and a half after starting the next day another soldier on horseback appeared. He brought a letter from the Moawin of Kuttum and a small quantity of rice and sugar. They were gratefully received, for once more we were on short rations and without sugar for our tea. I gave him a letter to take back to Kuttum. A little later we camped in the small valley of Boa. In the afternoon, soon after we had started again, it came on to rain with a strong south-east wind, and I thought it might be wise to camp until the storm was over. But through my glasses I made out ahead of us the row of straw huts of the Markas—the Government house—of Kuttum, and spurred on by the sight we drove the camels faster.

Soon a group of horsemen were seen approaching us and my Beduins impulsively raised a cheer. When I recognized the uniform of Sudanese troops, it was the most cheering sight that I had seen for many weeks. Riad Abu Akla Effendi and Nasr El Din Shaddad Effendi, the two Moawins of Kuttum, approached with a detachment of ten soldiers, the *Kadi*, the head clerk, and other officials and notables of Kuttum. I shook hands warmly with them all, and under their escort the caravan moved on through the village. As we approached, the Markaz women, clothed in white and beating drums, greeted us with singing and " lu-lias." We settled ourselves in and about the rest-house, and the women came again to offer greetings. In a long line they sang and danced, much to the delight of my Beduins, who asked permission to " empty gunpowder " in acknowledgment of the courtesy. I could not refuse my consent and one by one, beginning with Bukara, the men performed the ceremony of singeing the girls' slippers. The Sudanese women were not so accustomed to the Beduin manner of paying homage as the girls of the northern desert, and flinched a little as the powder flashed at their feet. But they accepted it all in good part, the whole line swaying and dancing to the rhythm of the drums, while one by one my men singled them out for the " slipper singeing honour." It was a wonderful reception and the pleasure of it dispersed like magic the fatigue and lassitude of the journey.

More hospitality was to come. Four sheep, butter and fresh vegetables, to say nothing of sugar, were brought to us as *diafa* from the Moawins and officials, and we spent a pleasant evening feasting.

Our arrival at Kuttum at this particular moment had seemed to the inhabitants there an especially auspicious one, for we came with the first rain of the season.

We stopped there for two days, entertained generously by the Moawins in the absence of the Inspector, Mr. Arkell, who was at El Fasher.

One afternoon we attended a Soccer match between two teams of soldiers. It was played with energy if not with *finesse*. At times a player, striving to give the ball an especially vigorous kick, would miss it and send his Sudanese slipper shooting high into the air. The *camaraderie* between officers and men playing this not exactly gentle game together was interesting to see.

Dinner that night with Riad Effendi and Nasr El Din Effendi, the Moawins, was the first meal I had eaten in a house since leaving Kufra. My hosts gave me Egyptian newspapers to read, the first I had seen in nearly six months.

We left Kuttum at 6 o'clock on the morning of June 17th, cheered by the generous hospitality we had enjoyed and the friendly send-off our friends gave us. The two days' journey to El Fasher was a joy-ride. We all felt the thrill and exhilaration of getting in touch with the world again.

But as I went to bed on the 18th I realized with a stab of regret that this was my last day in the real desert. I thought how I should miss my men and my camels, the desolateness and the beauty, the solitude and the companionship—in two words, the desert and its life. I thanked God for His guidance across this vast expanse of pathless sand, and found myself adding a prayer, half wistfully, that I might come back to it again.

I had given orders for an early start the next morning. In their eagerness my men somewhat exaggerated my idea of " early," but I was excited myself and did not mind getting under way at half-past 2.

Three hours' march from El Fasher we camped to make preparations for entering the place. We all shaved and put on our best clothes. Mr. Dupuis had sent a supply of white cloth to Kuttum for us, and my men were able to appear once more in decent raiment. They crowded around my remnant of a mirror to see how they looked. Rifles were cleaned, and the luggage, which was in a very shabby state, was tidied as much as possible. I wished that I might be able to do something for the camels as well, which were thin and dejected-looking. But rest and attention to their sore backs were what they needed, and we had no time or facilities for giving them that. Nevertheless, they too seemed to be infected with the spirit of eagerness felt by all of us, and walked forward briskly. Abdullahi and Zerwali got into their silks, and the caravan moved gaily towards its destination.

As we reached the outskirts of El Fasher, cheers of rejoicing rose throughout the caravan. A cavalcade of men in khaki was coming toward us. I put spurs to Baraka and he responded willingly. He saw the horses before us, pricked his ears forward and dashed toward them.

Mr. Dupuis came forward on his horse to meet me, and we shook hands warmly. The greetings were repeated by the English and Egyptian officers of his staff, and we went on to his house, a part of which he generously made over to me and the men of my caravan. The weary camels were promptly taken in hand by Bimbashi Andas, who gave them food, water and the medical treatment for their wounds they so much needed.

The officer in charge of the wireless station kindly got me the exact Greenwich time from Paris by radio. I was pleased to discover that my chronometer had lost only 23 minutes and 23 seconds in eight months.

For ten days I was the guest of Mr. Dupuis and was lavishly entertained by the officers and officials of the garrison, both English and my own compatriots, and the notables of the town. Hospitality was showered upon me and every kind of assistance that could possibly be needed was eagerly rendered. This was civilization again. I enjoyed once more the luxuries of life, especially vegetables and fruits. It is only when one has gone through the austere régime of the desert that one looks upon these things as luxuries and not necessities. There was, in particular, a brand of prunes, the pride of Major Smith, and of peculiar lusciousness. He called them "If Winter Comes," and I have never tasted their like anywhere.

At last the day came when I must take leave of my companions of the trek from Kufra. When Bukara and his brother, and Hamid and Senussi Bu Jaber came to my room to say good-bye, it was a moment full of real emotion and crowded with memories. These rugged men of the desert burst into tears and I found my own eyes wet. We had been through thick and thin together and came out fast friends. I could never wish for better companions on a journey into desolate regions, more able, more manly, or more loyal.

We read the Fat-ha, the sound of the familiar sacred phrases punctuated by Bukara's sobbing. I exchanged a final hand-clasp with each of them and we parted, to meet one day, I hope, in that desert that I love as much as they.

One more camel trek lay before me to El Obeid, 600 kilometres to the eastward. There I took train for Khartoum and thence home to Cairo, where I arrived on August 1st, 1923.

I had been away from home seven months and twenty-three days, having trekked 2,200 miles across the desert by caravan.

I had determined finally the position of the Zieghen Wells and of Kufra on the map of Africa, in the placing of which there had been hitherto errors of 100 and 45 kilometres respectively.

I had also had the great good fortune to put the "lost" oases of Arkenu and Ouenat definitely on the map of the Libyan Desert.

To A. M. H.

I crave no statue in a public street,
  Nor page of history to give my name :
A desert flower on my winding sheet
  Is all I ask to mark the way I came.

There were no jewels buried in the sand,
  The treasure that I sought was little worth :
I went—but oh, how few will understand—
  To tread an unworn carpet of the earth.

Wide spaces called me, and the way was free ;
  Feet falter not upon a road unknown :
How languish, one who, looking back, can see—
  A thousand miles—no footsteps but his own ?

Not half a hundred voyagings for gold
  Could make me rich as many times I've been
When, weary eyed, I've watched the dawn unfold
  And spread soft radiance o'er a desert scene.
Thoughts were my treasure ; where may thoughts be sold ?
  My world was empty, but my world was clean.

G. F. FOLEY.

EL FASHER,
June 30th, 1923.

Appendices

NOTE ON THE CARTOGRAPHICAL RESULTS OF HASSANEIN BEY'S JOURNEY

JOHN BALL, O.B.E., D.Sc., *Director of Desert Surveys, Egypt.*

1. Introduction.

The cartographical data brought back by Hassanein Bey consist of

(1) Note-books containing the records of astronomical observations for the determination of time, latitude, and compass-variation at nineteen principal camps, with records of watch-comparisons.

(2) A journal giving a continuous record of observed compass-bearings and estimated distances from Siwa Oasis to Lameina Wells, near El Fasher, a distance of about 2,430 kilometres.

The journal also contains a considerable number of observed compass-bearings to conspicuous features on either side of the route, with a few rough trigonometrical estimations of the altitudes of mountains passed, a large number of readings of an aneroid barometer and sling thermometer for the estimation of altitudes along the route, daily observations of maximum and minimum temperatures, observations on the character of the country passed through, and notes on the meteorological conditions.

These observational data have been reduced in the Desert Survey Office, Cairo, and utilized in the preparation of the map on a scale of 1 : 2,000,000 which accompanies Hassanein Bey's account of his travels. The object of the present note is, first, to give an account of the critical examination to which the records were subjected in the course of the reduction of the observations, so as to enable an estimate to be formed of the degree of precision which may be fairly assigned to the geographical positions, altitudes, and other results used in the construction of the map; and, secondly, to indicate the additions to existing geographical knowledge concerning a little-known region of north-east Africa which have accrued from the expedition.

2. Astronomical Determination of Local Time.

Theodolite observations of altitudes of the sun or of stars were made at all the principal camps for determining the error on local mean time of the half-chronometer watch which was used in the latitude observations. In all, thirty-four complete time determinations were made at seventeen camps. The observations were made with a 3-inch Troughton & Simms theodolite, the vertical circle of which could be read by two verniers to 1′, and which was provided with a sensitive level on the microscope arm. The theodolite was invariably set up in the magnetic meridian by its trough compass, and the method used was to note the times of passage of the sun's limb or of the star over each of the three horizontal wires of the stadia-graticule, reading the level and circle at each pointing, face-right and face-left. In the case of stars, the magnetic bearing of the star was also noted from the horizontal circle, and a note made of the colour and brightness of the star, for the identification of the stars subsequently in the office, and thus to free the observer from the necessity of knowing the stars' names. The barometer and thermometer were carefully read at each observation for calculating the refraction.

No difficulty was experienced in subsequently identifying the stars. In only a single case was it found necessary to reject an observation, and this because the observer had accidentally sighted different stars on the two faces of the instrument. On many days two or more observations were taken at the same place, and comparisons of the results at these places indicated that the observations are remarkably accurate for so small an instrument. In seven cases where the sun has been observed shortly before sunset and a star soon after sunset, for example, the maximum difference between the results given by the two observations is only seven seconds, while the average is under four seconds. It is thus apparent that the precision of the time observations is amply sufficient to ensure that no sensible error in the latitudes can be due to errors of the adopted local times.

As the only use made of the time observations in the preparation of the map has been in the determination of latitude, it would serve no useful purpose to give a list of the watch errors. But it may interest future geographers undertaking long desert journeys, to note some of Hassanein Bey's experiences in the transport of watches, and the hazard of relying on constancy of rate for long periods with even the best watch.

Of the six watches carried, only a single one remained in going order throughout the journey. The timekeeper which thus successfully resisted the vicissitudes of the seven months of desert travel was fortunately the one with which Hassanein Bey took all his observations, and was carried in his pocket during the entire journey; it was a large-sized half-chronometer "explorer's" watch of English manufacture, with a dust-proof cap to the winding mechanism. It had been awarded an "especially good" certificate at the National Physical Laboratory of England, and was consequently the most expensive of all the six watches taken on the journey. Even this watch failed to maintain a sufficiently constant rate to be of any service in the determination of longitudes though it amply sufficed for the latitudes, even in two cases when reliance had to be placed on the constancy of its rate for one or two days owing to latitude alone being observed without corresponding observations for local time. Thus, for instance, the following were the average rates of the principal watch deduced from local time observations at places of previously known longitude:

RATE OF PRINCIPAL WATCH.

Sollum to Siwa .	Dec. 29–Jan. 13	15 days	losing	5·8	seconds.
Siwa to Jaghbub .	Jan. 13–Jan. 20	7 ,,	,,	0·1	,,
Jaghbub to Furawia .	Feb. 14–June 5	111 ,,	,,	7·7	,,
Furawia to Um Buru	June 5–June 8	3 ,,	,,	6·6	,,
Um Buru to El Fasher	June 8–June 26	18 ,,	,,	9·4	,,
El Fasher to El Obeid	June 30–July 15	15 ,,	,,	9·4	,,

The above table fails, however, to bring out fully the actual variations of the watch. So long as the other five watches remained in order, Hassanein Bey made frequent comparisons with his principal watch, and between March 21st and 23rd there is strong evidence that the principal watch made an abnormal gain of about fifty seconds. A similar abnormal gain of twenty-nine seconds by the principal watch is evidenced in the twenty-four hours between comparisons of March 24th and 25th. Both these abnormalities occurred between Jalo and El Harrash, at an early stage of the journey, while all the watches appeared to be behaving tolerably well, and it is quite possible that other abnormalities occurred at later stages, when, owing to some or all of the other watches having stopped or broken down, no satisfactory control by comparison was possible.

Of the other five watches carried, one was an English half-chronometer, similar to the principal watch but of smaller size ; three were high-class Swiss lever (" Peerless ") watches with very tight-fitting cases ; and the fifth was a small Swiss lever watch with luminous dial, carried on the wrist for noting the times of marching. The small half-chronometer stopped on April 3rd, after going for over four months ; and though it was re-started, its rate changed considerably after the stoppage. The three " Peerless " watches, though they failed to continue going to the end of the journey, showed by no means a bad record. One was found stopping and unreliable on May 6th, after going for over five months ; the two others continued to go for over a month longer ; and so far as can be judged from the comparisons made on the route, their variations of rate were about of the same order as those of the half-chronometers. The wrist-watch, from the manner in which it was carried, was of course liable to much greater variations of rate, and was occasionally reset by the principal watch ; but it kept going till nearly the end of the journey.

As regards dust-resisting power, which must always be one of the principal aims in selection of watches for desert exploration, there appears to be nothing to choose between good English half-chronometers and the highest class of Swiss watches, the cases of the latter being remarkably close-fitting. The most probable cause either of stoppage or of abnormal changes of rate appears to be the sudden shocks which may arise either to a watch carried on the person when jumping on or off a camel, or to one carried in the baggage by sudden movements of the camel. The most likely explanation of the abnormal gains of the principal watch for short periods on the two occasions above noted would seem to be that owing to a jerk in mounting or dismounting, two contiguous coils of the hair-spring may have been made to touch each other for a short time, with consequent temporary shortening of the period of vibration of the balance-wheel. It is noteworthy that the watch which remained going throughout the journey was the largest of all those taken, and its greater resisting-power may have been to some extent due to its size permitting of greater strength in its component parts.

3. Astronomical Determinations of Latitude.

Observations for latitude by altitudes of the Pole-star were carried out on thirty-five nights at nineteen principal camps, using the same 3-inch theodolite as was employed for the time-observations. Three readings of altitude were made on each face, using each of the three horizontal stadia-wires in turn, the corresponding times being noted on a half-chronometer watch whose error on local time was accurately known from sun or star-observations carried out just before the latitude-observation. Particular care was taken with the level-adjustment, and the air-pressure and temperature at the time of the observation were recorded.

The following table gives the results of the observations:

Astronomical Latitudes.

				°	′	″	
Sollum	4	nights	Lat.	31	35	9	N.
Siwa	1	,,	,,	29	12	41	,,
Jaghbub	5	,,	,,	29	44	26	,,
Camp near Jalo	1	,,	,,	29	11	56	,,
Jalo (El Erg)	1	,,	,,	29	2	33	,,
Buttafal	1	,,	,,	28	54	26	,,
El Harrash	1	,,	,,	25	26	29	,,
Taj	6	,,	,,	24	13	47	,,
Arkenu	2	,,	,,	22	12	32	,,
Ouenat	1	,,	,,	21	52	29	,,
Erdi	1	,,	,,	18	35	39	,,
Agah	1	,,	,,	17	52	38	,,
Enebah	1	,,	,,	17	21	24	,,
Bao	1	,,	,,	16	28	24	,,
Furawia	2	,,	,,	15	21	51	,,
Um Buru	2	,,	,,	15	3	57	,,
Kuttum	1	,,	,,	14	12	15	,,
El Fasher	2	,,	,,	13	38	3	,,
El Obeid	1	,,	,,	13	10	51	,,

Of six of the above places (Sollum, Siwa, Jaghbub, Kuttum, El Fasher, and El Obeid) the latitudes are accurately known from the Egyptian and Sudan official surveys, and the agreement in these cases is very satisfactory, though a very close comparison is not generally possible owing to uncertainty as to Hassanein Bey's precise observation-spot. At Jaghbub, Hassanein Bey records that his observation-spot was 200 metres S.S.W. of the dome of the mosque. Applying the corresponding difference of latitude (−6″) to my own determination of the latitude of the dome in 1917 (29° 44′ 41″), we obtain 25° 44′ 35″, showing a difference of only 9″ from Hassanein Bey's observed latitude.

A further test of the degree of precision of the latitude-observations can be made by comparison of the latitudes found for the same camp by observations taken on different nights. The following gives the average deviation of a single observed latitude from the mean at all the camps where two or more observations for latitude were made :

Sollum	4	nights ..	Av. dev.	8
Jaghbub	5	,, ..	,,	40
Taj	6	,, ..	,,	12
Arkenu	2	,, ..	,,	6
Furawia	2	,, ..	,,	8
Um Buru . . .	2	,, ..	,,	23
El Fasher . . .	2	,, ..	,,	6

It thus appears unlikely that any observed latitude can be as much as 1′ in error, and consequently in the preparation of the map, Hassanein Bey's observed latitudes have been accepted as fundamental data for all the places for which no previous determinations are known to exist, viz. El Harrash, Taj, Arkenu, Ouenat, Erdi, Agah, Enebah, and Bao. His latitudes for Jalo (El Erg), Bir Buttafal, and Furawia have also been adopted for the map, the first because it is possibly better than that of Rohlfs, with whose mapped position it is however in very close agreement ; the second because while differing by about 2′ from Rohlfs' value (28° 36′ 22″) it is doubtless more exact, because it checks admirably well with Hassanein Bey's dead reckoning ; and the third because, although the position of Furawia is shown on the Sudan maps, it is outside the present limits of the Sudan triangulation and is possibly liable to some slight error.[1]

[1] Since the above was written, I have received information from the Director of Sudan Surveys that a recent extension of the Sudan triangulation-net includes Gebel Furawia as one of the points, and

4. Observations of Compass-variations.

For finding the Pole-star easily when the sky was not very dark or was partially obscured by clouds, and also for obtaining the approximate bearings of time-stars for their subsequent identification, the theodolite was invariably set up in the magnetic meridian by its trough-compass, and the magnetic bearing of the Pole-star was read on the horizontal circle after each latitude-observation and the time noted. In this way the approximate compass-variation was determined at each camp, with the following results :—

VARIATION OF THE COMPASS.

Place	Date	Observations	°	′	
Sollum	Dec. 1922	3 obs.	2	34	W.
Siwa	Jan. 1923	1 ,,	2	42	,,
Jaghbub	Feb. 1923	5 ,,	2	25	,,
Near Jalo	March, 1923	1 ,,	4	12	,,
Jalo (El Erg)	,, ,,	1 ,,	4	5	,,
Buttafal	,, ,,	1 ,,	—		
El Harrash	,, ,,	1 ,,	3	48	,,
Taj	April, 1923	6 ,,	3	32	,,
Arkenu	,, ,,	2 ,,	3	25	,,
Ouenat	,, ,,	1 ,,	3	32	,,
Erdi	May, 1923	1 ,,	3	57	,,
Agah	,, ,,	1 ,,	4	0	,,
Enebah	,, ,,	1 ,,	4	21	,,
Bao	,, ,,	1 ,,	4	59	,,
Furawia	June, 1923	2 ,,	4	32	,,
Um Buru	,, ,,	2 ,,	3	25	,,
Kuttum	,, ,,	1 ,,	4	26	,,
El Fasher	,, ,,	2 ,,	2	51	,,

The method of estimating the compass-variation with the

that the precise position found for the summit of the hill is lat. 15° 20′ 59″·9 N., long. 23° 36′ 48″·1 E., altitude 954 metres above sea-level. This position differs by about 2 kms. from that shown on the map above referred to ; but in view of the fact that the distance and bearing of Hassanein Bey's camp from the hill is unknown, though his observed latitude shows his camp to have been on a parallel about a kilometre and a half north of the hill, I have not thought it worth while to make any change in the adjustment of Hassanein Bey's data. The longitude adopted for the camp (p. 281) may be slightly in error, but it is unlikely that the error can exceed a mile or so. The difference of level between the top of the hill and Hassanein Bey's camp being unknown, the triangulation-level affords no control over Hassanein Bey's barometric value for the latter place, and consequently I have judged it best to use El Fasher as the south control point in adjusting the level-determinations.

theodolite is, of course, only rough; but the values found are probably correct at most places within half a degree, and they serve to show that there is no likelihood of any serious errors of dead-reckoning owing to local irregularities of the compass-variation. They have accordingly been utilized in reduction of the compass-bearings of the traverse to true bearings over the major portion of the route, where no previous determinations exist, and where in consequence the distribution of the isogonic lines is not known with any exactitude.

5. Longitudes.

The probability of some watches breaking in the course of seven months' travel had been foreseen, and from the outset it appeared improbable that any use could be made of the watches in the direct determination of longitude on so long and difficult a journey. We had decided accordingly to depend ultimately on dead-reckoning for longitude, making every effort to obtain an unbroken chain of compass-bearings and estimated distances between Jaghbub and some known place in the Sudan, the bearings to be taken with a good compass with all possible precision, at very frequent intervals, and the estimates of distance to be carefully made each day from the marching time of the baggage-camels, assuming a normal rate of 4 kms. per hour over average desert, and making allowance for the variations in speed over ground of varying character. The journey being predominantly north to south, the estimates of distance could mostly be well controlled by the latitudes, while errors of bearing would not be cumulative, and would tend to cancel out over any considerable stretch of route. The primary reason for taking six watches was therefore not to determine longitude, for which at best they could afford only somewhat uncertain values, but to make sure of at least one watch being available throughout the journey for latitude-observations, without which no proper control of the all-important distances could be obtained.

The doubts about the possibility of safely transporting the watches proved justified, for all but one broke down before the end of the journey. But fortunately on the one hand the watch which survived sufficed amply for the determination of latitude (though its rate was insufficiently constant for it to be used uncontrolled in finding longitudes), and on the other hand the programme of a continuous chain of very careful bearings and estimation of distances was scrupulously adhered to from the departure of the caravan from Jaghbub, the last known place in Egypt, to Furawia, the first known place in the Sudan—a journey of 2,430 kilometres—and from this chain of bearings and estimated distances, combined with the observed latitudes, it was possible to estimate the longitudes of all places on the route with a fairly high probability of accuracy.

For the estimation of the longitude of Jalo (El Erg), a slightly different procedure was followed from that adopted for the other principal camps on the route. It will be noticed from the map that the general direction of the march from Jaghbub to Jalo was predominantly from east to west, instead of from north to south as in the rest of the journey. Consequently the observed latitudes do not afford so good a means of correcting the estimated distances in this stretch as elsewhere. But fortunately the observed latitude at Jalo does enable us to correct the previous estimation by Hassanein Bey (in 1920) of the distance of that place from Jedabia, and this combined with the then observed bearings would lead to one value for the longitude for Jalo, while if we can assume the accuracy of the estimated distances from Jaghbub to Jalo, we may use the observed latitude of the latter place to correct the bearings and thus arrive at another value for its longitude.

From careful consideration of all the available data, the two methods appear likely to be about equal in degree of approximation. The position at present accepted for Jedabia (lat. 30° 48′ 10″ N., long. 20° 13′ 30″ E.) is open to a little uncertainty,[1] and the bearings taken by Hassanein Bey on his former expedition are probably a little less accurate than those of the present one. On the other hand, the estimations of the distances from Jaghbub to Jalo, as gauged by the latitude-control of the other portions of the route of the present expedition, are remarkably close to the truth, while a uniform correction to his bearings of less than half a degree would swing his dead-reckoning position for Jalo on to its observed parallel of latitude.

For the longitude of Jalo on the map I have therefore taken

[1] No observations are known to have been taken at Jedabia. The position given is that which I adopted for it in preparing a former map in 1921, and was arrived at by estimation from a car-and-compass traverse carried out by Captain Williams from Zuetina in 1918.

the mean of the two longitudes found (1) by assuming Hassanein Bey's bearings correct from Jedabia and correcting his distances by the latitudes, and (2) by assuming his distances from Jaghbub correct and using the observed latitudes to correct his bearings. The results are:

		°	′	″
(1) From Jedabia, long. of Jalo (El Erg)	.	21	29	48
(2) From Jaghbub ,, ,, ,,	.	21	26	19
Adopted mean .	.	21	28	3

It may be remarked in passing that the result places Jalo almost precisely where it is shown on Rohlfs' map of 1880.

As regards the longitudes adopted for the other principal camps along the route, the procedure has been as follows. The route was divided into the following nine sections between principal camps where latitudes had been observed: Jalo—El Harrash—Taj—Arkenu—Ouenat—Erdi—Agah—Enebah—Bao—Furawia, and the compass-traverse for each section was plotted on a scale of 1/500,000 from the recorded bearings and estimated distances. A true meridian was then drawn on each section from the mean of the observed compass-variations at its two ends, and the total difference of latitude of each section was scaled off and compared with the difference of latitude given by the latitude-observations. This comparison gave, of course, the average error of estimation of distance along each section, assuming the bearings correct. The results of the comparison for the various sections are tabulated below:

CORRECTION TO ESTIMATED DISTANCES.

Section of traverse.	Plotted difference of latitude. km.	True difference from latitude-observations. km.	True-plotted diff. lat. km.	Correction to estimated distances. Per cent.
Jalo–El Harrash	375·0	399·0	+ 24·0	+ 6·4
El Harrash–Taj	131·5	134·2	+ 2·7	+ 2·1
Taj–Arkenu	217·7	223·7	+ 6·0	+ 2·8
Arkenu-Ouenat	36·0	37·0	+ 1·0	+ 2·8
Ouenat–Erdi	369·0	363·2	− 5·8	− 1·6
Erdi–Agah	75·6	79·2	+ 3·6	+ 4·8
Agah–Enebah	57·0	57·5	+ 0·5	+ 0·9
Enebah–Bao	99·0	97·7	− 1·3	− 1·3
Bao–Furawia	124·2	122·7	− 1·5	− 1·2

Mean error of estimation of distances, per cent. . 2·6

The average error of distance-estimation in each section of the route having been thus found, the next step was to scale off the various departures from the plotted traverses, correcting for the errors of distance-estimation, and then to convert the departures into differences of longitude. When this was done, the resulting total difference of longitude between Jalo and Furawia was 2° 25′ 55″. But assuming the true longitude of Jalo to be that found above, and the true longitude of Furawia to be as shown on sheet 53 D of the 1/250,000 Sudan survey map of 1921, we have—

	°	′	″
Longitude of Jalo	21	28	3
Longitude of Furawia	23	38	10
Difference . .	2	10	7

so that the difference of longitude found by the dead-reckoning requires correction by 15′ 48″. This correction, which implies an average error in the observed compass-bearings of less than a degree, and a negligible correction to the adjusted distances, was distributed along the entire traverse in proportion to the difference of latitude between the principal camps, leading to the finally adopted longitudes shown in the following table :

CONCLUDED LONGITUDES.

	Dead-reckoning corrected by the latitudes.				Further correction.		Concluded longitude.			
	°	′	″		′	″	°	′	″	
Jalo . . .	—				—		21	28	3	E.
El Harrash. .	22	15	5	E.	4	10	22	10	55	,,
Taj . . .	23	29	5	,,	5	34	23	23	41	,,
Arkenu . .	24	52	10	,,	7	55	24	44	15	,,
Ouenat . .	25	2	34	,,	8	18	24	54	16	,,
Erdi . . .	23	22	34	,,	12	5	23	10	29	,,
Agah . . .	23	28	49	,,	12	54	23	15	55	,,
Enebah . .	23	27	58	,,	13	30	23	14	28	,,
Bao . . .	23	16	18	,,	14	31	23	1	47	,,
Furawia . .	23	53	58	,,	15	48	23	38	10	,,

In attempting to estimate the probable degree of accuracy of the concluded longitudes, we are faced with the difficulty that while we may be certain that the *average* error of the compass-bearings was less than 1°, which average error has been allowed for in the adjustment, we have no proof that in some of the individual sections the errors may not have been considerably greater. But in view of the great number of the observed compass-bearings (339) which make up the directional data of the 1,754 kilometres of traverse from Jalo to Furawia (an average of 38 observed bearings for each of the nine sections), and bearing in mind also the remarkable accuracy of the estimations of distance as evidenced by the latitude-observations, it would seem unlikely that any of the above-adopted longitudes for the principal camps can be in error by more than 3 or 4 miles. This implies a degree of accuracy which it would have been difficult to ensure by transport of even a considerable number of chronometers over a land journey lasting more than three months. It may, I think, be concluded that no better values for the longitudes can be obtained without the aid of wireless time-signals.

6. Altitudes above Sea-level.

For the barometric estimations of altitudes above sea-level, a 2-inch aneroid by Steward was used. This instrument, which was one of two specially made for the expedition, was very carefully compensated for temperature, and provided with a fairly open pressure-scale, a millimetre of pressure being represented by very nearly a millimetre of actual scale-length, so that estimations to half-millimetres of pressure could be readily made.

The aneroid was read morning and evening at each camp, and at numerous other points on the route, the air-temperatures being as a rule recorded at the same time, as given by sling-thermometer. The aneroid behaved very satisfactorily throughout the journey. There had, unfortunately, been no opportunity of testing the instrument before Hassanein Bey's departure, but it was in perfect order on his return, and was then tested in the laboratory of the Physical Department at Cairo, when it was found to require the following corrections (at about 25° C.):

Pressure, mm. .	760	750	740	730	720	710	700	690	680	670	660	650
Correction, mm.	− 2·3	− 2·3	− 2·3	− 2·1	− 1·4	− 1·1	− 0·1	+ 0·6	+ 1·7	+ 2·0	+ 2·8	+ 2·9

That the above corrections had remained sensibly constant throughout the journey is rendered extremely probable by the close agreement noted farther on (p. 287) between the levels found for Jalo directly from the aneroid readings (corrected, of course, on the assumption of constancy of the table) and those found indirectly from readings of the mercurial barometer in the meteorological station at Siwa.

The first step in the calculation of the barometric levels was to collect the whole of the readings of the barometer and sling-thermometer at each of the nine principal camps, where a halt of at least several days had been made, and a considerable number of readings taken. The means of all the recorded pressures and air-temperatures were taken for each of these principal camps, and the pressure corrected for instrumental error from the table above given. The readings being taken at various times of the day, the diurnal variation of pressure could safely be neglected, as it would most probably disappear on taking the mean of the readings. To allow for the annual variation, the mean pressures were next reduced to the mean of the year by applying a correction based on the mean of the normal annual variations at Siwa and El Obeid, as found from the recent volume of 'Climatological Normals' issued by the Physical Department of Egypt and shown in the following table:

CORRECTIONS TO REDUCE MONTHLY MEAN PRESSURES TO ANNUAL MEANS.

	Jan.	Feb.	March.	April.	May.	June.	July.
	mm.	mm.	mm.	mm.	mm.	mm.	mm.
Siwa . .	− 3·4	− 2·0	− 1·9	+ 0·9	+ 0·9	+ 2·7	+ 3·5
El Obeid .	− 1·2	− 0·7	+ 0·3	+ 1·2	+ 1·0	+ 0·6	0·0
Mean .	− 2·3	− 1·4	− 0·8	+ 1·0	+ 1·0	+ 1·6	+ 1·8

A further correction to allow for the distribution of the sea-level isobars over the region traversed was desirable, but no sufficient data exist for estimating its amount; the distribution is however probably nearly linear, and such a distribution was approximately allowed for by assuming the previously accepted levels at Siwa (—17 m.) and El Fasher (793 m.) to be correct and distributing any residual difference found by the otherwise corrected barometer readings between these two places uniformly among the different sections.

The difference of height corresponding to each difference of mean corrected barometer-readings was calculated by the tables of *Barometrische Höhenstufen* in Jordan's 'Mathematische and Geodätische Hülfstafeln,' for the air-temperature corresponding to the mean of the thermometer-readings at the two ends of the line.

The adopted levels of thirteen principal camps as found in the above manner are tabulated below. It is interesting to note that the residual difference of height which had to be distributed between Siwa and El Fasher, and which is presumably mainly due to systematic pressure-gradient, was 63 metres, corresponding to a normal fall of sea-level pressure between the two places of about 5 mm., and this is from other considerations probably very near the truth; also that the resulting adjustment which had to be made in the levels in any single main section of the route did not exceed 5 metres.

CONCLUDED ALTITUDES ABOVE SEA.

	Number of observations.	Mean pressure (corrected). mm.	Mean temperature. ° C.	Diff. of height from Jordan's tables. metres.	Diff. of height (adjusted). metres.	Altitude above sea-level. metres.
Siwa	4	762·6	12	—	—	− 17
Jaghbub	50	757·7	15	+ 54	+ 49	+ 32
Jalo	18	754·7	17	+ 34	+ 29	61
El Harrash	6	732·8	23	+ 254	+ 249	310
Taj	31	718·5	19	+ 170	+ 165	475
Arkenu	12	708·0	31	+ 128	+ 123	598
Ouenat	14	706·3	31	+ 21	+ 18	616
Erdi	7	683·3	31	+ 295	+ 290	906
Agah	3	695·2	34	− 157	− 162	744
Bao	5	677·7	33	+ 230	+ 225	969
Furawia	11	685·8	31	− 107	− 112	857
Um Buru	8	679·5	30	+ 83	+ 78	935
Kuttum	5	660·2	24	+ 254	+ 249	1184
El Fasher	5	689·7	31	− 386	− 391	793

After thus determining the levels for the principal camps, those of intermediate camps and other places were computed in a similar manner, adjusting each section to the adopted levels at its terminal points. The maximum adjustment which it was found necessary to apply to the difference of height given by the barometer between points a day's journey apart was 5 metres, and the average 3 metres.

An exception was made in the stretch between Jaghbub and Jalo, where no intermediate levels were adopted for the map, owing to the extremely unstable state of the atmosphere during the journey between these two places; sandstorms of great violence occurred on several days of marching, with such rapid fluctuations of air-pressure that no heights could safely be deduced from the barometer-readings.

As regards the degree of reliability of the deduced levels,

some little uncertainty exists in the levels adopted for the terminal points Siwa and El Fasher, while the temperature-compensation of the aneroid has not been tested and may not be quite perfect. Taking everything into account, it may be estimated that the levels of the principal camps are probably correct to within about 20 metres, while those of the intermediate camps and other points, for which only one or two readings of the barometer are available, may possibly be in error by twice that amount.

7. Summary of Principal Geographical Positions and Levels.

	Latitude N.			Longitude E.			Metres above sea.	Remarks.
	°	′	″	°	′	″		
Jaghbub (mosque) .	29	44	41	24	31	11	32	Position from previous determination by Dr. Ball.
Jalo (El Erg) . .	29	2	33	21	28	3	61	
Bir Buttafal . .	28	54	26	21	45	15	98	
El Harrash Well (Zieghen) . .	25	26	29	22	10	55	310	
Taj (Kufra) . .	24	13	47	23	23	41	475	
Boema (Kufra. Rohlfs' camp) . .	24	13	8	23	24	40	400	Short compass traverse from Taj.
Arkenu . . .	22	12	32	24	44	15	598	
Ouenat . . .	21	52	29	24	54	16	616	
Erdi (Camp 8 kms. north of well) . .	18	35	39	23	10	29	906	
Agah . . .	17	52	38	23	15	55	744	
Enebah . . .	17	21	24	23	14	28	1100	
Bao . . .	16	28	24	23	1	47	969	
Furawia . . .	15	21	51	23	38	10	857	Longitude from Sudan map.

8. Construction of the Route Map on Scale 1/Two Million.

In the process of utilizing the dead-reckoning for the determination of the longitudes of the principal camps, the whole route had been provisionally plotted on to a scale of 1/500,000 direct from the field-books, on a series of sheets each comprising one section of the route. To these plottings of the actual route were now added the computed levels of all camps, the geographical features fixed by cross-bearings on either side of the route, and notes on the nature of the ground.

The various sections thus provisionally mapped on 1/500,000 were then reduced to the scale of 1/2,000,000, allowance being made for the small departures of the original plottings from the 1/500,000 scale as found by the latitude-observations, and the various sections so reduced were drawn in on the final map between the finally adopted positions of the principal camps. It was found practicable to show all the principal geographical features on the final scale, though many notes on the nature of the ground had perforce to be omitted in order not to overcrowd the map. These notes are however carefully preserved on the 1/500,000 manuscript sectional maps in the Desert Survey Office in Cairo, so as to be available for future reference, while the principal of them are incorporated in Hassanein Bey's narrative of the expedition.

The main portion of the route, namely that from Jaghbub to Furawia, has been mapped entirely from Hassanein Bey's journals and note-books. The portions of his route from Sollum to Jaghbub in the north, and from Furawia to El Obeid in the south, have been copied from the latest official survey maps of Egypt and the Sudan, as being more accurate than any route survey could be.

The fixing of the positions of El Harrash and Taj by Hassanein Bey's observations had enabled the course of his former expedition to Kufra (with Mrs. Forbes) in 1920–21 to be delineated more accurately than was possible from the original records of that journey, which were unaccompanied by any astronomical observations; and the course of the former route, adjusted to newly determined positions, has been indicated on the new map by a dotted line.

9. Additions to Geographical Knowledge resulting from the Expedition.

JALO.—The first portion of Hassanein Bey's route from Jaghbub to Jalo appears to be identical with that trodden by Rohlfs in 1869. At Gara Matan Sidi, about half-way between Jaghbub and Jalo, the track forks, and Hassanein Bey went by the northern (Zawaiya) branch, which passes Hiseila Wells and enters Jalo from a more northerly direction than the southern (Majabra) branch taken by Rohlfs.

Hassanein Bey's position for Jalo is almost identical with that of Rohlfs, but peculiar interest attaches to the former's determination of its level at 61 metres above sea. Rohlfs, visiting the place in 1869 and 1879, had found the aneroid to indicate a level below the sea in 1869, and above it in 1879, and had ultimately concluded that both Aujila and Jalo lay about at sea-level.[1] Hassanein Bey's determination is based on ten days' aneroid readings and comparison with Siwa, and it is noteworthy that exactly the same altitude (61 metres) for Jalo results whether the comparison is made with the readings of the standard barometer in the meteorological station at Siwa during the same period, or with the readings taken by Hassanein Bey with the same aneroid on four days at Siwa two months earlier (allowance being made, of course, for the annual variation of pressure over the intervening period). There can, I think, be hardly any doubt of the greater accuracy of Hassanein Bey's determination, since it is unlikely that Rohlfs' readings extended over so long a period, and it is practically certain that no comparisons were made by him with simultaneous observations at a place of known level. It should however be mentioned that Hassanein Bey's level probably refers to a somewhat higher observation point than that of Rohlfs; for owing to sand-drifts enveloping the houses, the inhabitants of El Erg are gradually rebuilding their dwellings on higher ground, and his observations were taken in one of the most recently constructed of these. Another point worthy of remark is, that although Hassanein Bey's determination is to a certain extent checked by the exact agreement of the two methods of comparison above referred to, the day-to-day variations of pressure observed at Jalo are much in excess of those at Siwa during the same ten-day period. The extreme range shown by the aneroid at Jalo was 10 mm. against 5 mm. of the standard barometer at Siwa, and the 7 mm. average difference of pressure between the two places for the ten days of comparison which has been used to calculate the new value of the level, is the mean of difference ranging from 1 to 12 mm. on different days. The relatively great variability of atmospheric pressure at Jalo, which readily explains the discordant results noted by Rohlfs on different dates, may be closely connected with the sandstorms which are so frequent in the neighbourhood.

Bir Buttafal.—Bir Buttafal ("Battifal" of Rohlfs) is of importance as being the last watering-place for caravans proceeding on the weary desert march of nearly 400 kms. to

[1] Rohlfs, "Kufra," 1881, p. 226.

Zieghen. The position found for Bir Buttafal by Hassanein Bey agrees fairly well with that given by Rohlfs :[1]

	Lat. N.			Long. E.			Metres above sea.
	°	′	″	°	′	″	
Bir Buttafal, Hassanein Bey .	28	54	26	21	45	15	98
,, ,, Rohlfs . .	28	56	22	21	44	10	58
Difference . .		1	56		1	5	40

ZIEGHEN ("Sirhen" of Rohlfs).—Zieghen is the name of a district containing numerous wells. It is not inhabited, but is of great importance as lying on the main caravan route from Jalo to Kufra. The principal well used by the caravans is El Harrash. Rohlfs did not visit Zieghen; he travelled from Jalo to Kufra by the more westerly track through Taiserbo and Buseima, and the position shown for Zieghen on his map, which was based merely on his guides' statements, is about 100 kms. too far to the east-north-east.

As the journey from Jalo to Kufra by any future traveller is likely to be undertaken in the winter, when the question of fuel is second only to that of water, it is worth noting that the first "hatab" (firewood) is met with at about 342 kms. after leaving Bir Buttafal, and 52 before reaching El Harrash Well. In an emergency water may be got at Matan Abu Hosh, the old well of Zieghen, about 18 kms. before reaching El Harrash; but El Harrash yields better water, and being the regular halting-place of the caravans, the water can usually be obtained there without digging; hence, unless the caravans are very thirsty they usually prefer to go on to El Harrash rather than make a halt at the old well. Excellent water can be got anywhere in the neighbourhood of El Harrash by digging to a depth of 3 or 4 feet. From El Harrash to Buseima is about 54 kms. in a direction a little east of south, and from El Harrash to Taj, the principal town of Kufra proper, is 182 kms. in a south-easterly direction.

TAISERBO.—Taiserbo, the most north-westerly oasis of the Kufra group, has not, so far as is known, been visited by any traveller since Rohlfs' day. Its position was however indicated to Hassanein Bey as lying between 70° and 80° west of north from El Harrash, at a distance of 60 to 70 kms. This indication would place Taiserbo very nearly in the position

[1] *Mitt. Afrik. Ges.*, Band ii., 1880–1881, p. 17.

which Rohlfs assigned to it. Rohlfs' position for his camp at Kasr Djrangedi is probably therefore substantially correct, though it is likely that the oasis is in reality less extensive than shown on his map.

BUSEIMA.—Although Buseima was not visited by Hassanein Bey on this occasion, his fixation of the position of El Harrash, in combination with his former rough compass-traverse from that place to Buseima with Mrs. Forbes in 1921, permits of a fair approximation for its position. Hassanein Bey's estimates of distances and bearings on his former journey (adjusted by his recently observed latitudes at El Harrash and Taj) give his camp in Buseima as being 60 kms. from El Harrash in a direction of 5° east of true south, and from his camp to that of Rohlfs (Ain el Nusrani) was roughly about 15 kms. in a true west-north-westerly direction. Adopting Hassanein Bey's recently fixed position of El Harrash, this would give a position for Rohlfs' camp about 30 kms. south-west by south of where Rohlfs placed it, as is shown by the following comparison :

	Lat. N.			Long. E.		
	°	′	″	°	′	″
Buseima (Rohlfs' camp) from Stecker's observations	25	11	42	22	15	0
Buseima (Rohlfs' camp) from Hassanein Bey's estimation	24	58	11	22	5	46
Difference		13	31		9	14

It would hardly seem possible that Hassanein Bey can have made so large an error as 25 kms. in his former estimation of the distance of Buseima from El Harrash, and hence it would appear reasonable to think that there was some error either in Stecker's observation or (what is more likely) in his reduction of it. This point is referred to farther on in the discussion of the position of Boema (p. 290).

KUFRA (Kebabo of Rohlfs).—The name "Kufra" is now generally applied, not to the whole of the Kufra group of oases as was done by Rohlfs in 1879, but specially to the area called Kebabo by that traveller.

The seat of local government and principal settlement is the walled town of Taj, situated on a rocky cliff overlooking the depression of the oasis proper which lies to the south and contains the villages of Jof, Buma, Boema, El Zurruk, Talalib, and Tollab. Hassanein Bey carried out latitude observations at

Taj, and proceeded 3 kms., on a bearing of 16° west of south, to Jof, from which place he made very careful estimations of the distances and bearings of the other villages of the oasis, which has enabled their relative positions to be plotted on the map with much closer approximation than had hitherto been possible.

Considerable interest attaches to the position of Boema, the easternmost village of Kufra, for it was here that Stecker camped with Rohlfs and made his observations for latitude and longitude in 1879. Hassanein Bey found Boema to lie 2 kms. from Taj, in a direction 54° east of true south. Accepting his determination of the position of Taj, this leads to the following position for Boema as compared with that given by Rohlfs:

	Lat. N.			Long. E.		
	°	′	″	°	′	″
Boema, according to Hassanein Bey .	24	13	8	23	24	40
,, ,, Rohlfs [1] . .	24	31	38	23	12	40
Difference		18	30		12	0

Hassanein Bey thus places Boema some 40 kms. south-south-east of the position assigned to it by Rohlfs from Stecker's observations. The remarkable thing about this large discrepancy is that it is chiefly in the latitude, which was directly observed by Stecker at Boema itself, and by Hassanein Bey at Taj, only 2 kms. away from Boema. I have not been able to find any details of Stecker's observations, except that they were carried out with a "prismatic circle." But I have subjected the original records of Hassanein Bey's observations for time and latitude at Taj to very careful examination, and there is overwhelming evidence that his latitude for that place cannot be in error by more than 1′. He observed the altitude of *Polaris* at Taj on no fewer than six different nights, with a watch whose error on local time was accurately known from sun and star observations carried out on the same dates. From the internal evidence of the observations themselves, the watch-error at the time of sighting *Polaris* cannot on any occasion have been uncertain by more than two seconds, which would not, of course, sensibly affect the latitude found; the recorded magnetic bearing of the star sighted, as well as its rate of apparent motion, proves that the star used for

[1] *Mitt. Afrik. Ges.*, Band ii., 1880–1881, p. 25.

latitude in each case was really *Polaris*; and the greatest difference of any single observed latitude from the mean of the six nights' observations was only 15″, the average departure of a single observation from the mean being 12″. Hassanein Bey's latitude of 24° 13′ 47″ for Taj can therefore be unhesitatingly accepted as correct within 1′; and since there is not room for an error of even this amount in his estimation of the short distance of Boema from Taj, it becomes absolutely certain that Rohlfs' latitude for Boema is over a quarter of a degree too high.

It is curious to notice that in the case of Buseima (p. 289) the discrepancy of 13′ 31″ between Rohlfs' latitude and that estimated from Hassanein Bey's recent work is of the same order and of the same sign as that found at Boema; and that a negative correction equal in amount to the sun's semi-diameter would in each case bring the results of the two observers into fairly close agreement. The explanation hence suggests itself that Stecker may have determined his latitudes by observation of the upper limb of the sun at noon, and both at Buseima and Boema failed to correct the measured altitude for the semi-diameter, thus making both latitudes 16′ too great. A mistake of this kind, as every scientific traveller knows, is very easily made in hurried reductions in the field; and at the time when Stecker carried out his observations and calculations in Kufra, both he and his brave leader were in imminent peril of losing their lives at the hands of treacherous Badawi.

A similar explanation may account to a large extent for the discrepancies of longitude at the two places. Thus, according to Hassanein Bey's work, Rohlfs' longitude for his camp at Buseima is 9′ too far east, and that for his camp at Boema 12′ too far west. We have only to assume that Stecker observed the sun's lower limb in the morning at Buseima, and the upper limb in the afternoon at Boema, for finding the local times, and in each case omitted to correct the observed latitude for semi-diameter, to account pretty completely for both discrepancies of longitude.

The puzzling thing about the above explanation of the errors of Rohlfs' map is that Rohlfs actually travelled the distance between Buseima and Boema, and estimated it at 120 kms.,[1] whereas Hassanein Bey's positions would indicate

[1] *Mitt. Afrik. Ges.*, Band ii., 1880–1881, p. 23.

that the true distance is 40 kms. greater. But as Rohlfs' statement of the distance was obviously written after Stecker had determined the positions of the places astronomically, it is probable that he obtained his 120 kms. by calculation from the astronomical positions, rejecting any rough estimate he may have made of the distance from his times of marching. Both Hassanein Bey and Mrs. Forbes had considered that the true distance was much greater than 120 kms. when they traversed it in 1921 ; but as on that occasion no observations for position were taken, it remained uncertain whether either Buseima or Boema had been wrongly placed on Rohlfs' map. It is now practically certain that both were wrong.

As regards the level of Kufra, it is satisfactory to notice a very close agreement of Hassanein Bey's observations with those of Rohlfs. Hassanein Bey's barometer-readings at Ezeila, to the south of Jof, give 389 metres for the level of that place, and he estimates that Boema lies some 10 metres higher; this would give about 400 metres for the altitude of Boema, a figure identical with that found by Rohlfs. Taj, which has been built on the cliff north of Jof, since Rohlfs' day, is found to be 475 metres above sea-level from a series of aneroid-readings extending over a fortnight. The outlying villages of Kufra which lie north of Taj are lower than Taj itself, but substantially higher than the southern villages of Kufra; Awadel is 434 metres above sea, and Hawari and Hawawiri are about the same altitude.

There is also fairly close agreement as to the extent of Kufra from north to south. Rohlfs' map makes the extent in latitude between Hawawiri and Tollab to be about 35 kms., while Hassanein Bey makes it 30 kms. But when we come to the distance over which the villages extend from east to west, there is a much graver discrepancy. Rohlfs makes the extent from east to west (Buma to Tollab) about 40 kms., while according to the latest estimations by Hassanein Bey the true extent is only about 21 kms. As Rohlfs appears to have located many of the villages on his map merely from Arab statements, and not from careful personal estimation as did Hassanein Bey, we need have no hesitation in accepting the latter's relative positions as by far the more nearly correct, and hence concluding that Rohlfs' map gives an east-and-west extension which is nearly double the truth.

The error in east-and-west extension (so far as concerns the placing of the villages, not the extent of the vegetation) is even greater on the map prepared by me and published by Mrs. Forbes in 1921.[1] This is due to the distance between Jof and Tollab having been much overestimated on the former journey; it was given to me as about 42 kms., while according to Hassanein Bey's latest estimation it is only 20 kms.

A matter which will at once strike the eye of anyone who compares Hassanein Bey's latest map of the Kufra villages with that published by Mrs. Forbes is that in the later map a place called Ezeila is shown south of Jof, while in the earlier map (which was prepared from Hassanein Bey's own data and rough sketches) Ezeila is shown north of Hawawiri. The explanation is that there are *two* Ezeilas. The name "Ezeila" is applied locally to any outlying well (usually with a clump of palms) which forms the last watering-place for caravans leaving the oasis. Thus the northern Ezeila is the last well for a traveller leaving Kufra to go north-eastwards towards Jaghbub, while the southern Ezeila is the last well in Kufra for anyone going south towards Wadai.

From the southern Ezeila of Kufra to Arkenu is 266 kms. in a nearly south-easterly direction, and there is no water or grazing on the way. From Arkenu to Ouenat is a further 42 kms. in a slightly more southerly direction.

THE OASES OF ARKENU AND OUENAT.—One of the most interesting and important results of Hassanein Bey's expedition is the confirmation of the real existence of the Oases of Arkenu and Ouenat, and a fairly exact determination of their positions and altitudes. There has long been a tradition that two oases existed in or near the south-western corner of Egypt. Thus the map of Africa on a scale of 1/4,000,000 published by Justus Perthes of Gotha in 1892 shows an unnamed small oasis and well in lat. 21° 51′, long. 23° 3′, and another "uninhabited oasis," also unnamed, about 48 kms. due east of it in lat. 21° 50′, long. 23° 29′. Both these oases were doubtless placed on the map from vague Arab statements; they appear not to have been previously visited by any explorer, and indeed their very existence was so doubtful that they have not been shown on the maps either of the English or of the French General Staff.

I have not been able to trace any published reference to the existence of Arkenu, but that of Ouenat has been mentioned

[1] *Geographical Journal*, vol. 68 (1921), p. 248.

in recent papers by Mr. Harding King and Lieut.-Col. Tilho. In Mr. Harding King's paper of 1913[1] on "The Libyan Desert from Native Information," he states that he heard of a place called "Owana" or "Owanat," about halfway along a road from Merga to Kufra, where there is a well and green grass after rain. The map appended to his paper shows that Mr. Harding King's estimate of its probable position was lat. 21° 37′, long. 24° 45′, which differs by nearly 130 kms. from the nearer of the two oases shown on the above-mentioned German map.

Lieut.-Col. Tilho, who carried out exploratory work in Tibesti, Erdi, Borkou and Ennedi in 1912–17, mentions[2] "the still unknown massif of El Aouinat, situated approximately between the 22nd and 23rd degrees of latitude north and the 24th and 25th degrees of longitude east" and a route he heard of from Aouinat to Merga.

Hassanein Bey's observations give for the positions and altitude of his camps at Arkenu and Ouenat:

	Lat. N.			Long. E.			Metres above sea.
	°	′	″	°	′	″	
Arkenu . .	22	12	32	24	44	15	598
Ouenat . .	21	52	29	24	54	16	616

Thus Ouenat is only some 34 kms. from where Mr. Harding King guessed its position to be from his guide's statements, but it is outside the somewhat wide limits of latitude indicated by Lieut-Col. Tilho, and is nearly 150 kms. from the place marked "uninhabited oasis" on the German map; while Arkenu, which is presumably the small oasis marked to the west of the "uninhabited oasis," is now proved to be some 180 kms. from where it is shown on that map.

It may be remarked that Arkenu is well within the boundaries of Egypt, while Ouenat is a short distance over the boundary, in the Anglo-Egyptian Sudan.

The principal interest in these places lies in the possibilities they open up for further exploration of the south-west corner of Egypt, which has hitherto been inaccessible to military patrols, and even to the boldest of explorers, by reason of the absence of any certain knowledge as to the existence and position of permanent water-supplies. Now that Arkenu and Ouenat

[1] *Geographical Journal*, vol. 42 (1913), p. 282.
[2] *Geographical Journal*, vol. 56 (1920), p. 98.

are exactly located, and the existence of drinkable water in reasonable quantities, it may be possible for a traveller from Egypt to reach them and procure the necessary water-supplies for his return journey. I say it *may* be possible, for there are still great difficulties about access to Arkenu and Ouenat from Egypt, although both the compilers of the German map and Mr. Harding King were informed that an old track to Egypt runs from Ouenat. According to Mr. Harding King's informant, the track runs to Dakhla Oasis, which is a distance of some 600 kms. through a waterless desert, and consequently the journey between the two places is a very formidable undertaking for camels, even in winter; while the suitability of the ground for motor cars, especially in the mountainous region round the oases themselves, is as yet unknown.

An interesting feature of Arkenu and Ouenat is that they are not depressions with underground water-supplies, like all the other oases of the Western Desert of Egypt, but mountainous areas where the water is dependent on local rainfall and collected in natural basins in the rocks.[1] The Nile Valley in the same latitudes has practically no rainfall, but here, some 700 kms. westward into the Sahara, there is sufficient rain to maintain perennial though limited supplies—at Ouenat even sufficient for the needs of a settlement of some 150 Badawi—and at certain seasons to provide grazing for animals in the valleys and lowlands. The ground-level in this region is high (600 metres above sea-level), but the mountains near the oases rise to heights of over 1,100 metres above the sea, and it can hardly be doubted that the rainfall is connected with the orography, the mountains attracting or helping to form clouds. In this connection it is worth noting that in the more open country further south, as well as in that to the north, the absence of vegetation shows that rainfall is evidently much scarcer than in the mountains around the oases; also that Ouenat, where the mountains are higher than at Arkenu, possesses better and more abundant water. The conservation of the water through the dry season is partly conditioned

[1] Though rare in the Western Desert of Egypt, these rock-basins are common in the mountains of the Eastern Desert near the Red Sea, where they are called "galts." See my "Geography and Geology of South-Eastern Egypt" (1912), p. 240. They are also abundant in the Erdi and Ennedi regions of French Equatorial Africa, as we know from the explorations of both Lieut.-Colonel Tilho and Hassanein Bey.

by the almost impermeable nature of the crystalline rocks composing the mountains, and partly by the sheltered position of the pools in the rocky gullies, which diminishes evaporation.

The full extent of the mountains of Arkenu and Ouenat is not yet known, but they cover at least 1,000 square kms. Hassanein Bey's main route lay along the western feet of the masses, so that their western limit is ascertained, as also their north-and-south extension; but their eastern limits in Egypt are unknown, and it is not yet certain whether there may be a continuous chain of hills connecting the two masses to the east. Hassanein Bey made a round reconnaissance extending some 40 kms. eastward of his camp at Ouenat, without reaching the limits of the mass. The mountains are visible from great distances from the north and south, Arkenu having been sighted from at least 60 kms. north, and Ouenat remained visible for at least the same distance on the track southward from it. There is a possibility that the mountains may be less conspicuous to a traveller approaching from the east, owing to their breaking up into smaller hills and the ground on that side of them being higher and falling away gradually towards the Nile; but this must remain uncertain until further exploration is undertaken.

From Ouenat to Erdi "well" is a journey of 430 kms. in a south-south-westerly direction, the first 284 kms. being in the Anglo-Egyptian Sudan, the remaining 146 in French Equatorial Africa. There is no water in all this stretch, but patches of dried grass were met with at intervals in the latter half of the journey, and some 25 kms. before reaching Erdi the valleys were full of green grass. Thus the northern limit of the equatorial rain-belt hereabouts is approximately in lat. 18° 50′.

ERDI.—Erdi appears to be the name given to an extensive tract of country stretching between the 21st and 24th meridians of east longitude, rising gradually southwards and ending in a broken east-and-west escarpment in about lat. 18° 30′. The water-source visited by Hassanein Bey, called by the guide "Erdi Well," is in lat. 18° 31′, long. 23° 10′, and is 958 metres above sea-level. It is not really a well, but a rock-pool, similar to those of Arkenu and Ouenat; the water is good.

Hassanein Bey's "Erdi Well" is close to the locality marked "Erdi-ma" on Lieut.-Col. Tilho's map of 1920, but it appears not to be the same water-source as the one visited by that traveller. Erdi well is at the head of a small valley draining northwards, and one has to ascend the hills to a height of 1,020 metres above sea and cross a stretch of broken plateau before reaching the southward drainages which cut back into the scarp. Over this broken plateau Hassanein Bey proceeded in a south-easterly direction, descending the scarp in lat. 18° 25′, long. 23° 20′. The level at the foot of the scarp was 790 metres, so that the scarp hereabouts is some 230 metres in height.

After descending the Erdi scarp, Hassanein Bey's track southwards across the great sandy depression which separates the Erdi plateau from that of Ennedi, to Agah (88 kilometres from his camp north of Erdi Well), appears to have been almost parallel to, and some 20 kilometres east of, that followed by Lieut.-Col. Tilho in 1914.

AGAH.—The water-source of Agah is a rock-pool similar to that at Erdi; but the water is bad, owing to fouling by animals. The pool is some 6 kms. up a valley cutting back northwards into the scarp which faces that of Erdi. The position found for the pool at Agah lies some 24 kms. from the "Aga Spring" shown on Lieut.-Col. Tilho's map. There are possibly several springs and pools among the hills in this neighbourhood, all bearing the same name, which would explain the apparent discrepancy.

From Agah the track to Enebah (65 kms.) runs in a rather zigzag course with a general southward trend. For the first 10 kms. beyond the pool, the track ascends the valley; then, mounting rapidly, it soon reaches altitudes of over 1,000 metres on the plateau.

ENEBAH.—Here is a small settlement of Badawi and a well of good water about 28 kms. east of the wells of Keita shown on Lieut.-Col. Tilho's map, on the same high plateau.

From Enebah to Bao is 120 kms., by a rather zigzag track in a general south-south-westerly direction over an undulating and hilly plateau. The greatest altitude recorded by Hassanein Bey during his entire journey, 1,184 metres above sea, was reached at a point on the road about 18 kms. from Enebah. This altitude (3,884 feet) is slightly higher than that (3,600) feet which Lieut.-Col. Tilho records as his maximum on the same (Erdebe) plateau at a point further west; so that the plateau probably increases in height to the eastward. The Kaptarko Valley was crossed about 47 kms. farther on, and it is interesting to note that Hassanein Bey's data give a position for this which is very close to the " Kapterko " of Lieut.-Col. Tilho's map.

Bao.—Hassanein Bey's Bao is not the " Bo " visited by Lieut.-Col. Tilho, which lies over 100 kms. further north, but the place called " Orobo " on Tilho's map and " Bao " on the map of Wadai and Darfur which was attached to the Convention between the British and French Governments at Paris in 1919; this is evident from the following comparison of Hassanein Bey's position with those scaled for the abovementioned places from the maps referred to:

	Lat. N.			Long. E.		
	°	′	″	°	′	″
Bao (Hassanein Bey) . .	16	28	24	23	1	47
Orobo (Tilho)	16	30	0	22	59	0
Bao (Convention map) . .	16	28	0	23	4	0

The wells of Bao are at the head of a small valley draining northwards, in which shrubs and trees are plentiful. There are several wells, with perennial supplies, though the water becomes scarce in the dry season and the wells have then to be deepened.

From Bao to Furawia is 145 kms. in a south-south-easterly direction, over ground partly covered with grass and small trees. About 55 kms. before reaching Furawia, Hassanein Bey passed close to a hill called Tameira, on which is a signpost, formed of a dead tree, marking the boundary between French and Anglo-Egyptian territory. No astronomical observations were taken here, but Hassanein Bey's adjusted traverse-data indicate the approximate position of the hill to be lat. 15° 48′ N., long. 23° 27′ E. The Wadi Hawar (" Howa " of the Anglo-French Convention map) was crossed about 7 kms. beyond Tameira Hill.

Conclusion.—In concluding this analysis of Hassanein Bey's results, the reduction of which has occupied a large part of my time for over two months, I may be permitted to remark that his expedition appears to me to be an almost unique achievement in the annals of geographical exploration. The journey of 3,345 kms. from Sollum to El Obeid, most of it through inhospitable deserts sparsely inhabited by fanatical and predatory tribes, is one which, without a strong military escort, could have been undertaken only by a Moslem, and by one of remarkable grit, tact, and perseverance. But Hassanein

Bey has not only accomplished this difficult journey and brought back interesting descriptions and photographs of the country through which he passed. Before setting out from Cairo he had applied himself strenuously for several weeks to acquiring facility in the use of the theodolite, and instruction in the particular methods of reconnaissance-survey best adapted for exploration of the kind on which he was to embark; and throughout his travels he made excellent use of the surveying knowledge thus acquired. How complete and accurate were his observations will be obvious from the foregoing analysis; and the really remarkable thing is that he managed somehow to carry out all this observation single-handed, and to maintain the continuity and accuracy of his measurements and records over the distance of more than 2,000 kms. which separates the points on his route whose positions were previously known. Thanks to the detailed and systematic character of his observations, their reduction has been a pleasant labour, and it has been comparatively easy to map his route and the newly discovered places along it with a high degree of accuracy.

The principal additions to our knowledge of North-Eastern Africa which have resulted from the expedition are:

(1) The true positions of Zieghen and Kufra, resulting in changes of about 100 and 40 kms. respectively from the positions hitherto assigned to these places on maps of Africa.

(2) The discovery of the Oases of Arkenu and Ouenat, previously unknown, and the determination of their positions and approximate extent, thus opening up possibilities of new desert travel from Egypt into regions of the Libyan Desert still unexplored.

(3) The discovery of a route from south-western Egypt across the Erdi and Ennedi plateaux of French Equatorial Africa into Darfur, and the positions of the water-sources along it. Incidentally, this establishes a connection with, and extension of, Lieut.-Col. Tilho's recent brilliant explorations in the French Sudan.

(4) The determination of careful barometric levels along the entire route, affording valuable information on the orography of a vast region of which little was previously known, and confirming Lieut-Col. Tilho's conclusion that there is no possible drainage-outlet from Lake Chad in an easterly direction.

CONCLUSIONS DERIVED FROM THE GEOLOGICAL DATA COLLECTED BY HASSANEIN BEY DURING HIS KUFRA-OUENAT EXPEDITION

W. F. HUME, D.Sc., *Director, Geological Survey of Egypt.*

Before dealing with the facts ascertained I would desire to congratulate Hassanein Bey on the successful accomplishment of an expedition which has given us knowledge of a large tract of country hitherto unknown to geographical science. Those of us who have a slight acquaintance with desert travel will appreciate the fact that he should have covered 3,500 kms. over an almost waterless waste in a region which from religious or political causes is practically closed to a European explorer. It has often meant weariness of body and anxiety of mind, though no doubt he has been compensated by the freedom of feeling engendered by free wind-swept spaciousness and by the constant interest of new discovery.

Hassanein Bey has shown a keen desire to obtain data which would be of scientific value, and consequently has collected specimens and taken photographs which might enable those familiar with the desert geology in Egypt to arrive at conclusions as to the geological nature of the country traversed. Mr. Moon has examined these specimens in my absence, and his notes and conclusions are attached.

The following points are those which have struck me most forcibly in looking over the specimens and photographs brought back by Hassanein Bey:

(1) Between Siwa and Jaghbub large specimens of petrified trees were noted and photographed. This is of interest as showing the wide extension to the west of the so-called "petrified forests." It emphasizes the desirability of extending the examination of the southern edge of the Cyrenaic scarp to the western boundary of Egyptian territory, including the portion now marked "unexplored" on the 1 : 1,000,000 geological map of Egypt.

(2) The beautiful specimens of the Miocene oysters *Ostrea Virleti* and *Ostrea digitalina* indicate clearly that Jaghbub is on the same formation as that of Siwa, viz. Middle Miocene, while the further continuation of these strata towards Jalo is indicated by Specimen No. 3.

(3) At a point a little south of lat. 28° N., a collection was made of hard limestones. A very shelly piece among them may be Miocene, but the others might well form part of the Eocene or Cretaceous members which are so well developed on the same latitude to the east of the Egyptian boundary. The absence of type fossils in the rocks renders further identification impossible.

(4) Between March 20th and 24th Hassanein Bey was crossing a flat plain. The question arises whether this might not be due to erosion of the finer clays and sands which so often lie between the hard Cretaceous limestone and more compact members of the Nubian Sandstone series.

(5) Be this as it may, as indicated by Mr. Moon, the Nubian Sandstone proper was met with in typical form a little north of El Harrash (Zieghen). The specimens obtained from this point onward to the junction with the igneous rocks, about 30 kms. north of Arkenu, are all varied members of the same sandstone formation which in Egypt proper and the Sudan spreads over enormous areas.

(6) Great interest attaches to the discovery of typical granite in the Oases of Ouenat and Arkenu. The main rock is of pegmatitic type, being composed of well-shaped felspars, glassy quartz, and hornblende. A point brought out by the photograph is the intense action of temperature variation on these igneous rocks. The whole of the hillside is strewn with gigantic boulders, some of which have been split into large pieces which obviously once formed part of the same block.

As regards the nature of the relations between the granite and the Nubian Sandstone, it is to be noted that the granite range rises high above the sandstone which surrounds it. This difference of level might be explained (*a*) by the existence of a fold, (*b*) by the presence of a fracture line or fault, (*c*) by intrusion of the granite when in a molten condition into the overlying sandstone.

After conversation with Hassanein Bey, and a closer examination of his photographs from this point of view, one is led to the following conclusion :

(1) A fold seems possible, because the sandstone (which dips or slopes off the granite in certain folds in the south of Kharga Oasis) is seen to be obviously dipping towards the spectator in the cinema photograph of camels coming through the valley of Ouenat. Taking (*c*) first, we have no proof anywhere in Egypt that granite has been intruded into the Nubian Sandstone, in all cases where the relations are clearly displayed, the granite having obviously been worn down before the sandstone was deposited on it.

(2) We are consequently disposed to adopt the view, pending further study, that the differences of level may be due to the existence of a fold. The alternative would be the presence of a fracture line, along which the granite has been pushed up in a solid form to a higher level than the sandstone which normally overlies it, or the sandstone has been let down along the line of weakness against the granite.

A very interesting feature is the presence of well-made drawings of giraffes and ostriches on the sandstone walls. As Hassanein Bey points out, the camel is absent, and it is to be regretted that there are no pictures of human beings. These "graffiti" may be of ancient date, being drawn at a period when rainfall was greater in this portion of North Africa than it is at present.

Hassanein Bey's expedition has thus indicated that both the Miocene strata in the north and the great Nubian Sandstone formation further south continue well to the west of the western Egyptian boundary with unchanged characteristics, while the discovery of the granitic oasis, as I understand within the boundaries of Egyptian territory, opens up the possibility of developing alternative routes to Darfur from Dakhla Oasis, and also indicates a water base of great importance in connection with the exploration of the unknown territory lying west of the route followed by Hassanein Bey. Its further study from the geological standpoint would be of great interest.

NOTES ON THE GEOLOGY OF HASSANEIN BEY'S EXPEDITION, SOLLUM–DARFUR, 1923

F. W. Moon.

Having been requested by Hassanein Bey, in the absence of Dr. Hume, to report upon the interesting geological specimens collected by him on his recent exploratory tour through the Western Desert from Sollum, on the southern shores of the Mediterranean Sea, to Darfur in the Sudan, I have much pleasure in submitting the following short summary of the main features of the journey from a geological point of view, as deduced from the specimens collected.

Although the specimens are small and, in the case of the igneous rocks, much weathered, yet for all intents and purposes they are quite sufficient to enable one to make deductions and conclusions as to the main geological formations passed over.

As the explorer explains, there was not the freedom of transport he would have desired for making a larger collection of full-sized specimens, nor did he wish to incur the displeasure of those who formed his escort by seeming to do anything that might appear in any way suspicious, such as the constant breaking and collecting of stones.

From the tabulated list of specimens herewith appended, it may be seen that the beginning of the journey was made over Miocene formations indicated by fossil oysters and pectens (identified as *Ostrea digitalina*, *O. Virleti*, *Chlamys Zittteli* and others), of which there are seven valves of the former, two of the second, two of the third, and five which resemble *Chlamys sub-malvinæ*.

The Miocene formations continue through Siwa, Jaghbub, and Jalo, and far southwards to a point about 180 kms. to the south of Jalo (see specimens 1–4), where the last Miocene specimen (No. 4) was picked up.

At this point begins a wide barren stretch of flat and desolate country, devoid of rocks of any particular geological interest beyond the thin covering of " sand and alluvium " which extends for nearly 200 kms. (four days of monotonous marching) along the route to the south.

Then, when about 50 kms. north of Zieghen, the explorer noticed that the aspect of the country took a sudden change; the light yellow of the Miocene limestones and desert sands gave place to brighter, more varied and highly coloured scenery, which the specimens show was due to the approach of the Lower Cretaceous " Nubian " Sandstones, which, wherever they occur, add beauty to the landscape in unbelievable brilliancy and variety of colouring.

Although greens and blues are sometimes observed, red is the dominant colour, all shades of pink, terracotta, maroon and brick-red are blended together, and umbres and ochres are sometimes present.

Thus we are provided with a point well westward of any hitherto known on the northern limits of the " Nubian " Sandstone; in other words, the evidence suggests the continuation westwards by some 600 kms. of the " Nubian " boundary shown on the existing 1/1,000,000 coloured geological map of Egypt (1910).

Mention may here be made of the apparent absence of specimens definitely representing the younger Cretaceous rocks which are shown coloured green, on the map just referred to, to the east; but this may be readily accounted for by the presence of the expansive plain passed over between Jalo and Zieghen, the " sand and alluvium " covering of which is quite sufficient to hide all evidence of the younger rocks of that age.

Another question rendered obscure by the presence of this large flat expanse of " sand and alluvium " is the exact position of the southern limits of Miocene formations. If we assume (which seems to be the case) that the point, 180 kms. to the south of Jalo, where the last Miocene specimens were collected, be the southern boundary of the Miocene, then we find that the distribution of that formation as now suggested is of particular interest as (1) indicating a western extension of the general outline of the ancient Mediterranean Ocean in Miocene time; and (2) adding extra weight to our conceptions as regard the period (in geological chronology) of the Egyptian-Sinai uplift which caused the elevation of land involving a considerable portion of Egypt in pre-Miocene times, and ultimately defining the shore of the Miocene Sea more or less as we now follow it from this newly discovered spot between El Harrash (Zieghen) and Jalo to a short distance east of Siwa from where it runs north-eastwards to the 30° lat. along which it continues with little variation to Suez.

It would appear that all Egypt lying between the Miocene Gulf of Suez in the east and the Siwa–Zieghen Miocene shoreline in the west and southwards was dry land in Miocene times, and therefore exposed to denudation extending over a vast geological period during which the "Nubian" Sandstone and younger Cretaceous rocks were laid bare and in a position to have Miocene strata laid down upon or against them.

The "Nubian" Sandstone, as indicated by the specimens 5–10, shows identical characteristics to those exhibited wherever it occurs in Egypt or Sinai. It is a sandstone consisting in the main of more or less fine rounded grains of pure quartz, through which is distributed, in greater or lesser proportions, larger grains or pebbles. In cases where the latter predominate a pudding-stone or conglomerate results; where the larger grains are sparsely distributed a porphyritic appearance is suggested.

The cementing material, which may be either calcareous, siliceous, or ferruginous, is the colour-imparting medium, the depth of colour depending upon the amount and composition of iron oxides present in it, and when this material is weathered, washed out, and accumulated into pockets it becomes when finely ground suitably adapted for the manufacture of paints.

The "Nubian" Sandstone continues south of the Miocene–Nubian boundary above referred to, to a point some 15 kms. north of the Arkenu Mountains.

Approaching this point, still another change in the general aspect of the country met the eye of the explorer: the brighter colouring of the sandstones gave place to the duller browns, greys, and blacks of an abrupt range of igneous hills, the position on the ground where the igneous rocks come up through the "Nubian" Sandstones being approximately 25 kms. north of Arkenu.

The changes of scenery in passing from one formation to another are strikingly seen in the excellent collection of photographs procured by Hassanein Bey, who is to be highly complimented on the success he obtained under great difficulties and inconveniences.

Judging from the specimens 11–22 submitted for examination, the igneous rocks, of which the Arkenu–Ouenat hills are composed, consist mainly of coarsely crystalline granites and syenites varying in texture and appearance, and through them run intrusive veins of finer-grained dyke rocks.

The Arkenu hills are mostly composed of rocks represented by specimens 12 and 14, which are really somewhat similar in composition.

No. 12 consists of a holocrystalline aggregate of large crystals of a light grey (possibly a decomposed or kaolinized orthoclase) alkali-felspar, which constitutes the main bulk of the rock. No quartz is visible in the hand specimen, which is greatly weathered, and only gives a specific gravity of a little over 2·5. Small crystals of dark greenish hornblende are well formed, and occur in fewer numbers than in specimens 17 and 21, which are representatives of the rock-mass of the Ouenat hills to be described presently.

Specimen 14 is an unweathered grey rock chiefly composed of a mottled grey alkali-felspar, with hornblende crystals in similar numbers to those in specimen 12.

The microscopic examination of a rock-section made from specimen 14 corroborates the above description, but introduces the possibility of the presence of nepheline in granular-like patches in the slide, which correspond to darker slightly lustrous areas in the hard specimen; however, no nepheline has been actually identified.

Specimens Nos. 12 and 14 may therefore be called *syenites*.

Running through the syenites of the Arkenu hills are veins of intrusive rocks represented by specimens Nos. 11, 13, and 15, and no doubt many others occur.

Specimen No. 11 represents a vein of a hemicrystalline, hard dark green rock weathering brown on the outer surface, with innumerable small dark specks which are scarcely discernible in the unweathered portion of the specimen.

Under the microscope this rock is found to be of considerable interest. It consists of an aggregate of small phenocrysts of idiomorphic felspar, which in places assumes the appearance of a crypto- or microcrystalline felspathic matrix crowded with acicular crystals of a green mineral resembling ægirine. The latter are in places irregularly distributed, but in areas where the felspar occurs in roughly rectangular or lozenge form, the ægirine microlites are crowded round the edges of the latter.

No quartz is noticeable in the rock-slide, and the rock may be tentatively determined as an *ægirine-felsite*, apparently similar to a rock described and figured in Harker's "Petrology for Students."

A second vein in the Arkenu hills is represented by specimen No. 13, which is a brownish *quartzite*.

The third vein is indicated by specimen No. 15, which is a dark grey laminated rock, weathering to reddish-brown, very fine in texture, with small clear crystals of phenocrysts sparsely disseminated through the groundmass. The rock-slide shows, under the microscope, a great similarity to specimen No. 11 as described above. The felspar here, however, forms a much finer crypto-crystalline groundmass than in the former, and the ægirine microlites are smaller, tapering, and not so well formed. This rock may also be tentatively called a fine *ægirine-felsite*.

The Ouenat hills are mainly composed of rocks represented by specimens 17 and 21, the chief constituent of which is a grey alkali-felspar (possibly orthoclase with some microcline). Quartz is well represented in idiomorphic forms; no mica is noticeable in the hand specimens, but many well-developed prismoidal crystals of very dark or dark green hornblende are thickly distributed throughout the mass.

No slide was made of these specimens owing to their fragile condition due to weathering, but the rock may be determined as a coarsely crystalline grey *hornblende-granite*.

Specimen No. 18 is another representative rock from, and constitutes a considerable bulk of, the Ouenat hills. It may be termed a *red granite*, approximating to an aplite with very little mica, which decomposes and forms oxides of iron which have stained the rock a brownish-red; quartz and felspar form the main bulk of the rock.

As in the case of the Arkenu syenites, so here in the Ouenat granites we find other examples of endogenous veins running through the parent rock, represented by specimens 16, 19 and 22.

Specimen No. 16 represents a vein of purplish *felsite*, in the felsitic groundmass of which occur phenocrysts of idiomorphic felspar.

Specimen No. 19 represents a vein of pure white granular *quartz rock* which occurs in and may have been the cause (through denudation) of the cave found in the foothills of the Ouenat range.

Specimen No. 22, found at Garet Shuzzu, is a typical *quartzite* which may also occur as a vein in the granites.

Two specimens found inside the cave in the Ouenat oasis are of particular interest. These specimens are Nos. 20 and 21. The former, a laminated *travertine*, could only have been deposited from running water, as the formation of ripple-markings confirms; and from notes made by the explorer at the time of his inspection, we learn that there was quite a lot of it lying about on the floor of the cave. Under the microscope spheroidal structure is displayed, representing the ripple-markings, and in the matrix of calcite many fragments of quartz, felspar, etc., are conspicuous, these having been derived from the denuding granites. No organic remains were observed.

The second specimen (No. 21) is a fragment of the hornblendic-granite of which the Ouenat hills are chiefly composed, and which forms the roof of the cave; this is coated on one side with a thin black iron-manganese film, similar to the well-known deposit on the rocks in the Nile at or near the Aswan dam.

This whole igneous area, which includes the newly discovered mountains and oases of Arkenu and Ouenat, is possibly of limited extent, and occurs in, and is possibly surrounded by, a much wider expanse of "Nubian" Sandstone, in a similar manner to several other such areas already shown on the one-million geological map of Egypt.

Judging from other known similar occurrences where igneous rocks appear surrounded by "Nubian" Sandstones, we may infer that the latter were deposited upon the ancient igneous rocks which subsequently rose vertically, bending the super-incumbent strata over and round them, possibly only to a slight degree in this instance, as none of the photographs show very highly dipping rocks.

On leaving Ouenat for Erdi the igneous area is soon left behind. The actual junction between it and the "Nubian" Sandstone (which again forms the surface rock) occurs at a point about 20 kms. south of Ouenat, and the aspect of the country again changes from the more uneven weathering of the igneous range of greys and browns to brilliant colourings of the "Nubian" Sandstone which forms a long series of prominent escarpments rising to heights bordering on 1,000 metres above the sea between Enebah and Kuttum, after which the ground begins to fall, until El Fasher is reached, where the ground-level is only about 700 or 800 metres in height.

SUMMARY.—The several interesting geological features suggested by the recent expedition may be summarized as follows:

1. That Miocene rocks extend southwards, to or near the 27th degree of north latitude, forming a large bay bordered by older rocks.

2. That the Miocene rocks, resting here apparently upon or against "Nubian" Sandstones, seem to follow the same conditions noticed first by Dr. Hume in the Gulf of Suez region, namely, that they rest upon older and older formations the further southwards they are found; in other words, that prior to the deposition of the Miocene there was a time of denudation which was more effectual in the south than in the north, owing to the fact that in the south was an area of greater uplift.

3. That a large area of "Nubian" Sandstone (Cretaceous) exists south of this latitude.

4. That a newly discovered range of igneous rocks in the Arkenu hills exists well inside Egyptian territory, and possibly entirely within this "Nubian" Sandstone area, or connected as a tongue to a larger igneous massif lying in the south.

5. That the Cretaceous rocks (younger than the "Nubian" Sandstone) which appear on the coloured Geological Map of Egypt farther to the north-east, possibly do not occur along the route traversed, having been concealed beneath "sand and alluvium" areas.

LIST OF SPECIMENS COLLECTED BY AHMED MOHAMMED HASSANEIN BEY IN HIS EXPEDITION FROM SOLLUM TO DARFUR.

No.	Date. 1923.	Locality. (As taken from descriptions on labels.)	Determination of Specimens.
1	—	Siwa.	Three crystal fragments of selenite; one pecten and two oyster shells (possibly of Miocene age).
2	—	Jaghbub.	One pecten in a shelly limestone (possibly indicating Miocene age).
3	—	Surface rocks on the way from Jaghbub to Jalo.	One piece of fossilized wood; three loose siliceous pebbles; two long concretions of calcareous grit, and fibrous salt crystal (curved, five inches long).
4	March 20	In Wadi, in small patches.	Two loose pebbles of calcareous grit with quartz grains.

No.	Date. 1923.	Locality. (As taken from descriptions on labels.)	Determination of Specimens.
5	March 24	Getting near El Harrash (Zieghen), patches of this strewn (broken) before reaching Halab.	Nubian Sandstone (one specimen).
6	March 28	One day's journey from El Harrash (Zieghen), on way to Kufra.	Hard ferruginous bands from Nubian Sandstone (five specimens).
7	March 29	Garet el Sherif.	Nubian Sandstone (three specimens).
8	—	Gebel el Neri, the garas nearing Hauari.	Ferruginous bands (colour maroon) from Nubian Sandstone (three specimens); one black ferruginous "bomb."
9	—	Kufra (Taj) hills.	Blocks of Nubian Sandstone (three specimens).
10	April 22	Between Kufra and Ouenat; specimens from chain of hills crossed that day.	Nubian Sandstone (one specimen); and ferruginous bands from Nubian Sandstone (two specimens).
11	April 24	Arkenu Mountain.	Igneous rock (ægirine felsite).
12	— 24	From patches of Arkenu Mountain. There are big hills formed entirely of it . . . on the outside of the mountain.	,, (badly weathered syenite).
13	— 24	From big patches north of Arkenu Mountain.	,, (quartzite vein in).
14	— 25	From Arkenu Mountain itself.	,, (grey syenite).
15	— 25	Found in big blocks buried in the ground on the border of Arkenu Mountain, in the Arkenu Valley.	,, (ægirine felsite).
16	—	Specimen from formations (in layers) found in Ouenat big valley.	,, (felsite).
17	—	Ouenat Mountain is mostly of this stone.	,, (badly weathered hornblende-granite).
18	—	Stone of which Ouenat is generally formed.	,, (badly weathered granite).
19	—	Found inside the water cave at Ouenat, near the water-level; plenty of it in small patches.	,, (quartz vein).
20	—	Found inside the water cave at Ouenat.	Calcareous deposit from running water (travertine).
21	—	Found inside the water cave at Ouenat, in the roof. Most of the stone of the cave and mountain is of this kind.	Igneous rock (badly weathered hornblende-granite, coated with polished film of iron which may have come from the water).

No.	Date. 1923.	Locality. (As taken from descriptions on labels.)	Determination of Specimens.
22	May 8	From Garet Shezzu, near Ouenat.	Igneous rock (fine quartzite).
23	May 10	Between Ouenat and Erdi.	Nubian Sandstone (one specimen).
24	May 13	Found strewn on red sand, getting near Erdi. Nothing but red sand and this stone.	Ferruginous band (containing hæmatite) from Nubian Sandstone.
25	May 16	Erdi hills.	Dark red clay, with small percentage of quartz sand (grinds up into dark brick-red powder).
26	May 16	Stone of Erdi hills.	Brick-red clay, with small percentage of quartz sand (grinds easily into bright brick-red coloured powder).
27	May 19	Agah hills.	Soft, fine, yellow to red, slightly calcareous micaceous sandstone.

Index

Abdullahi El Sahabi, 94
Abid, Sayed El, 168
Adam Bu Gmaira, 71–5
Agah, valley of, 238, 297
— bad water at, 242
Altitudes, 282–5
Ants, white, 246
Arkell, Mr., 264
Arkenu, 191–6, 293–6
Astronomical determination of latitude, 275
— — of local time, 272
Aujila, 94–7

Baggage, blessing of the, 34–6
Ball, John, D.Sc., 184
— Note on the cartographical results of Hassanein Bey's journey, 271–99
Bao, 298
Bather, Lieut., 49, 257
Beduin chivalry, 259
— law of murder, 100
— marriage customs, 101
— powers of observation, 242
— songs to camels, 124–5, 198
— songs, 87–8
— suspicion, 109, 148–9
— women, 106–7
Bidiyats, 243
Bir Buttafal, 287
Blessing of the baggage, 34–6
Boema, 290
Bu Gmaira, Adam, 71–5
Bukara, a Beduin servant, 207–9
Bu Seif Bu Gmaira, 73
Buseima, 289
Bu-Zafar custom, 89, 106

Camels, 28, 90, 103, 115, 136, 230, 248, 266
— cleverness of, 130–5
— dates as food for, 41, 103, 134
— flesh as food, 141–2, 193
— songs to, 124–5
Cartographical results of Hassanein Bey's journey, by John Ball, 271–99
Chronometer, author's, and Greenwich time, 266
Clothing required, 44–5
Compass saves party, 214–16
Compass-variations, observations of, 277

Dates, 41, 51
— as food for camels, 41
— as omens, 53
Desert, charm of, 23–9
— etiquette, 249
Dining customs, 76–9
Drawings at Ouenat, 203–5
Dupuis, Charles, 261, 262, 265–7

El Fasher, 265
" Empty gunpowder " custom, 113, 181, 220, 258, 264

Enebah, 244, 297
Equipment, 37–46
Erdi, 228, 296–7
Etiquette of desert, 249
Ezeila, 293

Fasher, El, 265
Food, want of, 254–7
Forbes, Mrs. Rosita, 32, 286, 289, 292, 293
Fouad I., 16, 33, 39
Furawia, 257

Game, unable to follow, 240–1
Geographical positions and levels, 285
Geological data collected by Hassanein Bey, Conclusions derived from, by Dr. W. F. Hume, 300–2
Geology of Hassanein Bey's Expedition, Notes on, by F. W. Moon, 303–11
Gmaira, 71–5
Goran tribes, 193, 244–7
Guide loses way, 214–16

Hardships of the march, 253–5
Hassanein Bey, Ahmed Mohammed.
— arrives home, 267
— as a fencer, 14
— blessed by his father, 34–6
— cartographical results of journey, 271–99
— clothing taken, 44–5
— decides to go to El Fasher by Ouenat, 166
— discovers Arkenu, 195
— dresses in Beduin costume, 52
— enters Sudan, 255

Hassanein Bey, Ahmed Mohammed (*contd.*).
— equipment required for journey, 37–46
— extracts from *Diary*, 128, 129, 141, 143, 145, 148, 150, 152, 158, 187–8, 211, 213, 216, 218, 222, 247, 251, 252
— geographical results of journey, 286
— guide loses way, 214–16
— hardships of the march, 253–5
— leaves for Sollum, 36
— "Lost" oases no longer lost, 257
— plans journey, 31–3
— plots against, 256
— prevents serious quarrel among his men, 230–3
— reaches end of journey, 265
— receives warning before journey, 47
— says good-bye to his men, 267
— staff for journey from Kufra to Sudan, 187
— starts for the "lost" oases, 187
— suffers from excess of hospitality, 175–6
— supplies taken for journey, 37–46
— unable to follow game, 240–1
— uses serum for scorpion-bite, 157–8
— want of food, 254–7
— want of tobacco, 261 and *passim*
Hawari, 156
Herodotus, 93
Herri, Sheikh, 206–7
Hospitality, 76
— excess of, 175–6

Hume, W. F., Conclusions derived from the geological data collected by Hassanein Bey, 300–2
Hyena visits the camp, 247

Idris El Senussi, Sayed, 31–2, 53–5, 66, 91, 174
Ikhwan, 57, 67, 70–4

Jaghbub, 61–2, 68–75
Jalo, 91–110, 279–82, 286–7
— higher to-day than in 1879, 109

Kamel Effendi, 51
Kaptarko Valley, 297
King, Harding, 294–5
Kufra, 155, 161, 175–84, 289
Kuttum outpost, 256, 263–4

Latitude, astronomical determination of, 275
Lawler, Lieut., 51
Library of Sayed Idris, 174–5
Lizards, 223
Longitudes, 278
"Lost" oases no longer lost, 257. *See also* Arkenu, Ouenat
— — starts for, 187

Majabra tribe, 97–8
Marriage customs, 101
Marriages, 181
Maxwell, Sir John, 14
Meals, 76–9
Medicine, 79–82
Mirages, 122–3
Moon, F. W., Notes on the geology of Hassanein Bey's Expedition, 303–11
Mosque services, 171–2
Murder, Beduin law of, 100

Ostriches, 239–40
Ouenat, 197–209, 293–6
— rock drawings, 203–5

Perthes, Justus, 293
Plots against Hassanein Bey, 256
Prayer, 201–2
Provisions required, 40–3

Quarrel among Hassanein Bey's men, 230–3

Ramadan, 58
Rock drawings at Ouenat, 203–5
Rodd, Francis, 32
Rohlfs, Gerhardt, 13, 31, 109, 149, 155, 175, 178, 184, and references in appendices.

Sahabi, Abdullahi El, 94
Sandstorms, 83–6, 153
Saville Pasha, 254, 256, 261
Scorpion bites, 157–8
Senussis, The, 56–67, 94–6
Serum for scorpion-bite, 43, 157–8
Servants for journey from Kufra to Sudan, 187
Siwa, 50–2
Slaves, price of, 179–81
Slaves and black women compared, 259–60
Smith, Major, 267
Sollum, 36–7
Songs to camels, 124–5
Staff of men for journey from Kufra to Sudan, 187
Stecker, 184, 290–1
Supplies taken, 40–6

Taiserbo, 288
Taj, 156–7, 160
Talbot, Col., 31
Tea-making, 126
Tebus, 129, 139–40, 151
Ticks, 192
Tilho, Lieut.-Col., 294, 295 (*note*), 296, 297, 298, 299
Time, astronomical determination of local, 272
Tobacco, want of, 261

Wakil, 58
Water, carrying of, 42
— want of, and its effects on men, 212–13
Weddings, 181
Wells in the desert, 145–7
— method of approach, 226
White ants, 246
Widows, 51
Williams, Captain, 279 (*note*)

Zawia, 57, 59, 61
Zieghen, 148–51, 288
Zwaya tribe, 62, 64, 98–100